ALSO BY ELAINE SCIOLINO

Persian Mirrors: The Elusive Face of Iran

The Outlaw State: Saddam Hussein's Quest for Power and the Gulf Crisis

La Seduction

La Seduction

How the French Play the Game of Life

Elaine Sciolino

TIMES BOOKS HENRY HOLT AND COMPANY NEW YORK

Times Books
Henry Holt and Company, LLC
Publishers since 1866
175 Fifth Avenue
New York, New York 10010
www.henryholt.com

Library of Congress Cataloging-in-Publication Data

Sciolino, Elaine.
La seduction : how the French play the game of life / Elaine Sciolino.—1st ed.
p. cm.
Includes bibliographical references and index.
ISBN 978-0-8050-9115-1
1. France—Social life and customs. 2. Seduction—France. I. Title.
DC33.7.S36 2010
302.3'4—dc22 2010049572

Henry Holt books are available for special promotions and premiums. For details contact: Director, Special Markets.

First Edition 2011

Designed by Kelly S. Too

Printed in the United States of America
5 7 9 10 8 6 4

To Alessandra and Gabriela

CONTENTS

PART FIVE: THE END OF THE AFFAIR?

•PART ONE•

So Very French

1

Liberté, Égalité, Séduction

. . .

It is not enough to conquer, one must also know how to seduce.
—Voltaire, *Mérope*

Le plaisir... is something so much more definite and more evocative than what we mean when we speak of pleasure.... To the French it is part of the general fearless and joyful contact with life.
—Edith Wharton,
French Ways and Their Meaning

The first time my hand was kissed *à la française* was in the Napoléon III salon of the Élysée Palace. The one doing the kissing was the president of France.

In the fall of 2002, Jacques Chirac was seven years into his twelve-year presidency. The Bush administration was moving toward war with Iraq, and the relationship between France and the United States was worse than it had been in decades. I had just become the Paris bureau chief for the *New York Times*. Chirac was receiving me and the *Times*'s foreign editor, Roger Cohen, to make what he hoped would be a headline-grabbing announcement of a French-led strategy to avoid war. When we arrived that Sunday morning, Chirac shook hands with Roger and welcomed me with a *baisemain*, a kiss of the hand.

The ritual—considered old-fashioned nowadays by just about everyone under the age of sixty—was traditionally a ceremonial, sacred gesture; its history can be traced to ancient Greece and Rome. In the Middle

Ages, a vassal paid homage to his lord by kissing his hand. By the nineteenth century, hand kissing had been reinvented to convey a man's gallantry and politesse toward a woman. Those men who still practice it today are supposed to know and follow the rules: never kiss a gloved hand or the hand of a young girl; kiss the hand only of a married woman, and do so only indoors.

Chirac reached for my right hand and cradled it as if it were a piece of porcelain from his private art collection. He raised it to the level of his chest, bent over to meet it halfway, and inhaled, as if to savor its scent. Lips made contact with skin.

The kiss was not an act of passion. This was not at all like the smoldering scene in Marcel Proust's *Swann's Way* in which the narrator "blindly, hotly, madly" seizes and kisses the hand offered to him by a lady in pink. Still, the kiss was unsettling. Part of me found it charming and flattering. But in an era when women work so hard to be taken seriously, I also was vaguely uncomfortable that Chirac was adding a personal dimension to a professional encounter and assuming I would like it. This would not have happened in the United States. It was, like so much else in France, a subtle but certain exercise in seduction.

As a politician, Chirac naturally incorporated all of his seductive skills, including his well-practiced *baisemain*, into his diplomatic style. He kissed the hand of Laura Bush when she came to Paris to mark the return of the United States to UNESCO; she turned her face away as if to prevent giving him the satisfaction of her smile. He kissed the hand of Secretary of State Condoleezza Rice—twice in one visit. He kissed the hand of Angela Merkel the day after she became Germany's chancellor, fondling it in both hands; she repaid him by announcing the importance of a "friendly, intensive" relationship with France.

It turned out that Chirac was too ardent a hand kisser. Catherine Colonna, who was Chirac's spokeswoman, told me later that he did not adhere to proper form. "He was a great hand kisser, but I was not satisfied that his *baisemains* were strictly executed according to the rules of French savoir faire," she said. "The kiss is supposed to hover in the air, never land on the skin." If Chirac knew this, he was not letting it get in the way of a tactic that was working for him.

The power kiss of the president was one of my first lessons in understanding the importance of seduction in France. Over time, I became aware of its force and pervasiveness. I saw it in the disconcertingly intimate eye contact of a diplomat discussing dense policy initiatives; the exaggerated, courtly politeness of my elderly neighbor during our serendipitous morning encounters; the flirtatiousness of a female friend that oozed like honey at dinner parties; the banter of a journalist colleague that never ended and never failed to amuse. Eventually I learned to expect it, without quite knowing why.

Séduction and *séduire* (to seduce) are among the most overused words in the French language. In English, "seduce" has a negative and exclusively sexual feel; in French, the meaning is broader. The French use "seduce" where the British and Americans might use "charm" or "attract" or "engage" or "entertain." Seduction in France does not always involve body contact. A *grand séducteur* is not necessarily a man who easily seduces others into making love. The term might refer to someone who never fails to persuade others to his point of view. He might be gifted at caressing with words, at drawing people close with a look, at forging alliances with flawless logic. The target of seduction—male or female—may experience the process as a shower of charm or a magnetic pull or even a form of entertainment that ends as soon as the dinner party is over. "Seduction" in France encompasses a grand mosaic of meanings. What is constant is the intent: to attract or influence, to win over, even if just in fun.

Seduction can surface anytime—a tactic of the ice cream seller, the ambulance driver, the lavender grower. Foreigners may find themselves swept away without realizing how it happened. Not so the French. For them, the daily campaign to win and woo is a familiar game, instinctively played and understood. The seducer and the seduced may find the process enjoyable or unsatisfying. It may be a waste of time and end without the desired result. But played well, the game can be stimulating. And when victory comes, the joy is sweet.

That's because seduction is bound tightly with what the French call *plaisir*—the art of creating and relishing pleasure of all kinds. The French are proud masters of it, for their own gratification and as a useful tool to seduce others. They have created and perfected pleasurable ways to pass the time: perfumes to sniff, gardens to wander in, wines to drink, objects of beauty to observe, conversations to carry on. They give themselves permission to fulfill a need for pleasure and leisure that America's hard-working, supercapitalist, abstinent culture often does not allow. Sexuality always lies at the bottom of the toolbox, in everyday life, in business, even in politics. For the French, this is part of the frisson of life.

Even though France is the fifth-largest economy in the world, for many decades the French have bemoaned and documented the decline of their country from its lofty position as a once-mighty power. The trend line was fixed forever when the Germans invaded the country in 1940 and the French succumbed. Ever since then, the French have struggled with an inferiority complex even as they proclaim their grandeur. "Declinism" has become a national sport.

These days, the sense of decline extends far beyond the spheres of military or imperial power. The French way of life itself is under fire. Globalized capitalism means everything is faster, more efficient, less thorough, and less personal. The French landscape has fewer family-owned farms and more industrial warehouses. Designer bags once hand-crafted in small ateliers are made en masse in China. Perfumes once blended by artisans in Grasse are produced according to market research specifications in laboratories in New York. Billboards on the highways leaving Paris advertise instant rice. A chain of supermarkets stocks nothing but frozen food. A restaurant on the Île de la Cité in Paris serves what it calls traditional onion soup made from freeze-dried packets. The art of intricate French-style back-and-forth diplomacy built on refined language and form is threatened by e-mail, Facebook, Twitter, and the twenty-four-hour news cycle. The French are being pulled into a world that devalues their expertise and celebrates things they do badly.

There is much that is unlovable about France: the sclerosis in its educational system; the blindness and unwillingness to acknowledge and embrace ethnic, religious, and racial diversity; the emphasis on process and form rather than completion; the inelegant and often brutal behavior that sometimes surfaces in prominent political figures.

And yet the French still imbue everything they do with a deep affection for sensuality, subtlety, mystery, and play. Even as their traditional influence in the world shrinks, they soldier on. In every arena of life they are determined to stave off the onslaught of decline and despair. They are devoted to the pursuit of pleasure and the need to be artful, exquisite, witty, and sensuous, all skills in the centuries-old game called seduction. But it is more than a game; it is an essential strategy for France's survival as a country of influence.

The insight that led to this book came in the spring of 2008. It was a particularly uneasy moment in France. Nicolas Sarkozy had been president for just a year, and a recent poll had determined that the French people now considered him the worst president in the history of the Fifth Republic. His failure to deliver quickly on a campaign promise to revitalize the economy was perceived as a betrayal so profound that a phenomenon called "Sarkophobia" had developed. There was little in Sarkozy's clumsy personal style to help him counter it.

Around this time I read a new book written by a thirty-four-year-old speechwriter at the Foreign Ministry named Pierre-Louis Colin. In it, he laid out what he called his "high mission": to combat a "righteous" Anglo-Saxon-dominated world. The book was not about France's new projection of power in the world under Sarkozy but dealt with a subject just as important for France. It was a guide to finding the prettiest women in Paris.

"The greatest marvels of Paris are not in the Louvre," Colin wrote. "They are in the streets and the gardens, in the cafés and in the boutiques. The greatest marvels of Paris are the hundreds of thousands of women—whose smiles, whose cleavages, whose legs—bring incessant happiness to those who take promenades. You just have to know where to observe them."

The book classified the neighborhoods of Paris according to their women. Just as every region of France had a gastronomic identity, Colin said, every neighborhood of Paris had its "feminine specialty."

Ménilmontant in the northeast corner was loaded with "perfectly shameless cleavages—radiant breasts often uncluttered by a bra." The area around the Madeleine was the place to find "sublime legs."

Colin put women between the ages of forty and sixty into the "saucy maturity" category, explaining that they "bear witness" to "an agitated or ambitious sex life that refuses to lay down its weapons."

The book was patently sexist. It offered tips on how to observe au pairs and young mothers without their noticing and advised going out in rainstorms to catch women in wet, clingy clothing. It could never have been published in the United States. But in France it barely raised an eyebrow, and Colin had obviously had fun writing it. The mild reaction to a foreign policy official's politically incorrect book tells you something about the country's priorities. The unabashed pursuit of sensual pleasure is integral to French life. Sexual interest and sexual vigor are positive values, especially for men, and flaunting them in a lighthearted way is perfectly acceptable. It's all part of enjoying the seductive game.

The sangfroid about Colin's book made for a striking juxtaposition with the hostility toward France's president. To be sure, the flabby economy was one reason Sarkozy was doing so badly at the time; another was that he hadn't yet mastered the art of political or personal seduction.

But he was trying. Sarkozy's second wife, Cécilia, had walked out on him a couple of years earlier, returned before the election, and dumped him for good after he took office. As president of France, he couldn't bear to be seen as lacking in sex appeal. Nor could he afford to. In the United States, mixing sex and politics is dangerous; in France, this is inevitable.

In the weeks after Cécilia's final departure, Sarkozy had presented himself as lonely and long-suffering, but that had seemed very un-French. Then he had met the superrich Italian supermodel-turned-pop-singer Carla Bruni and married her three months later. On the anniversary of his first year in office, Sarkozy and Bruni posed for the cover of *Paris Match* as if they had been together forever. Sarkozy looked—as he wanted and needed to—both sexy and loved.

• • •

My understanding of the rules and rituals of the game of French seduction did not come suddenly but evolved over the years. It began with my very first day in France when I was a college student. I arrived in Paris late on a summer night in 1969, armed with a backpack and two years of high school French. America had landed on the moon that day, and the newspaper seller at the train station celebrated the event—and my arrival—by kissing me on both cheeks.

Later, I lived and worked for many years in France, first as a foreign correspondent for *Newsweek*, later as bureau chief for the *New York Times*. I covered stories in cities, in small towns, on farms, in poor immigrant housing projects and well-appointed drawing rooms. In time I came to see the extravagant attention given to seduction in France as a manifestation of something deeply embedded in French culture. Seduction is an unofficial ideology, a guiding principle codified in everyday assumptions and patterns of behavior so well established and habitual that they are automatic. It comes so naturally that often it isn't acknowledged or even understood by the French. But when seduction's role in their lives is called to their attention, they are often fascinated by the idea and eager to explore it.

Armed with the realization that seduction is a driving force in French life, I felt as if I had put on a special pair of 3-D glasses that made confusing shapes snap into sharp focus. It suddenly became clear that the French impulse to seduce applies to many features of French life. The tools of the seducer—anticipation, promise, allure—are powerful engines in French history and politics, culture and style, food and foreign policy, literature and manners. Like much else in France, the power and influence of seduction are profoundly centralized. Paris, the capital of France and home to French corporations, media, fashion designers, and intellectuals, is also the place where seduction and its hold on French life are most palpable. Wherever I go in the country, all roads seem to lead back to Paris, and in much the same way, the cultural imperative of seduction that is nurtured in Paris remains a potent force even in the grim suburbs and the distant countryside.

A key component of seduction—and French life—is process. The rude waiter, the dismissive sales clerk, the low-ranking bureaucrat who demands still another obscure document is playing a perverted version of a seduction game that glorifies lingering.

When I decided to explore the meaning of seduction *à la française* more systematically, as the French themselves might do, I began with words. I set up a Google alert for the words *séduire*, *séduction*, and *séduit* in the French media. I sometimes got as many as a dozen hits a day.

Then I did an analytical study of these alerts over a three-month period. My researcher and I found 636 occurrences of the words falling into nine categories. Some were predictable, like love/sex, fashion/style, and tourism; others were more unexpected, including the seductive powers of presidents, commerce, gastronomy, the arts, "anti-seduction" (people and items lacking in seductive techniques), and the military-sounding *opération séduction*. (In English, *opération séduction* becomes something tamer: "charm offensive.")

The two largest categories, with more than ninety articles apiece, were *opération séduction* and commerce (the selling of "seductive" items). These were closely followed by the arts (seduction of the general public), with eighty entries. The love/sex category had a meager thirty-four, tourism twenty-five, fashion fifteen. "Anti-seduction" tied with gastronomy at eleven. The presidents category was quite small, with Barack Obama accounting for ten and Nicolas Sarkozy with just two.

Seduction appeared to be omnipresent in the French consciousness. During a trip to Israel in May 2009, the pope was said to have "seduced the Palestinians" with his call for the creation of a Palestinian state. Museums wanted to "seduce" new visitors. Sarkozy's political strategy was to "seduce the young." The milk producers of northern France were not simply on strike; they were on a "seduction mission" to negotiate with milk processors and to explain to consumers why they were blocking trucks and collection points. The interior of the Citroën DS automobile was filled with the "spirit of seduction." The Iranian presidential candidate Mir-Hossein Mousavi "knew how to seduce in using all of the modern techniques" of politics. By far the most "seductive" selling items were computers and phones; when the sales of Dell laptops declined, it was because the company had "a hard time seducing."

The word is also deployed ironically, sometimes with dead-serious effect. The left-leaning newspaper *Libération* once ran a two-page article illustrated with a photo of a French soldier in full battle gear and pointing a large automatic weapon under the headline "Afghanistan: The French in Seduction Mode." I thought nothing would top that headline until another one popped up in the same newspaper about the mass execution of eight thousand Bosnians by Serbs in Srebrenica during the Balkan wars of the 1990s. It read, "Srebrenica: Serbia Offers Its Apologies to Seduce the EU."

As for *opération séduction*, it surfaced in the broadest range of topics—from golf to high schools, from agriculture to doctors, from the environment to business. One newspaper headline read, "*Opération séduction pour draguer les sédiments*" from polluted harbors. Literally, it means, "*Opération séduction* to extract sediments." The article opened with the sentence, "Not sexy, sediments?" It explained that the region was trying to sell its dredging and land treatment plan to the central government. But *draguer* also means "to flirt with," so the headline could be read as: "*Opération séduction* to flirt with sediments."

The word *séduction* no longer surprised. It overwhelmed.

I reached out to French writers and thinkers and quickly found that my new subject had special hazards—like the time I interviewed Pascal Bruckner, the philosopher and essayist who has written extensively about the disorderly state of relations between men and women. We were in the café of a grand Paris hotel, and the closeness of the encounter coupled with the word *séduction* created unexpected intimacy. I put on reading glasses and a serious look, clenched my knees together, rested my hands in my lap, and asked him about his daughter. I wanted to avoid the appearance of flirting. (I shouldn't have worried. I ran into him months later at a private film screening, and he didn't even recognize me.)

When I told French women about my investigations of seduction in their culture, they got it right away. And they joined in with complicity and lightness. When I described my project to French men, by contrast, there were two reactions. Some got a deer-in-the-headlights look, as if to say, "Get me away from this pathetic, crazed American woman of a certain age." Others jumped in with a bit too much enthusiasm.

One morning I uttered the words "seduction" and "France" to a museum curator as we were walking down a curving staircase. He stopped short, grabbed the banister, and leaned over me so excitedly that I had to step back. "Seduction—maybe it's chance!" he exclaimed. "You can find the man of your life, the woman of your life, in a restaurant, in a café. It starts by an innocent, stupid sentence. 'Can you pass me the salt?' 'Can you pass me the carafe of water?' And then, a look!"

Early in my research, I was dealt a cruel blow. I was informed that while I could try to play the game, I was destined to lose. The bearer of this grim message was a former president of France, not Chirac this time but one of his predecessors, Valéry Giscard d'Estaing.

Our meeting at his home on a quiet street in the sixteenth arrondissement of Paris was for the most part pleasant. He tried to establish common ground between us. He told me the story of his visit to my hometown of Buffalo, New York, when he was twenty-three. He had met "a nice, very sweet girl" on the *Queen Mary* crossing the Atlantic. She went to Vassar College and lived in Buffalo. She had become his girlfriend and at one point, he had visited her home. They had toured Niagara Falls. Giscard confessed his love for America. He said little about its inhabitants but professed an attraction to its vast open spaces. He even fantasized about buying a ranch someday in the Southwest.

That gave me the opening I was looking for. I knew I couldn't be so brazen as to ask a former president to explain France through the prism of seduction. So I took a more indirect route. Suppose he was having dinner on such a ranch with a group of Americans, and one of them posed the question, "Mr. President, could you explain to us how we can understand your country?"

Giscard is now in his eighties, and age has made him ever more certain that he possesses the truth. He resisted the temptation to play the game with me. "My answer is clear—you cannot," he said. "I have never met an American, never, who has really understood what drives French society."

France, he said, operates as "an extremely strange system, impenetrable from the outside, rather agreeable to live in, but totally different from anywhere else."

"The French do not practice hospitality at all," he went on. "No. They can be generous. They can say, 'There are Americans here. We have to do something. Let's invite them over.' But after one time, it's over. You've done your duty. The idea that an American is going to penetrate the system? No. Ours is an old, extraordinarily fragmented society, with thousands of small strata in which everyone is inferior to someone and superior to someone else. There can be reciprocal acceptance but not the desire to come together. The French want to stay in their cultural and educational milieu and certainly do not want to change."

I was *déstablisée*—shaken.

When I later told Charles Bremner, the veteran Paris correspondent for the *Times* of London, about the conversation, he urged me not to be discouraged. "Maybe the French aren't as perceptive about themselves as outsiders are," he said. "Seduction is so much a part of them that maybe they don't think about it. Like goldfish not knowing what water is like."

And so, I dared to venture on.

For centuries, the most perceptive experts on seduction in France have been its female courtesans. More important than their youth, beauty, and sexual performance have been their experience and maturity. Therefore, I sought advice from the two women I consider to be France's icons of the modern world of courtesans (without the sex part): Arielle Dombasle and Inès de la Fressange.

The women have a lot in common. They have Latin roots: La Fressange's mother is Argentinian; Dombasle lived in Mexico as a child. That has given them the air of outsiders who had to master the rules. Both are past fifty and have been performing for more than three decades. They move with the swiftness and fluidity of cats—Dombasle as an actress, singer, and dancer, La Fressange as the former supermodel for Chanel. Both are impossibly tall and thin, with bodies that long to be stared at. Both are smart businesswomen who understand the need to continue to market their allure and their beauty. They are professionals: aware of their power and how to use it. And they are national treasures: each has been awarded the Legion of Honor.

The main difference between them is the way each has chosen to promote her look. Dombasle seems to have been worked on and is always done up. Her allure comes from her resemblance to a gorgeous alien. La Fressange, a mother of two, often wears jeans and loafers, and she smokes. She has retained the innocent air of a much younger woman.

Over tea one afternoon, Dombasle compared seduction to a battlefield of communication. "Seduction is largely transmitted through words—what you say and when you keep quiet," she said. "That's the key. Voilà."

I had no idea what she meant. I asked her to explain. "You must choose your words carefully as you would in a war," she said, "The way you seduce depends on whether you want to win or you want to lose."

It could be a campaign to weaken your opponent by injecting an element of surprise, for example. "You could play against type to throw your adversary off balance," she said. "Seduction is not a frivolous thing. No. It's war."

I was encouraged. "I know war," I said. "I was a war correspondent. I don't understand seduction, but I understand war."

Dombasle and I had found common ground. She explained that this war is nonviolent. The woman warrior must avoid the sort of traumatic exposure that comes with vulnerability in front of the adversary. Dombasle has not hesitated to bare her breasts for a *Paris Match* cover or for a revue in front of hundreds of people at the Crazy Horse cabaret. But she insisted that nakedness is a vulnerability that must be used with care. Apparently, on the battlefield of the bed, the rules are different. "Nudity is extremely violent to gaze at," she said. "I would never walk naked in front of my husband. Never, never, never."

"So you're only nude in the shower?" I asked.

"I'm nude when I'm alone, and I'm nude when I'm in his arms, but never in a sort of casually stupid gesture of the morning or whatever. Never."

"So nudity is not something trivial?"

"Of course not. But we know that."

How do you know something like that? I wondered.

I told her how different it was in the United States, where many women feel liberated and sexy walking around the bedroom in the nude. I thought that perhaps her insistence on the value of concealment was an affectation of an aging sex symbol struggling to cling to her youth. A young French journalist from my office was with us, so I turned to her and asked, "If you were in a love relationship, and you were getting out of bed to go into the bathroom, you would not be totally nude?"

"No," she replied. "It's not only prudishness. It's just, you know . . ."

I too should never be nude in front of my husband, Dombasle advised. "You shouldn't," she said. "Otherwise, he won't buy you lunch."

She had now warmed to the subject. "The relationship to nudity, the relationship to love, the relationship to men, the relationship to women—all this carries great complexity and great danger," she said. "I have felt my whole life that it is extremely positive to engage in combat and rule over one's own life."

Her advice about my work was similar: I should be a modern-day courtesan who makes full use of the weapons of my profession. "You are a serious journalist, truly a journalist who represents strength after the liberation of women," she said. "You have succeeded with weighty work about politics and diplomacy, with solid things. So now it will be very interesting for you to reveal that there is another woman inside of you, who was born once you came into contact with France."

But I have never been one of those women who dreams of taking a dizzying carousel ride of passion and learning colloquial French with the help of mysterious Gallic men. I love to read those fictional and real-life romantic confections about leaving a job and a bad relationship behind in the United States and discovering good sex and even better coffee with an experienced, long-waisted, velvet-voiced, poetry-spouting French man. That doesn't mean I can do it.

Dombasle was simply too sexy for me. So I turned to Inès de la Fressange. I had first met her when she was a fresh-faced yet flirtatious runway model and I was covering the Paris fashion shows for *Newsweek*. Even then La Fressange was not just any ordinary fashion model. She was the daughter of a French marquis and off-the-charts wealthy.

Thirty years later, in a 2009 Internet poll, she was voted "La Parisienne," the quintessential Parisian woman. It's hard not to be attracted to a woman with the long limbs of a runner, the raspy voice of a cabaret singer, the impish look of a coquette, the sense of humor of a stand-up comic, the smile of Audrey Hepburn.

La Fressange told me my subject was so vast and so serious that I needed firsthand experience. "You have to be conscientious," she said. "You can't talk about seduction, fashion, politics, beauty without a French lover. Yes, yes! For the final touch!"

"But I'm in love with my husband and I have kids," I protested.

"Even better—an American woman in Paris who doesn't want to get married and have kids and is sure to leave France!" she replied.

I told her I had no need to find a French lover; back in the 1970s, I had briefly had a French boyfriend, whose family owned a château with horses and servants.

That was beside the point, she said. "It's all about attitude," she said. "If you decide to be like a nun in Paris, who does American-style journalism with all the information, all the statistics, well, that will be interesting. But there will be no romance."

To get off to the right start, she said, I needed to invest in a new haircut, new clothes, and a visit to a Turkish bath to "feel some pleasure." Then she said, "You go to the terrace of a café. You say to yourself, 'Voilà, something is going to happen.' And you'll see. Something will happen."

I thought about the scene in the film *Clair de femme* when Yves Montand literally bumps into Romy Schneider as he gets out of a taxi, and then they sit together at a café. A bit later, he's in her bed.

"You have to stroll the streets of Paris at night with your lover, go to Montmartre, walk along the Seine, eat soup in a bistro," she said. "Then you go to Deauville and walk along the sea and eat shrimps until four a.m. And when your husband calls you, you say, 'But, no! You're just imagining you hear the sound of waves in the background.' "

She insisted that all would be fine as long as the affair remained secret. "Tell him absolutely nothing. There's no reason to make him miserable. You have your foundation as a couple, a history, a marriage. You've built something you can be proud of, and this tiny romance in

Paris is not going to disrupt it. Write about it in a way that the reader can feel things but not know them."

Eventually, we compromised: I could take a virtual lover, a French man who would be my soul mate but only playact with me. "It doesn't have to be torrid and frenetic," she said.

Then came the coup de grâce. Because of my age, she said, I had no time to waste. "It's your last chance!" she told me. "Pretty soon, you'll be thinking only about your cats, your dogs, your knitting, and your garden. Your arthritis will make it hard to take long walks at night."

The next morning, at breakfast with my husband, Andy, I started making a list of possible candidates: my downstairs neighbor, a white-haired, retired business executive who wears perfectly knotted cashmere scarves and elegant tweed sport coats, even when he rides his bicycle to the supermarket; a writer and radio talk show host who is very smart and safely gay; a famous stage and film actor who I feared might take the role too seriously; a colleague who said he would be happy to help, but alas, he is British; a former diplomat with a passion for nineteenth-century paintings whom I ruled out as dangerous because his wife lives in a foreign country. I asked Andy for his advice. He took a break from his Special K and put on his glasses. "I somehow don't think you're supposed to be telling me about this," he said.

Now that I was concentrating on seduction, I began to see it in places where I had never noticed it before. Making coffee one morning, I looked at the Carte Noire coffee bag and saw that it described itself as "A Coffee Named Desire."

Andy found nothing surprising in it. "Chock Full o'Nuts called itself 'the heavenly coffee,' " he said drily.

"Heaven means celestial and pure and virginal," I replied. "Desire is carnal."

Seduction was like a neon light that never stopped blinking. On a road from Paris to Compiègne, there was an oblong, one-story prefabricated building with a small sign that read, "Auto Séduction." I assumed the enterprise was some sort of kinky private club for personal sexual satisfaction. No, it was a garage for car repairs. Its website explained that it had "only one objective: your satisfaction." I called Sylvain Chidiac, the garage owner, who said he had intended nothing suggestive in choosing the name of his company. He had initially wanted to call it Auto Prestige, but that name was already taken. "Auto Seduction," he explained, "just imposed itself naturally in my mind."

Even the French style of conducting elections in two rounds rather than one could be seen as an exercise in seduction. French voters are said to vote their hearts in the first round and their beliefs in the runoff. The final competitors must attract a fraction of the opponents' voters without losing their own. "Seducing to reduce," is how the magazine *Valeurs Actuelles* defined the phenomenon.

I found seduction in France's idea of itself, and the connection is an old one. The characters in Jean de La Fontaine's *Fables*, the seventeenth-century morality tales taught in French schools, often demonstrate the supremacy of cunning over force. The French believe that their country (about the size of Texas) is able to project power around the world not because of brute force or military might or a robust economy but because of its imagined mythical power, its ability to lure others to want to be like France.

France is also a nuclear power with a colonial past and troops deployed in far-off places like Afghanistan and the Ivory Coast. Its philosophy as a colonizer was not manifest destiny but a *mission civilisatrice*—France's civilizing mission. Unlike British colonialists, who also talked of "civilizing" far-flung lands but habitually regarded their subjects as "the other," the French claimed their mission was assimilation. They taught their subjects that by adopting the French language, culture, and value system, they eventually could become perfect—that is, French themselves (as if those factors could truly determine nationality).

In foreign policy, France is a global case study in "soft power," the ability to influence others through "attraction" rather than "coercion." The term was coined by an American, Joseph Nye of Harvard University, but the concept is very French. In an interview with Nye that was translated into French, the concept of "attraction" under his soft power formula was rendered as *séduction*.

• • •

Jacques Chirac's *baisemain* became emblematic of what I needed to understand about the French. No French person to whom I told the story thought I should be offended; everyone expressed amusement. The writer Mona Ozouf described it as "a slightly theatrical gesture with a touch of irony." Sophie-Caroline de Margerie, a jurist on the Conseil d'État, the highest administrative court in France, and an author herself, explained that the Polish aristocracy did it much more sensually. She took my hand but only half-showed me. Perhaps the kiss itself would have been too intimate for her.

But not for Maurice Lévy, the chairman of the French advertising giant Publicis. He gave me the definitive lesson in hand kissing.

Lévy is tall and strongly built and gives off an air of calm and nonchalance. He greeted me in his headquarters on the Champs-Élysées, in a reception area bathed in white. I prodded him into speaking a few sentences in English. I had been told that he carefully preserves his strong French accent and then apologizes for it, part of what his aides call his "French touch." He doesn't do hard sell. When he wants to make a point, he slowly closes his eyes, parts his lips, and leans back in his chair. But his greeting—a big, hard handshake and a command to get down to business—underscores what others had told me about him. Deep down he is a killer businessman, a cunning predator who built Publicis into the world's fourth-largest advertising and public relations empire.

He had been well briefed on my book project and my interest in the themes of seduction and sensuality in French life. The intermediary who had arranged the interview must have told him about my fascination with hand kissing, because Lévy suddenly shifted the subject from the globalization of the advertising market to focus on my right hand. "You have evoked the *baisemain*," he said, even though it was he, not I, who had raised the subject. He told me that a man's lips should never *effleurer* the hand. *Effleurer* is hard to translate. It means "to skim" or "to brush lightly." The sound and spelling of the word is similar to the French word for "flower," *fleur*. That led me to think, the first time Lévy said it, that it might have something to do with the petals of a flower, a sort of delicate act involving a touch of something fragile.

"You must not *effleurer* the hand! You must not!" he said. "When you *effleurez* the hand, you are sending a special message."

He stood up and ordered me to stand as well.

"The real *baisemain*, it's like this," he said, as he bent down from the waist, took my hand, and came within a hair of touching his lips to my skin. There was a barely perceptible squeezing of my hand before he returned it to me. "I must not touch, but you should feel that I am close enough."

"If I do it this way," he said, drawing back, "I am too far. I must do it close enough. You must almost feel my breath."

I was getting nervous that one of his army of assistants would walk in and find us in midkiss.

Then his second kiss came. He pressed his lips gently to my hand. He defined that kiss as *affectif*—with emotion. "There, this is someone I like quite well, with whom I have a good relationship, and she knows it," he said. "There we go."

"And the last," he said, "it's to *effleurer*. I do it like this."

So we were going to *effleurer* after all.

His lips opened slightly and moved up and down, teasing my hand. The kiss could not have lasted more than two seconds. I felt the warmth of his breath and a slight tickling, as if I were being touched by a butterfly's wings. I marveled at the mastery of the simultaneous double movement of opening and closing and up and down. The memory of the gesture lingered like the scent of an exotic perfume.

"In this one, I try to say that you please me," he explained. "And if I brush my lips lightly, it means—"

I interrupted: "I might have intentions that are more complex and mysterious—"

"No, no, no, no, no, no," he replied. "It means, 'Will you sleep with me tonight?'"

"Ah. More direct!" I said.

"No, wait. It's not more direct," he said. "It simply means—it's the final goal."

I was at a loss for words. How do you respond to the chairman of one of the largest corporations in the world who has just shown you how a French man, without saying a word, can ask a woman to sleep with him?

So I changed the subject to Jacques Chirac. "Okay, but I have a fourth *baisemain*," I said. I told Lévy I had been at an event hosted by Chirac that week and saw how he had greeted a dear friend, the former minister Simone Veil. Chirac had stretched out his arms and extended his hands three times as if he were rushing out from the wings onto center stage in a Broadway musical. Then he had grabbed Veil's hand and smacked it. Loudly.

"And maybe that's the *baisemain Chiraquien*?" I asked.

"No," Lévy replied. "When I see Simone, who is a friend, this is the way I do it. Come—ah—So, here."

And Lévy planted a big loud kiss on my hand. "Really *affectif*," he said.

2

The Seductive Country

. . .

> History, this great seductress, proves every day to the French people that France quite rightly holds the monopoly of reason and civilization.
>
> —Friedrich Sieburg, *Dieu est-il français?* (Is God French?) (1930)

> I have a deep instinctive awareness of France, of physical France, and a passion for her geography, her living body.
>
> —François Mitterrand, 1977

One morning in the 1990s, Alain Baraton, the chief gardener at Versailles, was making his rounds of the vast palace grounds when he came upon a young Japanese tourist. Her beauty was so absolute that it took his breath away. She was distraught: it was Monday and Versailles was closed. Baraton, who lives in a small house on the grounds, expressed regrets and moved on.

Then, in the afternoon, he saw her again, this time wandering in a garden. He discovered that she spoke French. With the keys to the château in his pocket, he offered to unlock the doors for her. "We were all alone," he told me as we toured the gardens one morning. "I showed her the Galerie des Glaces. I showed her the bedrooms of the king and of Marie Antoinette."

He took her into the Petit Trianon, the neoclassical mini-château built by Louis XV and intended for his favorite mistress, Madame de Pompadour. She already owned a big house in Paris: the current Élysée

Palace. Decades later, Louis XVI would give the Petit Trianon to his teenage bride, Marie Antoinette, as a wedding present. "This pleasure house is yours," the young king is said to have told his queen. At that point during Baraton's tour for his unexpected guest, champagne in the gardens seemed to follow naturally.

"If you want to seduce a woman at a swimming pool, it's best if you know how to swim," he told me as he recounted the story. "If you want to seduce a woman at a nightclub, you should know how to dance. At a ski resort, you should know how to ski. But I, I have Versailles! And to drink champagne in the Versailles gardens with no one else around late in the afternoon, she was conquered!"

Baraton took her to his house and cooked dinner. And sometime after midnight, he invited her to stay the night rather than head back to her hotel. He made up a bed for her in the second bedroom.

"At that moment," he recalled, "perhaps this woman said to herself, 'I came to Versailles. I am sleeping at Versailles. And now, this man who has invited me is rather nice.' Maybe she said to herself, 'If I can make love at Versailles as well, well, this doesn't happen every day!' "

And so, she stayed.

I didn't ask him what happened next. He didn't say.

He didn't have to. Versailles is France's national monument—to love and to power. It bears witness to an era when a goal of royal life was pleasure, and it serves as the centerpiece for the national romance that the French have with their history.

Baraton has written a book laced with stories of modern lovemaking at Versailles, in which most of the couples are French. But it makes perfect sense that in his favorite personal anecdote, his conquest is a foreigner.

It is easy to imagine her position—awed by the grand château and an atmosphere that seems to cry out, "Pleasure is here for the taking. Enjoy it." For centuries, foreigners have heard this message as France's siren song.

Modern travelers come to France seeking to be seduced by graceful surroundings, excellent food and wine, beautiful objects on display, stylish people to watch on the street and in the cafés. The fantasies of the visitors may not extend to the high of a romantic or sexual adventure, but almost universally, they expect to experience a sexy country. That is fine with the French, who expect to live in one. France's status as the most visited country in the world and its aura of glamour and allure are international clichés. What visitors may not understand so well is that the French love to be seduced as much as they love to play the seducer. So they too have a stake in being charmed by their country.

The French did not introduce sex to the Western world, and they did not invent sexual seduction. But France was the first European country to create a culture of love in the Middle Ages. Marriage had little to do with love, and the sex act was considered brutal and vulgar. Among the nobility, the ideal of courtly love was created and expressed in poetry. The man declared himself a vassal to the lady, who was by definition rich, powerful, beautiful, of a higher status, seemingly indifferent to his charms, and usually married to someone else. Lust was sublimated to romance, and complex rituals, ceremonies, and entreaties were used, even in pursuit of such modest outcomes as the touching of her hand. As the French perfected other arts of enjoyment and sensuality, seduction evolved into a high art.

The word *séduire* derives from the Latin *seducere*, which means "to lead astray." First used in the Middle Ages, it had a deeply religious and moralistic cast. Seduction was branded as "trickery, engagement in error, or in sin." An early French dictionary defined *séduire*: "To abuse someone, persuade one to do evil, or indoctrinate a spirit with evil beliefs. The wife of Adam said to the Lord, as an excuse, that the Serpent had seduced her." But in time the meaning changed, as seduction became linked to the pain and ecstasy of romantic love.

In the seventeenth century, the moral ground shifted again. The culture of the court of Louis XIV at Versailles ushered in a new era of freethinking. The pursuit of pleasure for its own sake was accepted and even encouraged. The nonchalant, unrestrained libertine who engaged in pleasurable sex appeared on the scene. Seduction became a campaign—often a game—to overpower the will of the other.

It was even codified, on a map. To illustrate her novel *Clélie* published in 1654, Mademoiselle de Scudéry drew the Carte de Tendre, a map of an imaginary country called Tendre, an allegory for the stages of love. The Bibliothèque Nationale in Paris has a leather-bound first edition, including a hand-colored version of the *carte*. Jean-Marc Chatelain, the curator of seventeenth-century books, offered to show it to me. He unwrapped a large brown baize cloth to reveal a leather-bound volume with gold-leaf trim. Close to the book's end was an insert. It unfolded into a twelve-by-nine-inch map, with a gentle river called Inclination, a Lake of Indifference, a Dangerous Sea representing passion, and peaceful villages with names like Pretty-verse and Love-letter. The map is still alive in French culture today: A few years back the lingerie maker Princesse tam.tam used it as the pattern on women's pajamas. It reappears regularly in French books on sex and romance.

By the late eighteenth century, seduction became a virtuous skill, an invitation to erotic playfulness and political strategizing. In other words, the French managed to transform seduction from a force for evil into a force for good. Seduce me with a delicious meal and a glass of excellent wine, a promise of romance, an intoxicating scent, and a lively game of words. Have you done me harm, or have you led me to a place where I find freedom to enjoy and savor the best life has to offer? And if in the process you also serve your own purposes, isn't it—as long as I understand the transaction—a fair trade?

Many foreigners have thought so, from the Romans who came to conquer but stayed and planted vineyards and made good wine, to twentieth-century expatriate writers and artists lured by sexual and intellectual freedoms.

Certainly President Barack Obama looked at France as a destination for pleasure seeking. During his visit to France in 2009 to commemorate the anniversary of the Normandy landings, he did no touring and declined an invitation to dine at the Élysée Palace with President Sarkozy and his wife, Carla Bruni. Asked at a news conference why he was spending so little time in Europe, Obama said he was too busy to enjoy himself.

"I would love nothing more than to have a leisurely week in Paris, stroll down the Seine, take my wife out to a nice meal, have a picnic in the

Luxembourg Gardens," he said. "Those days are over, for the moment.... At some point, I will be the ex-president, and then you will find me in France, I'm sure, quite a bit, having fun."

The French themselves take the permission for enjoyment and play as a basic right. This does not mean they live in the moment. On the contrary, they manipulate the moment, planning ahead for pleasure and seduction with a well-laid dinner table or plan of romantic attack. And they like to be prepared for unplanned opportunities as well, confronting the world armed with attractive dress, careful manners, and practiced conversational skills.

Leisure time is a right guaranteed in French culture. The preamble of the 1946 Constitution, which is recognized in the 1958 Constitution of the Fifth Republic, guarantees "to all, notably to children, mothers and elderly workers, protection of their health, material security, rest and leisure." In our own time, the French resist initiatives to raise the retirement age or add hours to their thirty-five-hour workweek. Most businesses and shops are banned from opening on Sundays. Poll after poll shows that the French prefer more time off to higher wages.

The pleasure principle is clearly visible in French medicine. Medical insurance doesn't come cheap here; workers and employers pay for it through direct contributions and steep taxes. But coverage can entitle you to all sorts of medical pleasures.

I found one example in Évian-les-Bains, the Alpine haven of 7,500 people on Lake Geneva, whose natural spring is world-renowned. In 1926, the French government declared the source of Évian's spring in the mountains to be in the "public interest," and its purity is now protected by a nature preserve twelve miles in diameter. In the center of town stands a small pavilion partly hidden under a balcony, where a red marble fountain with a brass spigot spews Évian mineral water at a constant temperature of fifty-three degrees, a free public amenity required by law.

At a state-subsidized curative spa in Évian, I met Pierre Lewandoski, a car mechanic from Arras in northern France. Dressed in tiny, skin-tight swim trunks in shades of ocean blue, he lay still in a deep tub in a small treatment room. Évian mineral water, heated to ninety-five degrees, bubbled and swirled, gently massaging his soft, middle-aged body. He seemed eager to explain what he was doing in a bathtub five hundred miles from home.

"I'm here on doctor's orders, for rheumatism in my neck," he said. "I have no idea if this is going to work." But French social security was paying 65 percent and his boss approved a paid leave, so there he was. The spa and health club overlooking the lake is not ashamed of what it is doing at taxpayer expense. On the contrary, its brochure boasts eighteen-day "thermal cures" to treat ailments like urinary tract infection, irritable colon, arterial hypertension, gout, postfracture trauma, and tendonitis. Clients can swim in an exercise pool filled with Évian water (lightly chlorinated) or take a twelve-jet shower with hot and cold Évian.

Years later, I longed to go to Évian after I slipped and fell on the avenue Montaigne, one of Paris's poshest streets. The sidewalk had just been polished to look prettier. I found myself on crutches but with a prescription for massage therapy. For months, Jean-François, the physical therapist, made house calls three times a week. The French health care system paid for most of it.

A vital part of living in this seductive country is France's romantic history. The French are at once stuck in their past and charmed by their national stories and myths. There is a perpetual fascination with the Old Regime, and the kings and queens of France regularly grace the covers of magazines. Few seem troubled that a permanent obsession with monarchy coexists so easily with the ideals of the Republic.

The romantic story line of French history goes like this: First there were the Gauls, who were vanquished by the Romans and then conquered their occupiers with the force of their artistry and sophistication. The two cultures intertwined as many Gauls became Roman citizens and Rome looked to Gaul for silver, glass, pottery, food, and wine. Then came the medieval era, with its troubadours and the twelfth century's star-crossed lovers, Abélard and Héloïse. Later, literature and art began to focus on the romantic and sexual intrigues of the royal family. At last came the Revolution and the French Republic, born and reborn in heroic resistance and gallant marches to the barricades.

The stories don't have to be faithful to reality. History may weigh on the French like a guilty conscience, but not enough to force an exploration of its darkest corners. The extent of French collaboration with the Nazi occupiers in World War II was revealed not by a French historian but by an American scholar, Robert Paxton of Columbia University. An example of France's amnesia is a plaque affixed to the wall of the Hotel Lutetia, an Art Deco landmark on the Left Bank in Paris. It identifies the hotel as the reception center for returning deportees and prisoners of war in 1945; it says nothing about its sinister role between 1940 and 1944 as the Paris headquarters of the German Army's intelligence operations during the Occupation.

This airbrushed version of history provides the French with protective shelter. The past is both celebrated and continually reinvented and improved. No anniversary is too minor to celebrate. In recent years, France has marked the 200th anniversary of the high school baccalaureate diploma, the 60th anniversary of the bikini, the 100th anniversary of the brassiere, the 150th anniversary of the twenty arrondissements of Paris. When Dim, the hosiery maker, celebrated its 50th anniversary as a period of "freedom for women," *Le Monde* ran an article illustrated with photographs of the legs of three women, their skirts flying up à la Marilyn Monroe in *The Seven Year Itch*.

The affection for a certain version of the past helps explain why so many French citizens with ethnic Arab and African roots feel alienated from the country's history. They don't relate to the romantic story line, and they don't even feel French. They remain a people apart in the present, facing discrimination and treated like outsiders on many levels. It also explains why the French government in late 2009 felt compelled to launch debates in cities and towns throughout France on the country's "national identity." The French are taught a particular view of history, one that celebrates not diversity but an idealized secular republic that is color-blind and ethnically indifferent; this vision is considered essential to the French sense of identity.

Because the past is romantic and can be viewed through the lens of pleasure rather than power, women play key roles in its retelling. For Alain Baraton, the Versailles gardener, French history has been driven by romance, seduction, sex, and love. "Ours is a country that built itself on love stories," he said. "But for many historians the idea that sex has decided everything is unbearable. There always has been a refusal to accept that women and seduction might have transformed the French political landscape. And yet they have."

At the top of the list of these transformative women is Marie Antoinette, the last queen of the Old Regime. During her lifetime, she was portrayed as spoiled, wasteful, promiscuous, and immature. But of all the royals, she is the one who most inflames the imagination of present-day France.

If I were a Marie Antoinette fan, I could join the Marie Antoinette Association; eat macaroons from a Marie Antoinette "collection" made by the Paris confectioner Ladurée; splash on the perfume created by Francis Kurkdjian in her honor; wear Lalique crystal earrings and a pendant inspired by one of her portraits; eat from copies of her royal dishes made by the Raynaud porcelain house; buy a Marie Antoinette Barbie doll; and cut with a limited edition jackknife made of wood from Versailles's fallen trees and engraved with the initials MA.

It was front-page news when Versailles broke with precedent and allowed the American director Sofia Coppola to rent its premises for her $40 million film *Marie Antoinette*. When the film was released in France in 2006, the newspaper *Le Figaro* published a special 112-page glossy magazine on the queen's life as "princess, icon, rebel." The women's magazine *Atmosphères* examined her "secrets." The weekly *Le Point* put her portrait on a cover with the caption, "Misunderstood, decapitated, Marie Antoinette, the remorse of the French."

France's national obsession with a glittering past weighs most heavily at Versailles. Outsiders tend to approach the château as a historical monument, a collection of stones, paintings, mirrors, objects, gardens, but for the French, its power derives from both reality and myth. The authority of the actors and actions that have marked Versailles over the centuries makes it a permanent celebration of the past. Versailles is a never-aging center of power (the monarchy), beauty (the aesthetics, the architecture), and sexuality (the wives, the mistresses). It is a symbol of France as a glorious nation, and the French state has spent vast sums to restore it. "Versailles deserves it, so let's not haggle over restoring its grandeur," Charles de Gaulle said in justifying costly renovations in the 1960s. During his presidency, a wing of the Grand Trianon was reserved for the president's use. When President Sarkozy decided to break with tradition and address France's Parliament in 2009, he did so not at the Élysée Palace or the National Assembly or the Senate but at Versailles. America doesn't have anything that comes close to it.

The gardener Alain Baraton has written a number of books on Versailles, including his most recent one on love at the château. He is a moderately attractive man in his fifties, with a slightly rounded belly. He wears pointy shoes, chain-smokes, and stares at beautiful women. We talked about his book, which is chock-full of stories about sex at Versailles: the famous actress who loved to visit there to expose herself; the older politician who had sex in the garden with a young woman whom he had tied to a tree; the elderly couple who complained when one of Baraton's gardeners fell from a tree, landing on them as they were in the throes of lovemaking.

"I think I lack imagination," I told him. "I can't believe that people make love in the gardens of Versailles."

"Of course!" he replied. "It's one thing if you have a discussion around a table in a café at Versailles as we are doing now. It's another thing if two people are sitting on a marble bench in the park as dusk falls with the sculptures and the fountains perfectly aligned. When there are no more disruptions, no more street noise, no more light and aggression, when you feel secure with someone who understands you and who only wants one thing in the end: to spend the evening with you and to give you pleasure.

"You might not say yes right away, but there will be hesitation because the site becomes enchanting! I'm not saying you are going to crack. I'm not saying you're going to accept. I'm just saying that at a given moment, you yourself risk being swept up in this dynamic and saying to yourself,

'If I begin to put up a barrier, I risk depriving myself of this magical moment.'"

Baraton explained the different ways Versailles can be used to seduce visitors. It becomes a multifaceted creature that can adapt, providing various possibilities, playing with its attributes. For men of power and money, Baraton shows the grounds from the kingly, manly perspective, with the château, the formal gardens, and the statuary straight ahead. For passionate gardeners and environmentalists, he goes to Marie Antoinette's "domain" surrounding the Petit Trianon with its gazebos, bridges, benches, hidden pathways, and luscious informal English garden with dandelions and wild roses. Her estate does double duty as a place to take a potential lover. An artificial grotto, where she held private encounters on a curved bench cut into stone, is constructed with two doors to better allow discreet entrances and exits. "Look on your right," Baraton commanded, as we drove along the pathways. "There is even the Temple of Love! When you have a temple devoted to the glory of love, it's not innocent. There are many structures here to let you isolate yourself, to talk, to reflect. There are small rivers. There are lakes, animals, birds. It's a place of seduction. Do you believe now that one single man needs such a big garden only for himself? No he doesn't. If you built so much, it's in order to seduce, to show your strength, your power."

The Petit Trianon itself and its surrounding fields and gardens work best. Baraton explained how. We drove through a set of iron gates along a winding dirt road, past fountains and elaborate flower beds and through another gate. He parked his car in front of a small château, the Pavillon Français. He introduced me to the caretaker, whom he referred to as "the king's first valet." The caretaker's lips curled up ever so slightly, a signal, perhaps, that he had heard it all before.

Baraton continued to spin his tale. "Let's say there are only the two of us. I'm Louis XV, and you're a young lady from a good background. And then, at some point it starts raining," he said. He led me into a small room with enormous gilt-framed mirrors and urged me to let go, to use my imagination to relive history. "You can see yourself in the mirrors with the king!" he said. He pointed out the moldings with their farm animals, musical instruments, and arrows of love. "Those are not war symbols!" he said.

"Now imagine, you're with Louis XV. You find yourself here. He has arranged for chocolates and tea to be set up. There's a fire in the fireplace. You must admit the temptation is here! I may be wrong, but the king is pleasant; the place is wonderful. Voilà! You see, this a place built for seduction. It's not a place built for power. It's not a place built for friends."

I asked him whether there are strategies to protect oneself from seduction. Apparently, it's not easily done. There is only one way.

"You must get away!" he said. "Flee!"

Seduction, he added, is a game. "It's danger. It's charm. It's conviction. And then, don't forget one thing: this is the essence of life! It's the motor."

"So you truly believe seduction is the motor driving society?"

"Of course it is," Baraton replied. "Driving everything. You can live only to seduce. I'm convinced of it."

The sex-charged nature of Versailles has been undermined in recent years by natural and man-made developments. Fierce wind storms in 1999 felled trees and destroyed landscaping, and, despite replanting, the gardens have been deprived of many of their hidden spaces. Cell phones and cameras have driven off exhibitionists. And technology has transformed the quest for companionship.

As Baraton said, "I have lived through a time when a very beautiful woman would walk in the gardens in the afternoon, would stop at a bench, and after half an hour a very elegant man would come sit down next to her, and they would start with, 'This place is really nice. Do you often come here?' and that was it! Nowadays, I'm afraid the same guy is on the Internet at night, starting with, 'I want her tall, blond or brunette.' The art of courting has changed, completely."

France has always been a woman. When Clovis, the first king of the Franks, was baptized at the end of the fifth century, France won the title "eldest daughter of the Church." Despite the strict separation of church and state, the late Pope John Paul II reminded the French of that status during his papacy, and France's two most recent presidents, Jacques

Chirac and Nicolas Sarkozy, used the phrase during their respective visits to the Vatican in 1996 and 2007.

In sculptures, paintings, engravings, medals, and coins dating from the Renaissance, the French nation has been portrayed as female and draped in the robes of antiquity. She has been depicted as a nurturing protector and as a loving mother surrounded by children.

Today, a fantasy woman is France's national symbol. She is Marianne, the personification of the French Republic and the idealized embodiment of freedom. She was a daring choice, not so much because she was feminine and often portrayed as sexually appealing but because she was a commoner. Some even called her vulgar. In the eighteenth century, the name "Marie-Anne" was one of the most popular in France and often found in the lower social classes. According to the American historian Paul R. Hanson, "To call the Republic Marianne was to characterize it as little better than a peasant, or more derisively, as a common whore." But she was adopted with pride by the republicans, and since then Marianne is the closest thing France has to Uncle Sam, if Uncle Sam had breasts.

The most recognizable Marianne is that of Eugène Delacroix's 1830 painting *Liberty Leading the People*. Barefoot, with muscular arms, she leads the rabble over the barricades, a bayoneted rifle in one hand, the revolutionary tricolor flag in the other, her bonnet firmly on her head. She does not seem to notice that the bodice of her dress has fallen to her waist. In the years since, Marianne has been reenvisioned in the image of France's most beautiful actresses and fashion models.

A far more important female figure in French history is the fifteenth-century teenage virgin-warrior Joan of Arc, who is memorialized throughout the country. Almost every city and town is graced with a statue or painting of Joan, almost every church and cathedral has a stained glass window or plaque. Thousands of novels, plays, biographies, films, songs, even operas and video games have told her story. Her image has been used on labels for mineral water, liqueurs, and cheese. A navy officer training ship was named after her. She is France's national hero.

Physically strong, psychologically independent, Joan vowed to stay sexually pure because she took her orders from God. Though she was an illiterate girl from the country, she was intelligent enough to convince her parents that she was hearing voices from heaven. She left home and made her way to the side of the dauphin, fighting to restore his kingdom. Using some unknown power of persuasion, she sweet-talked him into giving her money, horses, weapons, and soldiers so that she could rid France of its English invaders.

She led the siege against the English at Orléans and paved the way for the dauphin to be crowned King Charles VII at Reims. Then she was captured, sold to the English, tried for witchcraft and heresy for communicating with God directly instead of via the church, and burned at the stake in Rouen in 1431 at the age of nineteen. Asked during the trial why she was commanding an army rather than keeping to "other womanly duties" like raising children, she said, "There are enough other women to do those things."

Because so little is known about Joan's life, she has become one of the most myth-generating true-life characters in French history. A virgin, she is pure. A warrior, she is fearless. A free spirit, she is liberated. A military commander, she is a leader. A patriot, she is the incarnation of France. There is pleasure, amusement, and passion in the way the French debate details about Joan's story.

Jules Michelet, the great nineteenth-century historian, argued that Joan was responsible for the country's transformation into a woman worthy of love. Because of her heroism and sacrifice, he wrote, "for the first time, one feels, France is loved like a person. . . . Until then, it was a coming together of provinces, a vast chaos of fiefs, grand landscapes, a vague idea. But from that day on, by the force of the heart, she has been a *patrie* . . . this ravishing image of *la patrie*. . . . Remember always, Frenchmen, that *la patrie* is born from the heart of a woman, from her tenderness and her tears, from the blood she has shed for us."

France has not consistently embraced her. The kings tended to ignore her. Voltaire mocked her as an "unfortunate idiot." But French soldiers in World War I prayed to her, and the Vatican made her a saint in 1920. In World War II, the Germans and the Vichy regime used her as a martyr of national unity who had confronted the English invaders; the anti-Nazis saw her as a symbol of opposition to the Occupation.

Many in contemporary France view Joan with distaste because of her identification with right-wing extremism. Since the 1980s, she has been the icon of the far-right National Front party, which celebrates her every year as the personification of Gallic purity in the face of invading immigrants. For others, she is a well-worn cliché. Yet, stripped of centuries of overlay, Joan's story is enduringly romantic, even when she herself was far from the typical image of the romantic heroine.

Joan was neither feminine nor sexy. There didn't seem to be anything subtle or playful about her. In French art, she has been cast as a simply dressed shepherdess with long braids, a flat-chested tomboy, a warrior-goddess on horseback brandishing a sword and carrying the emblem of France. A nineteenth-century engraving by Fortuné Méaulle of a full-figured Joan tied to the stake in a flowing white dress with a plunging neckline robs her of beauty: her hair has been cut off. According to Colette Beaune, a medieval historian and Joan's most recent biographer, she ate and drank little, was anorexic, never menstruated, hated physical contact, and was terrified of being raped. Beaune noted the speculation that Joan was a lesbian, but she gave no credence to those claims.

I asked François Demachy, the creative perfumer at Dior, what scent he would invent to evoke the spirit of Joan of Arc. His answer was schizophrenic. "There would be a metallic note, because she is in armor in most of the images we have of her," he said. "But there would need to be something very flowery because she was a virgin."

I then turned to Jacques Séguéla, one of the impresarios of French advertising. He is the man who introduced Nicolas Sarkozy and Carla Bruni at a dinner party at his home in 2007 and who helped catapult François Mitterrand to the presidency in 1981 with a catchy slogan and advice about changing his wardrobe, haircut, and teeth.

Even Séguéla couldn't make Joan physically seductive. But he gave it a good try. I told him to imagine that I was his client and that I wanted to use the image of Joan of Arc to get consumers to buy my new product. What would be the ideal product and what would be the pitch?

He laid out his answer as if it were a mathematical formula. When you use a star to advertise a product, he said, the star must match up with the product's selling points. Marilyn Monroe and Brigitte Bardot equal sex, John Wayne the classic American hero, Catherine Deneuve the ideal Parisian woman. "We have to find the product that shares the same qualities as the star who promotes it," he said. "What are the qualities of Joan of Arc? One is purity, but there is also sacrifice and a kind of invulnerability. The only way to get her to disappear is to burn her at the stake. So, I would use her to launch an electric car."

"C'est pas vrai!"—"Not true!"—I said.

"Why an electric car?" Séguéla continued. "Because people are afraid of electric cars. They are afraid that they are not solid, that they are too light. Now, in her armor, Joan is solidity itself."

"And then," he continued, "the electric car has purity! It has zero CO_2, it has zero emissions, zero waste of energy, zero gasoline. So I have the purity and the solidity of Joan of Arc. And then, the electric car, it's a revolt against the normal car! So I can explain this revolt. And then finally, the electric car, it's young. And Joan of Arc is young."

He could sense my skepticism. In the next breath, he acknowledged, "So, you will say to me, 'But Joan of Arc was burned at the stake.' Well, the ideal myth does not exist! Even God isn't an ideal myth. So, we could come up with a different product!"

With that, he smiled. It was the smile of a man who had used the same lines a thousand times before and was confident that they would continue to work.

Before I let the subject of Joan drop, I went to Orléans one May, during the weeklong annual celebration of her victory over the English.

Dozens of groups in costume representing all corners of France (even its territories in the Caribbean and the Indian Ocean) sang, danced, and marched their way through the streets. Brass bands competed with church bells and bagpipes. A sound-and-light show projected photographic images of Joan's victory onto the facade of the cathedral. The bronze statue of Joan on horseback, her face looking upward to heaven, her strong body encased in armor, was ringed with baskets of flowers. Among the celebrators were 680 French troops, including horsemen from the Republican Guard in ceremonial uniform. During the parade, a formation of planes flew overhead. Joan was still the darling of the French military, as powerful a hero as Napoléon.

The star attraction was "Joan" herself, seventeen-year-old Charlotte

Marie, who was chosen to be that year's Joan of Arc for her spiritual devotion and her good works. I found her in a makeshift dressing room at a school. She wore twenty-five pounds of armor and a brass sword strapped to her belt. She was ready to mount a horse and ride around town.

I asked her if Joan was more like a man than a woman.

"Ah, like a woman!" she exclaimed. "Despite what everyone says, even if she was a warrior, I learned that she was a coquette! For the coronation of Charles VII, she had a dress made for herself. So she was a woman."

Except for the dress, Charlotte had no evidence that Joan was a coquette. I found it hard to believe. Later that day, I met Marie-Christine Chantegrelet, the president of the Joan of Arc Association, which serves to keep Joan's memory alive. Chantegrelet herself was Joan of Arc in May 1968, so while students in Paris were throwing cobblestones in the streets, she was riding a horse in full battle armor. She confirmed the coquette story.

"From the books I've read and the 'Joanists' I've talked to, I have the image of a young woman warrior who was a coquette on the side," she said. She also told me the story of the dress made for the coronation, adding that when Joan traveled through certain towns, she asked for lengths of fabric so dresses could be made for her.

"I love this story about her," Chantegrelet said. "I love that in addition to her faith and her service to God, to the king and to France, et cetera, et cetera, there was a small touch of femininity that got her excited."

So could she seduce? I asked.

"In the broad sense of the term, yes, she was a seductress, someone who has the aura, the charisma, to make people follow her," Chantegrelet said. "Everyone fell under her spell."

If I were to follow a hero of French history, it probably would not be a military leader like Joan of Arc but an adventurer. In fact, I have one in mind: the late Jacques Cousteau, the undersea explorer and television showman. For many years in the 1960s and 1970s, ABC television presented *The Undersea World of Jacques Cousteau*, a docudrama starring

Cousteau and a crew of divers with good looks, French accents, sleek diving gear, and a research ship called the *Calypso.* Cousteau is remembered for his patient style and slow, deeply accented speech that mesmerized Americans with stories about hidden treasure and sea creatures of the deep. And the silences! Cousteau wasn't all talk. He lured us in but then often left us alone, to dream. What American kid didn't want to quit school, run away from home, and go off to explore the sea with Jacques Cousteau?

And then one day I found Luc Long, Cousteau's modern-day incarnation. An archeologist and scuba diver, he digs up secret ancient Roman treasures from the bottom of the Rhône River. He works on the edge of the city of Arles, which two thousand years ago was a major colonial town. Long is lean and tanned, fast moving and fast talking, with wraparound sunglasses and locks of hair that spill onto his forehead and curl up along the nape of his neck. He works for the French state, on assignment for the Ministry of Culture, but he still speaks with the coarse twang of the south.

For twenty-five years, he has struggled to tame the river, one of the deepest and most dangerous in Europe. It pushes him away by turning black from currents and pollution; it sends out its one-hundred-pound bottom-feeders to sting his skin and bite his hands and feet. It serves as a massive garbage dump, a final resting place for busted motorcycles, rusty shopping carts, tree trunks, slabs of concrete, electric cables, car tires, and ordinary household garbage. It welcomes cargo-carrying ships that seem oblivious to the divers in their way. It is a depository for uranium waste, pesticide residue, and raw sewage—the ideal breeding ground for bacteria that fell the divers with urinary, lung, and ear infections. The river is even a resting place for dead bodies.

Luc Long has been nicknamed "the Serpent" by the river pirates who monitor his moves and who are, in turn, secretly monitored by French domestic intelligence police. The pirates are after the same prizes he seeks—long-submerged amphorae, pots, plates, funnels, oil lamps, bits of pillars, carved capitals, broken statuary—but for sale on the black market or for their private collections, rather than for preservation of the nation's *patrimoine*, or heritage.

Long and his team of divers and archeologists are romantics, reveling in Gallo-Roman history. They work in shifts from morning until early evening every summer and early fall from their command center: a wooden boat that sits on the edge of the river. In 2007, they pulled up a treasure that shook the archeological world. It was a marble bust dating from around 49 B.C., believed to be the oldest representation of Julius Caesar made during his lifetime. Long called it "a living portrait," so human that all of Caesar's flaws are exposed: a slight depression in his skull, small eyes, deep lines extending from the bottom of his nose to his mouth, wrinkles on his neck, a prominent Adam's apple, a receding hairline. Caesar haunted Long. "Did the people of Arles know him well?" he asked himself. "How did he get to the bottom of the river? Was he thrown in?"

On the day of my visit, the divers pulled up a chunk of white marble—an animal's foot with sinewy veins—and a tiara that could have belonged to a head of Artemis. Long cradled the tiara in his hands, but, possibly overtaken by the excitement of the moment, he let it slip from his fingers. It plunged deep into the water. Xavier, a retired naval officer on the crew, whipped off his clothes and stripped down to his skivvies. He was not at all self-conscious about his soft, round body that contrasted with the lean torsos of his fellow crew members. He didn't waste time suiting up. "It's yours, my commando!" shouted Long. Xavier dived. When he came back up, the tiara was in his hands.

For Long, the Rhône is an untamed lover. "She's very complicated," he said. "She is used to doing what she wants. She gets upset and breaks all the plates and bowls. She suddenly turns off the lights and leaves you in the dark. She keeps her treasures hidden and reveals them only when she feels like it. She has a good memory and can be protective of what is hers. She will hurt you by sending out her surrogates to bite. She is a domineering mistress, too, because she demands all your time. You can lose everything because of her: your home, your wife, your children."

But the river always lures him back. This is not Versailles, a man-made palace that celebrates power, but a sweep-you-off-your-feet adventure of unpredictability, a repository of treasures hidden in the mud and sludge and black waters. It is romanticism in the most unlikely place, beauty from ugliness, heroism on a small scale in a remote patch of nature. "Life is just one long story," said Long. "I'm not particularly religious or mystical, but sometimes I feel a connection with all these objects, as if they're calling to me"—like the voices that called out to Joan or the ghosts of the kings and queens hovering over Versailles. Or maybe Long, like the former president François Mitterrand, has "a deep instinctive awareness of . . . [the] physical France, and a passion for her geography, her living body." He desires to be seduced as much as he plays the seducer, using the ancient treasures he pulls from one of her rivers to dazzle the state, the art world, and the people.

I went to the Arles museum one day to see Caesar before he was put on public view. I was led up a flight of stairs to a private, locked work room. Inside a tall, blue metal cabinet was a Styrofoam box holding the head of Caesar, a man no younger than fifty, small-eyed, balding, with deep lines around his mouth. I looked into his eyes and he looked back at me, with an expression of pride dimmed by weariness.

Even though it was a symbol of the Roman invasion and conquest of Gaul, the Caesar marble was celebrated by the French state as part of the country's grand past. The weekly news magazines put Caesar on their covers, as if he were a living hero, just as they do with other heroes of history.

In 2009, on the day each year when the buildings of the state are opened to the public, culture minister Frédéric Mitterrand (the nephew of the former president) feted the country's heritage by introducing Caesar to the French people. He caressed the head, called it beautiful, and announced that for one full week he was able to keep it in his office. For that brief time, Caesar belonged to him. The gesture reinforced the idea of France as a global center of culture and beauty. It was part of the continuum of France's seduction of itself.

3

It's Not About the Sex

. . .

> You'd have a ball! You'd go to a party every night, drink nothing but champagne, swim in perfume, and have a new love affair every hour on the hour!
>
> —Fred Astaire telling Audrey Hepburn about the pleasures of Paris in the 1957 film *Funny Face*

> The law of seduction takes the form of an uninterrupted ritual exchange where seducer and seduced constantly raise the stakes in a game that never ends. . . . Sex, on the other hand, has a quick, banal end: the orgasm.
>
> —Jean Baudrillard, *Seduction*

One year at Christmas, my husband and kids gave me a collection of twenty-two films by the late, great director Eric Rohmer. I thought *L'amour l'après-midi* (*Chloé in the Afternoon*) would be a good place to start.

Frédéric, the narrator, is a thirty-year-old married man with a stable job, a structured life, a pregnant wife whom he appears to love, and a young daughter. But he has a secret obsession: women. He fantasizes about beautiful, anonymous women: in his imagination they approach him on the street, and he easily seduces them and takes them home to bed.

After lunch one day, Frédéric returns to his office and finds Chloé, the ex-girlfriend of an old, close friend, waiting for him. They begin to spend their afternoons together, shopping, eating, drinking coffee, but mostly talking. Eventually, Chloé confesses to Frédéric that she plans to seduce him; he replies that he will try to resist. A series of increasingly erotic scenes follow: Chloé undressing down to black tights and a tight black top; Frédéric touching a curve of her body, commenting on her beautiful figure; Chloé kissing every part of Frédéric's face except for his mouth as they sit together on a park bench. In their final encounter, Frédéric arrives at Chloé's apartment as she is finishing her shower. He brings her a towel, and she asks him to dry her. He does so, tentatively.

"No, really dry me!" she insists. The camera cuts to a shot of Chloé's back. Frédéric moves the towel down her wet body. He tries to avert his eyes, but his face is at the level of her pelvis. Still looking at her, he kisses her neck. She runs into the bedroom. Just as Frédéric begins to take off his sweater, he catches a glimpse of the naked Chloé on the bed, waiting for him to join her. He looks at himself in the mirror, freezes, leaves without saying good-bye, and goes home to his wife. The movie ends without Frédéric and Chloé ever having sex.

I should have known this would happen. The title of the film suggested that the plot was driving toward an inevitable sexual liaison between a happily married man and a somewhat kooky force of nature. But Rohmer was a master in denying his characters sexual finality. The easy way out would have been for Frédéric and Chloé to have sweaty sex with enlaced limbs and rapturous orgasms. Instead, they engage in endless foreplay: long, drawn-out conversations, flirting, and *frôlements*, or slight brushings of their bodies. This is hard work, but hard work infused with eroticism and pleasure. Rohmer knew how to evoke the sexual without the sex.

The emphasis on what comes before, the anticipation, the progress, and even the setbacks separate this kind of storytelling from the classic American sexual fairy tale. In America, the goal is to conquer as efficiently as possible and, if you're lucky, to live happily ever after. In France, the excitement comes less from gratification than from desire. If we Americans were to put the words "seduction" and "France" together, we might come out with the word "sex." The French might come out with the word "pleasure." The game is not one of notches on the bedpost. It is a process, based on the concept that the players are entitled to pleasure and that while sexual intercourse is exciting, the rich, heady, tantalizing pursuit of it may be even more so.

The preoccupation with prolonged sexual play is rooted in French history. One of the pioneers was the seventeenth-century noblewoman Ninon de Lenclos, whose beauty, cunning, independence, and sense of humor made her the most powerful and successful courtesan of her time. While most young women sought security in a well-constructed marriage, she renounced the feminine condition, declaring, "From this moment on, I am becoming a man." She struck out on her own, opening an unusual business: a salon, and later, a school, which she ran for thirty years, to teach young men and women the art of seduction and love. Men had to pay to hear her lecture; women came for free. She celebrated her eightieth birthday by taking a new beau.

Her life lessons were strategic and unsentimental: "A sensible woman should be guided by her head when taking a husband, and by her heart when taking a lover," and "Much more genius is needed to make love than to command armies."

One of Lenclos's cardinal rules was to conceal one's intentions. When she was sixty-two, she decided to help the twenty-two-year-old Marquis de Sévigné win the heart of a beautiful but aloof countess. She told him, as Arielle Dombasle would tell me hundreds of years later, that seduction was war.

"Have you ever heard of a skillful general, who intends to surprise a citadel, announcing his design to the enemy upon whom the storm is to descend?" Lenclos asked the marquis. "Do not disclose the extent of your designs until it is no longer possible to oppose your success."

The marquis took several weeks to make his moves, but then he veered from Lenclos's orders and professed his love to the countess. The seductive spell was broken; the countess rejected him.

Some of the most unlikely characters throughout French history have valued the sizzle more than the steak. Georges Clemenceau is best known in the United States as the French prime minister who clashed with President Woodrow Wilson at the Paris Peace Conference after World War I. But he was also a medical doctor, a journalist, and a novelist. In his 1898 novel *Les plus forts*, he celebrated the supreme pleasure of the prelude. One of the book's characters, a ruined gentleman named Henri de Puymaufray, says, "The most beautiful moment in love is when I climb the staircase."

Jean-Paul Sartre, the twentieth-century philosopher and writer, felt that the sex act was more of an obligation than a source of pleasure. Simone de Beauvoir, his longtime lover and companion, quoted one of their conversations. "I was more a masturbator of women than a lover . . . ," he told her. "The essential, emotional relationship is that I kiss, caress, run my lips over the body. But the sexual act—it took place, I performed it, I even performed it often, but with a certain indifference."

The concept that the chase gives so much pleasure that it must be repeated again and again is embedded in one of the most celebrated figures of the French theater, the title character in Molière's seventeenth-century play *Don Juan*. Don Juan wasn't French, but Molière transformed him into a French creation by appropriating the myth of the archetypal French seducer, in this case one without scruples. Cynical, hypocritical, and cruel—but also intelligent, articulate, and polite—the nobleman Don Juan fools both noblewomen and commoners by disguising himself and lying to them. He is a transgressor, faithful to the original meaning of the seducer as one who turns another from the right path. Conquest alone interests him, and he abandons the women once they submit. As he says in the first act: "It's a delicious thing to subdue the heart of some young beauty by a hundred sweet attentions; to see yourself making some small progress with her every day; to combat . . . her reluctance to surrender, with tears and sighs and rapturous speeches; to break through all her little defenses . . . and gently bring her round to granting your desires. But once you are the master, there is nothing more to say or wish for: the joy of passionate pursuit is over."

In the end, Don Juan goes straight to the fire of hell. But his appetite for a challenge and his rejection of Christian religious principles intrigued the increasingly freethinking public of Molière's day.

A contemporary take on sex as the end of seduction is a line I heard from a young woman I know. Whenever a flower seller approaches her and a friend (male or female) in a restaurant, she responds with a straight face and a cutting line: "No thanks. We've already had sex."

So how to play the game? Several weapons need to be mastered.

The first is *le regard*, the look, the electric charge between two people when their eyes lock and there is an immediate understanding that a bond has been created.

The concept is a classic component of French seduction, rooted in antiquity and developed in the love poetry of the troubadours. "The look is like an arrow that enters the Other's body through his/her eyes and infects the body and soul of the person, rather like Cupid's arrow," explained Lance Donaldson-Evans, a French Renaissance scholar at the University of Pennsylvania. "It can have a spiritual dimension, but it is usually associated with erotic love."

There is something chaste and pure about the look, as there is no sullying of the body. But there is also something inherently unfaithful about it, because with the look, you never stop falling in love. Stendhal, the nineteenth-century master of psychological and historical realism, defined *le regard* as "the heavy artillery of virtuous coquetry." He explained why: "You can say everything in one look, and yet you can always deny the look, for it cannot be quoted word for word."

I learned about *le regard* one day during a visit to a small museum in the Paris suburb of Boulogne-Billancourt, which houses a permanent collection of art from the 1930s. I was with the museum's director, Frédéric Chappey, when we happened on a room with drawings and lithographs, including an advertising poster for the Salle Marivaux theater. I admired the poster's tranquillity and Art Deco composition. Chappey told me I had it all wrong.

"This, this is seduction," he said.

"What is?" I asked.

There was elegance, certainly, in the poster, which showed two couples in formal dress at the theater. The women were seated, and the men stood behind. But seduction?

Chappey explained that the men put the women in front of them so they could both look at the napes of their necks and search for other potential conquests. "They signal they are in pleasant company, but they are looking elsewhere," he said. "The message is, 'I have already had this one. I have already succeeded. What matters now is the next one.' It's saying, 'I am very elegant. We are very elegant. I am a great seducer, and because I am such a great seducer, I can seduce again.' I think it is full of humor!"

"This is too subtle for me," I said.

My ignorance encouraged Chappey to go further. "The couples are not talking to each other because they have already sinned," he said. "Seduction has already been tested and incarnated. So, the most beautiful victory is not this one but the next one. It's not today's; it's tomorrow's. He is saying, 'See what a seducer I am? Are you ready? Are you free? Tonight, I am busy, but tomorrow? Are you free tomorrow?' He doesn't say anything. He talks entirely through his *regard*. And you, you cannot help but give in."

"It's too complicated," I said. Seemed like too much of an investment of time and effort, too.

Still, Chappey's analysis was intriguing. I decided to learn more about *le regard*. I knew in advance I would never learn how to do it properly myself, as I am hopelessly nearsighted, which means that my eyeballs get reduced to the size of peas behind my glasses. But as a journalist, I'm a trained observer. And I discovered that one of the best ways to learn how the French do *le regard* was to watch French films.

In *Les amants*, the 1958 film by Louis Malle, Jeanne Moreau plays the character Jeanne, who has an officious husband, a sweet daughter, and a polo-playing lover. She falls in love with Bernard, a young archeologist she meets by chance. It takes only one look. They are in the moonlit garden of her house in the country late one night. He tries to kiss her. She resists. He runs after her. He firmly grabs her shoulders in order to prevent her from moving. Her back is pushed up against a tree, and she has no way to escape. They are now staring at each other passionately. Jeanne smiles with contentment.

"Love can be born in a single glance," we hear Jeanne say, speaking of herself in the third person. "In an instant, Jeanne felt all shame and restraint fall away. She couldn't hesitate. There's no resisting happiness."

Jeanne and Bernard hold hands and walk in the moonlight. She declares her love; they can't stop looking at each other.

The Coen brothers mocked *le regard* in their contribution to a collection of vignettes that became the 2006 film *Paris, je t'aime.* At the Tuileries Métro stop, an anguished American tourist (played by Steve Buscemi) ignores one of the surreal warnings in his Paris guidebook: "Above all, eye contact should be avoided with the other people standing around." The tourist cannot resist staring at a pair of quarreling lovers on the other side of the tracks. The girlfriend toys with him, caressing him with her eyes to make her boyfriend jealous; the boyfriend glowers. Suddenly, the girlfriend is sitting next to the tourist. She kisses him passionately. The boyfriend punches him.

In real life a sexually tinged *regard* may also be used to disarm. On a visit to Strasbourg, Carla Bruni found herself in front of a swarm of photographers calling her name. She decided to give herself to one of them. He was sloppily dressed but no matter. For five minutes she posed, looking only at him, ignoring all the others. He was gobsmacked.

Le regard is not done with an open, wide, American-style grin but mysteriously and deeply, with the eyes. Never with a wink. "French women don't wink," one French woman told me. "It disfigures your face."

Another told me she picked up the habit of winking from a classmate when she was about twelve years old. She worked hard in front of the mirror practicing her wink. Her father, a military intelligence officer, made her quit. "Only whores wink," he told her.

The word is the second weapon. Verbal sparring is crucial to French seduction, and conversation is often less a means of giving or receiving information than a languorous mutual caress.

The practice was perfected by Marivaux, the eighteenth-century playwright, who devoted more than twenty-five plays to the light and lively art of conversation in flirtation, courtship, and seduction. *Marivaudage* in contemporary French means "banter" and "wordplay." When words are used as a tool of sexual seduction, indirection and discretion may work best. The frontal approach can be considered brutal and vulgar. The French seducer should not be transparent.

"How seductive you are," a roguish Michel Piccoli tells the icily beautiful Catherine Deneuve in the 1967 film *Belle de jour.*

"Your compliments are too subtle," she replies sarcastically. By being so direct, he has crossed the line.

If talking is the way the word is expressed, then it's useful to cultivate the voice. Living in France, I have come to understand that the French speak more softly than Americans (one reason Americans sometimes attract attention in public places). Private coaches can be hired in Paris to teach professional women how to rid their voices of chirpiness and men how to cultivate lower tones.

Several years back, the French writer Alice Ferney wrote a novel about infidelity called *La conversation amoureuse*. It tells the love story of Pauline and Gilles. Pauline is a beautiful, happily married, twenty-six-year-old mother who is expecting her second child. Gilles is a worldly, successful, forty-nine-year-old writer of made-for-TV movies whose marriage is ending.

The most sensual passages in the novel are the phone conversations between them. "A voice can hold things just as a body can," Pauline says to herself. "It can enter deeper inside you than a man's sex. A voice can inhabit you, lodge in the pit of your stomach, in your chest, right by your ear, and nag away at that part of you that so badly needs love, stoke it, whip it up as the wind whips up the sea. Am I in love with a voice?"

If I were to fall in love with a voice, it would be the voice of Jean-Luc Hees, the chief executive of Radio France. When a profile is written about Hees, more often than not it refers to him as a *grand séducteur.* I asked him once what that meant, and at first he played coy and pretended not to know. Then he talked about the voice. "When I listen to the radio, I know who has the power of *séduction,*" he said. "It's the first thing I hear. I can feel that someone wants to be desired, wants to be listened to."

Hees's voice is deep and soft, like too many velvet cushions on a sunken sofa. When he arrived years ago as a young radio correspondent in Washington, which is where we first met, he knew only the most rudimentary English. His voice compensated. At a dinner one evening, he chatted with a beautiful American woman sitting next to him. When they said good-bye, she said to him, "It was like opera. I understood nothing. But the music, the music was wonderful."

The kiss, the next natural weapon in seduction, is subject to its own rules of engagement. The most social kiss is the *bise*, the kiss on each cheek. I always have considered the *bise* a straightforward ritual that the French feel compelled to use when saying hello and good-bye. It's so routine that children are required to give it when meeting the adult friends of their parents, even when they are perfect strangers. It drove my young daughters nuts.

But then Florence Coupry and Sanae Lemoine, my researchers, ganged up on me and explained how cheek kissing could come with extraordinary power. "Okay, you can give *la bise* to say 'hi' to people you know, and there would be nothing special about it," said Florence, trying to be deferential. "But what a potentially wonderful ground for a game! Let's say that one day, kissing a dozen friends hello, I also kiss someone I've been dreaming about. I feel my heart beating weirdly and I'm so close to him for a second and I think I'm going to faint, and it will be absolutely delicious and maybe troubling. Maybe only I know what's happening, or maybe I let him know. Or maybe he guesses it and then what could happen?"

Sanae chimed in: "Sometimes his lips will touch your cheek, or he'll try to come as close as he can to your lips and touch your waist lightly with his hand. *La bise* allows you to get intimate. It allows you to come close to someone you don't know at all, so close that you can smell the other."

Beyond the social *bise*, the French take their kissing seriously. In the Forum des Halles mall in central Paris one Saturday morning, shoppers were offered a lesson in cross-cultural kissing. Two actors, Lise and Gaëtan, were led through the demonstration by Sophie Kerbellec, their acting teacher. A crowd stood and watched.

"So now we are going to try the 'French kiss,' where you really put your lips together, one mouth on the other," Kerbellec said. "You've got to throw yourselves into this kiss." She told the couple to think of Jean Gabin and Michèle Morgan in Marcel Carné's 1938 classic, *Le quai des brumes.*

The couple kissed. Their lips locked and then explored, softly.

"Think about moving your heads! Voilà! *Très bien*!" Kerbellec continued. "See, hold her head. That's very good! The back of her neck!"

Their heads swayed. Their lips pressed. They seemed to be enjoying themselves.

Then came an American kiss. "Now, what we are going to do are kisses that are a little more technically welcoming to the camera. They are going to simply move their jaws. It's called 'mouth eating.' You have to have the sensation of eating the mouth. . . ."

As the couple opened their mouths and started chewing each other's lips, I couldn't help reflecting that in a mall in America on a Saturday morning, you would be more likely to find a demonstration of a device to cut potatoes in ten ways.

Finally, the deal must be clinched. There are no fixed rules for making it happen. Christophe, a French man in his midtwenties who is both clever and handsome, devised a strategy he shares with male friends when they ask for advice. "I always play by the rule of the three Cs—*climat, calembour, contact*," he confessed to a young friend of mine.

Climat is context. "You want to establish a specific atmosphere, which can be somehow magical," he said. "You should not be too friendly. This ruins your chance to have her in the end. What's important is to create a special ambiance. You can transform a random situation into an atmosphere where you feel you are going to kiss each other. *Climat donc.*"

Calembour, which literally means "pun," comes next. "You need to make her laugh," he said. "But it has to be subtle."

The clincher comes with *contact*. "At the fateful moment, you manage to establish physical contact," he said. "Not a big slap on the back. But when you're saying something—a joke for example—you touch her arm. Or crossing the street, you take her arm. This is a very strong signal. And if she does not reject it, you can almost be sure you can at least kiss her."

He told the story of an encounter at a pharmacy where he was buying a medication late one afternoon. "The pharmacist was a beautiful young woman, alone in her pharmacy," he said. "It was late. So there was *climat*! I asked her if I could see her again. 'Tomorrow?' She said no. I insisted. 'The day after tomorrow?' I insisted, then insisted again. By now she was laughing. So there was *calembour*. But she said no. I left. Then I called information, to get the number of the pharmacy. I called and she answered." He went straight to the point: "And tonight?"

They had dinner that evening. *Contact* came a bit later.

French magazines—news magazines as well as those aimed at women—regularly run articles decoding the mysteries of seduction, presumably with consummation as the ultimate goal. It is usually a multistep process, not unlike Christophe's with his three Cs. In a 130-page special issue on amorous encounters, the monthly *Psychologies* magazine revealed five "master cards of seduction" in the "great game." First, "detachment vis-à-vis the gaze of the other," or feigning indifference; second, "authenticity," or being audacious, sincere, and vulnerable all at the same time; third, "coherence," or inner harmony that rules out trickery; fourth, "self-confidence," which starts with self-seduction; and fifth, "openness," or giving of oneself with "abandon" so that others fall under one's charm.

For a more learned opinion, I turned to the sociologist Alain Giami, a French coauthor of a scholarly work from 2001 entitled "A Comparative Study of the Couple in the Social Organization of Sexuality in France and the United States." He told me it often takes only a kiss to move straight to the act. "The kiss is a very intimate act," he said. "Do not underestimate its power."

So what does this say about the sexual habits of the French?

Even today, in the American mind, it's a given that Paris is the city of love and the French are great lovers. That assumption is perpetuated in novels, memoirs, and films about American women who go off to Paris to discover their inner French selves. The French men who inhabit their lives may turn out to be cads in the end, but they never completely disappoint. In one typical novel, *Paris Hangover*, the thirty-four-year-old heroine abandons a glamorous job as a fashion consultant in New York to live in Paris. "What's with this city?" she asks. "I swear it's making me into a sexual predator. It's *not* my fault. If you've ever been to Paris you *so* know what I'm talking about. The second you get off the plane, you just get swept into this maelstrom of mad, wanton desire: for croissants, for shoes, for men."

There is anecdotal evidence to support the notion that France is an exceptionally good sexual hunting ground, especially for deprived Americans, male as well as female. A French friend told me about an American man she knew who was obsessed with sleeping with a lot of French women. "He was charming, and quite handsome and a bit lost," she said. "He would go walking by the Trocadéro Métro station at three o'clock in the afternoon. When he saw a pretty woman who looked married, he would ask, 'Madame, could you tell me where Balzac's house is?' He had great success. Two out of three of the women would end up in bed with him."

I told her I didn't believe it. I asked typically American questions: Did the women have children, and where were they? (The children were still in school.) Where did the couple have the liaisons? (In small hotels in the upscale neighborhood.)

"I believe the story," she told me. "Even if it was only one out of two."

Scientific polls suggest a more complicated picture. Durex, the best-selling condom manufacturer in France—and in the world—regularly publishes statistics about sexual habits. One of its polls questioned twenty-six thousand people in twenty-six countries and concluded that the French have sex about 120 times a year. That makes them only the eleventh most sexually active country, behind Greeks at 164 and Brazilians at 145, but way ahead of Americans at 85.

Strange as it may seem, the French can be more sexually conservative than Americans. According to the study that Giami coauthored, single French men and women under the age of thirty-nine are significantly more monogamous than Americans of the same age. Young single unattached French women are likely to be less sexually active than their American sisters. French men and women tend to have fewer sexual partners in their lifetimes. There are proportionally more long-term, committed, monogamous couples—both married and not—in France than in the United States. The French even seem to be more faithful to their extramarital lovers: their affairs last longer than those of Americans. "The metaphor I like to use is that Americans are sprinters," Giami told me. "The French run marathons."

There are two dramatic differences: the frequency of sex is "markedly higher" in France than in the United States. And French women over fifty are much more likely to be sexually active than their American counterparts. The study blames the victim: "It appears as if older women in the U.S. are less desirable sexually or are themselves less interested in sexual activity than French women of a comparable age."

On issues of who and when, the French seem to be a lot less invested in moralistic codes than Americans. "Dating" with its rules and rituals does not exist. The ground rule my generation grew up with (sleep with a guy on the first date and be branded a slut) was shattered by the 1968 cultural revolution and the pill. That code seems to be back with a vengeance, tormenting many young American women today. The French women I know just don't get it. They say that if they want to have sex, they just do it and enjoy it, but perhaps they are more discriminating and private about it.

The French seem to place greater importance on romance—the prelude—than Americans do. Books and the popular media in France blame Americans for the focus on performance and for "hygienic" and "scientific" improvements in sex. Viagra, sexual surgery, *Sex and the City* performance are all American imports. So are psychological problems like "hypoactive sexual desire disorder" and "persistent genital arousal disorder."

Pascal Bruckner, in his 2009 book, *Le paradoxe amoureux* (The Love Paradox), uses the subject of sex as emblematic of French cultural superiority over the United States. "While Americans in their movies and television shows say, 'Let's have sex,' the French say, '*Faisons l'amour*,'" he wrote. "The difference is not only semantic. It reflects two visions of the world. . . . Bestiality on the one hand, ceremony on the other."

Bruckner was short on evidence, long on theory, and I thought he might be exaggerating or stuck in a time warp. Then one of my researchers decided to survey her French friends who had spent time in the United States. The young men and young women agreed overwhelmingly that American women can be more guilt-ridden and confessional and American men more brutal and less romantic than the French. One young woman replied, "Americans are more direct about sex: They say 'Do you want to have sex?' or send a text at two a.m. saying, 'Let's see each other now,'" she said. "A French guy will be much more romantic. First he will start the foreplay at a restaurant—by looking at the girl. Some American guys I've met have trouble looking me in the eye, while for me it can increase sexual excitement. Then a French guy will spend much more time kissing the girl—smoothly, slowly, and then kissing her all over her body. Most French guys know the erogenous zones (neck, smooth kiss in the ears, sides of the back, behind the knee . . .) and know how to drive a girl crazy by playing with that. Americans don't enjoy the experience of driving the girl crazy first, and they go straight to the point! And the girl is not aroused enough."

Another French woman reported that she was shocked when the man she was seeing said, "'Let's have sex now' as if he was saying 'Let's watch the Super Bowl together.'"

A third French woman wrote that it was a matter of different perceptions of efficiency: the French are more inclined to mystery, the Americans to mechanics. "American guys learned somewhere that girls like it when their clitoris is touched, so they focus on it, earnestly and directly," she said. "Americans can be, well, so pragmatic."

Valentine's Day is not a big deal in France, certainly not as big as in the United States. But in 2010, the seaside city of Deauville celebrated the day by reenacting the famous embrace between Jean-Louis Trintignant and Anouk Aimée at the end of the 1966 film romance *A Man and a Woman*. The film is about fragile, tender, unpredictable romance—a paean to anticipation, expectation, and seduction. The embrace scene takes place on a cold and gray December morning. Aimée is on the beach near the sea. Trintignant has driven through the night to find her, and when he does, they run across the sand toward each other, arms outstretched. They embrace. He lifts her off her feet, holds her close, and twirls her in the air. We don't see them kiss, but we assume they will.

The film won the Academy Award for best foreign film and the Grand Prix, at the time the highest award at Cannes. Claude Lelouch, the director, who had never made a box office hit before, was suddenly an international star.

To recapture the magic, the public was invited to the beach at Deauville on Valentine's Day morning. Lelouch would be there to film the scene. I asked Andy if he wanted to come along. It would be Valentine's Day, after all. "You sure someone isn't putting you on?" he asked.

I assured him this was going to happen, that it was part of Deauville's official campaign to celebrate its 150th anniversary.

So as snow fell on a Saturday, we took the train from Paris to Deauville. I read newspapers and magazines during the two-hour ride. One article described the distress of parents over the decision of the public elementary school system to cut out Saturday morning classes, a change that apparently disrupted the parents' sex lives.

The next morning, ice-cold and brilliantly sunny, we headed to the beach. The sound track from the film blared from loudspeakers, and a vintage black Mustang similar to the one Trintignant had driven in the film was on display. We had expected about thirty or forty couples. Instead, there were several hundred: teenagers, middle-aged couples, grandparents in their seventies. Some had driven hours to be there.

We all lined up at the spot where the original embrace had taken place. The women and men faced each other, the women next to beach umbrellas lined up near the sea, the men near the boardwalk. Philippe Augier, mayor of Deauville, and his wife, Béatrice, still elegantly beautiful in their sixties, demonstrated how the running, kiss, hug, and twirl should be done. (No one, not even Lelouch, seemed to remember or mind that there was no climactic kiss in the original film.)

Then Lelouch picked up a megaphone and told the couples, "Run toward each other, exactly as in the film!" The men and women raced across the sand, found their partners, and kissed. The men picked up and twirled the women, some more deftly than others. Andy wasn't bad.

"It's lovely!" exclaimed Lelouch.

We played the scene a second time. "Oh, she's too heavy!" one man said as he picked up his partner.

For the third and last take, Lelouch gave us different instructions. "Attention, now!" he said. "This time you are going to switch partners!" He was joking, right?

"I can't see my husband," I said to the women on either side of me.

"What does he look like?" one of them asked me.

"He looks like every other guy who's wearing black," I said.

"Well, don't grab mine!" the woman on the other side said.

Then we all ran, embraced, kissed, and twirled, one last time.

When the kissing was over, couples lingered on the beach as if they were pondering how to find the nearest hotel room—or at least how to prolong the warm glow of romance. Some continued to kiss. Some had tears in their eyes.

Later, over lunch with the mayor and his wife, Lelouch said that when the event was over, a young couple came to thank him. Apparently, the young man had followed Lelouch's suggestion that they change partners at the third kiss. "I found a fantastic woman! I found the woman of my life," the young man told Lelouch.

The mayor found the story sweet and serendipitous. He urged Lelouch to tell the story of his own seduction. A few years earlier, while Lelouch was visiting Deauville, a woman named Valérie wrote him a three-page letter describing what his films had meant to her. She asked a friend to hand-deliver it. Lelouch read the letter that night and was thunder-struck.

"She said sublime things," he recalled. "She saw things I thought only I had seen. She left no photo or phone number. She only signed it 'Valérie.'"

Lelouch launched a search. He found her. Three months later, he was back in Deauville and met Valérie for coffee. It was a *coup de foudre*—a flash of lightning, love at first sight. Lelouch, who had been married several times and fathered seven children, left his wife. Valérie, the mother of two, left her husband. "We've been together since then," he said. "You'd say it's like a Lelouch film, no?"

Maybe. But wasn't it also a celebration of infidelity? I didn't say it, of course. To have done so would have exposed me as the worst type of American woman in the eyes of a French man: a puritan.

At the time of the Monica Lewinsky scandal in 1998, CBS News aired a lighthearted report on the French and their attitude toward infidelity. The report opened with footage of the Eiffel Tower. The writer Jean d'Ormesson was interviewed. He spoke in English, reveling in the role of the unfaithful Frenchman.

Excerpts from the CBS transcript of the interview:

D'ORMESSON: The whole French culture has love at its center, and perhaps cheating.

CBS REPORTER: Cheating is that important?

D'ORMESSON: Ah, cheating, cheating—let us say "looking elsewhere." . . . Each time you cheat, you marry the new woman in America. And we keep the same wife and we have several mistresses. Roughly speaking, that's the position between your culture and ours. . . . When you are well brought up, you try to cheat without too much harm, perhaps. . . . We cheat in so many, many, many hundred years that now you know how to manage. Don't try. It's very difficult, you know?

CBS REPORTER: You have to be French?

D'ORMESSON: You have to be French.

CBS REPORTER: Are you serious?

D'ORMESSON: Yes.

The report ended with footage of the Eiffel Tower.

D'Ormesson was playing to an audience steeped in stereotypes. The cliché about French sangfroid in dealing with infidelity has been perpetuated in American movies for more than half a century. In Billy Wilder's 1957 comedy *Love in the Afternoon*, Maurice Chevalier, playing a French detective, tells a client that his wife is in the Ritz Hotel suite of an American entrepreneur, played by Gary Cooper. The husband vows to kill the lover. Audrey Hepburn, the detective's daughter, overhears the conversation on the phone and calls the police so they can warn the couple. The blasé police officer tells her: "Paris has 220,000 hotel rooms and on any given night similar scenes are taking place in 40,000 of them. If we were to warn them all, we'd have to send the entire police force, the fire department, the sanitation department, and the Boy Scouts in their short pants."

The reality is more complicated. The French, like Americans, have not figured out a way to inoculate themselves against the pain of a partner's unfaithfulness. Jealousy and guilt are alive and well. Adultery is a major reason for divorce in France, as in the United States. When infidelity turns serious and the unfaithful spouse leaves to live with a lover, a scorned wife (especially if she is no longer young) can have a much harder time recovering than a scorned husband, even in France.

Yet American and French cultures do tend to judge the act of infidelity differently. A French woman friend put it this way: "In American culture, infidelity is often considered a sin. You are led astray. You may burn in hell because of it. Or you can confess and perhaps be forgiven—'*Est-ce que je lui pardonne?*' ['Do I forgive him?'] In France, seduction is a skill and infidelity is a willful act. And you can ask the question, '*Pourquoi il a fait ça?*' ['Why did he do it?'] Then come the answers. Maybe he was miserable. Maybe he doesn't love you anymore. Maybe it's just the way he is, and you love him the way he is."

I told her I saw it differently. For Americans, infidelity is betrayal, the violation of a contract. For the French, what Americans call infidelity is often the glue that keeps the order of things: parents stay together; the children are spared emotional trauma; property stays in the family; financial security is maintained; family history is kept; vacations are taken. The game often is not as serious or as destructive as it would be for those with an Anglo-Saxon worldview, particularly if it is played in secret and no one gets hurt. A poll in 2008 indicated that 46 percent of the French believe an infidelity should not be "confessed."

The habits the French develop in their personal relationships inform their conduct in other areas of life: the way they eat, do business, run the country. Exhortations to self-denial do not seem to resonate as they do in America, whether the subject is good food and wine, smoking, well-made clothes, leisure time, or the luxury of long conversations. From there, it's not much of a leap to what seems to be a burning question in France: If sex and romance have faded in a marriage, is it even fair to demand that the partners forgo them on the side? Must all of the pleasures of the long seductive run-up to sex, as well as the sex act itself, be forsaken for the cause of loyalty?

French literature and popular culture are full of suggestions that the answer is no, that infidelity, while perhaps not ideal, should probably be tolerated. Even advice-to-the-lovelorn columnists tend to take a holistic approach. The advice columnist of *Femina*, the women's magazine supplement of a popular weekly newspaper, is one of the most practical. One week, Anne B. from Alsace asked a straightforward question: "Should I leave my husband?"

"Married for thirty years, we haven't had sex for five years," she explained. "Recently, I met up with an old flame. We've had a secret affair for ten months. I am very happy with him, but he's married as well, and he can't leave his wife. I don't feel brave enough to leave my husband. I don't want to hurt him and financially, it's impossible for me."

The advice was to be romantic, self-indulgent, and mature—by being dishonest. "In fairy tales, heroes love each other passionately and exclusively in nights without end; in real life, it happens that you sincerely love your husband or wife at the same time that you have an affair for a while," the adviser wrote back. "That's what happened to you. . . . Live your relationship one day at a time, without rushing to make an irrevocable decision that you may regret."

If Dear Abby were answering, the response would be very different. You cannot live a lie. Leave the lover. If you don't, you will pay. That's what Abby wrote to a woman whose husband left her when he found out she was cheating on him and who signed herself "Woke Up Too Late in Little Rock." "I'm sorry, but there are no magic words that can turn back the clock . . . ," Abby said. "The only magic I can see is that in your hunger for excitement, you made your marriage disappear in a puff of smoke."

In the 2009 book *Les hommes, l'amour, la fidélité* (*Men, Love, Fidelity*), the psychologist Maryse Vaillant argued that infidelity is natural—for men. She put men into a number of categories, including the anxious polygamist, the rehabilitated polygamist, the captive monogamist, and the deceitful monogamist. I was most intrigued by "Ben," a deceitful monogamist: a handsome sociology professor in his forties, long married to "Amandine," the mother of their three children.

Ben created an "honor code of the unfaithful but loyal husband." I have no firsthand experience to judge whether or not his rules work, but here they are in full:

1. Take all necessary precautions to hide your affairs carefully.
2. Keep your little love affairs at a good distance from the big one.
3. Keep any sexual escapade as far as possible from your family life, from the friends you have in common as a couple, and from your wife's relatives and acquaintances.
4. Know how to be discreet; do not trust the neighborhood or well-intentioned friends.
5. Monitor the contents of your pockets, your mail, your e-mails, your cell phone.
6. Inspect your shirt collars, and look for possible hairs on your jacket.
7. Never find yourself in a situation where you have to choose between your girlfriends and your wife.
8. Never fall in love. Know how to keep your heart if not your hormones under control. Affairs don't count. With them, you relax. You don't fall in love.
9. Never start an affair with a colleague, a family friend, a neighbor, your wife's relative.

10. Never sleep or even flirt with the wife of a friend, a colleague, a neighbor, or a relative.
11. Always be safe. The condom is essential. It is out of the question to risk contaminating a wife and putting your health or your life in danger, or ever impregnating someone—out of the question to have children out of wedlock.
12. Never bring anyone home. The familial territory is sacred. It is unacceptable to frolic in the home of your wife and children.
13. Surround your wife with true, sincere, and loyal love. Give her lots of genuine attention.
14. Lie to her intelligently. Never underestimate her capacity for observation and deduction.
15. Never forget your wedding anniversary or any of the important dates involving the children.
16. Always celebrate Christmas with your family. All celebrations and familial social rituals are sacred. The absence of a father or a husband would make the whole family suffer.
17. Try hard to be a good father, a good husband, a good lover, so your wife won't complain about anything.

One morning over breakfast, I asked Andy what he thought of Ben's rules. "It's a pretty good primer for an adulterer," he said. "All the rules make logical sense. But what's striking is that it's a very French perspective."

I asked him to explain. "It's not just a list of dos and don'ts to avoid getting caught," he said. "It is revelatory that he puts so much emphasis on the importance of wife and family. He says the family is 'sacred'—he uses that word twice—and the wife is the one who deserves 'true love.' "

"You make it sound as if there's something noble about this guy's behavior," I said.

"Not at all," he answered. "It's just very different from what we're used to. An American version of this would focus on how to be really good at cheating so your wife won't find out about it."

We agreed that in the American version there also would have to be guilt if the husband were found out and either a rupture or begging for forgiveness. The French version was much lighter, as if somehow the stakes were not so high and the game could continue to be played and the pleasure prolonged, provided that secrets were kept and the family treated with respect. The story line might have been unrealistic, but the fantasy was rich, especially for the guy. Or maybe it was all a put-on, the product of an overactive imagination, designed to titillate and amuse.

I came away from the subject convinced that it doesn't matter whether the French are better at sex than Americans or Chinese or Germans or any other people. What matters is that they take so much pleasure in all that surrounds the sex act. They make the before and after, the process and the denouement seem just as important and thrilling and worthwhile as the climax. Maybe for the very reason that sex is biological, physical, utterly subjective. The French have no control over that. But what they can manipulate, eroticize, embellish, intellectualize, sensationalize, and transform into art is the journey up the stairs and then back down again.

•PART TWO•

Prolonging the Moment

4

La Belle France

...

> Can one think that because we are engineers, beauty does not preoccupy us or that we do not try to build beautiful, as well as solid and long lasting structures? Aren't the genuine functions of strength always in keeping with unwritten conditions of harmony? . . . Besides, there is an attraction, a special charm in the colossal to which ordinary theories of art do not apply.
>
> —Gustave Eiffel

> The French export as important as Renault cars.
>
> —Charles de Gaulle describing Brigitte Bardot

It was Roland Barthes who taught me that the Eiffel Tower is a woman. I was at a Paris literary festival listening to readings devoted to the tower, and then it happened: the world's most identifiable monument moved in my mind from male to female.

An actor read these words from Barthes, the twentieth-century philosopher and writer: "The Tower is a human silhouette; with no head, except for a fine needle, and with no arms . . . and yet it is a long torso placed on top of two legs spread apart." Barthes wrote that he discovered a new truth about the tower from a photograph taken from below: "that of an object that has a sex. In the great unleashing of symbols, the phallus is no doubt its simplest figuration; but through the perspective of the photograph, it is the whole interior of the Tower, projected against the sky, that appears streaked by the pure forms of sex." From this perspective, he concluded, she is a woman who protects and inspects, like a hen sitting on her eggs. That would make her a 1,063-foot *femme de Paris*, its presiding mother perhaps, or its female lover.

For most of the world, the tower has a more general meaning, which any perception of its sexual power can only enhance. As the symbol of France itself—and specifically Paris, a city whose captivating power is unquestioned—it is the emblem of France as a seductive nation. An intricate iron construction, its architecture open to view, it sends a message about all of the seductive arts in which France excels. These sensual delights are not gifts of nature, like San Francisco Bay or the Rocky Mountains. This beauty is man-made. Seduction takes planning and manipulation. The goal may be an enjoyment that wells up naturally from the senses, but to inspire it, artifice is at work.

When Gustave Eiffel began building the Eiffel Tower, the defenders of Paris leapt into action, seeing in the nascent structure a threat rather than an enhancement to the city's familiar allure. Many were convinced the tower would be ugly, a crude construction in pig iron spectacularly out of step with French refinement, the last structure one might identify with the standard of beauty traditionally embodied in the feminine form. In 1887, a group calling itself "Artists Against the Eiffel Tower" circulated a petition to prevent the tower from being built. "We come, we writers, painters, sculptors, architects, lovers of the beauty of Paris which was until now intact, to protest with all our strength and all our indignation, in the name of the understated taste of the French, in the name of French art and history under threat, against the erection in the very heart of our capital, of the useless and monstrous Eiffel Tower . . . this odious column of bolted metal," they wrote.

In the first sentence of his reply, Eiffel wrote, "I believe that the Tower will possess its own beauty."

After the tower was built, the writer Guy de Maupassant was so revolted by it, calling it an "omnipresent and racking nightmare," that he left Paris. The Eiffel Tower for him was more than a work of architecture. It was a symbol of the decline of civilization, a form of anti-seduction. "Today the seductive and powerful emotion of the artistic centuries seems to be dead," he wrote. Few would agree with him now, but his aesthetic passion still sounds familiarly French.

When I visited the tower during a recent refurbishing, Aderito Dos Santos Baptista, an architectural painter and a modern disciple of the tower's beauty, urged me to see Eiffel's creation as a woman of sophistication and grace. For nearly thirty years, Dos Santos Baptista has used color to rejuvenate *la grande dame de fer*—"the grand iron lady," as he and others call her. She moves and sways because of the wind and the heat of the sun. She has never been naked but is always dressed in color.

The tower has also been treated like a beauty worthy of adornment. Soon after she was erected for the Paris Exposition in 1889, she was illuminated by thousands of gaslights. In 1900 Paris celebrated another exposition by bathing her in electric light. In 1925 the carmaker André Citroën used her as a giant advertisement for his company, running the word "Citroën" down her spine, with stars, comets, and signs of the zodiac in colored lights. Since 1985, more than three hundred sodium lamps set inside her lacy pig-iron structure have given her a bronze hue at night.

To mark the millennium, she started blinking, with a temporary light installation that made her sparkle like the whitest diamonds. The spectacle was so successful that a few years later, it was replicated in a permanent installation. Forty mountaineers, architects, and engineers endured high winds, sudden snowstorms, pigeon droppings, and bats to bolt and wire her with a complex system of lights. Nothing frightened them more than the possibility that a piece of equipment would slip, fall, and cause injury or death to the tourists below, all for the sake of glitter.

The transformation cost $5 million and required seventy tons of new materials. Pyramid-shaped glass fixtures had to be mounted in forty-two varieties of lead-free galvanized steel casings to fit every angle of her body. In all, she was dressed in twenty thousand lights strung on twenty-six miles of metal wiring. Since then, she has dazzled in white every night, for ten minutes every hour on the hour from dusk until after midnight.

But she was suffering—from corrosion, peeling paint, and rust—so the city of Paris decided to clean and repaint her. The tower could not be spray-painted because the wind would disperse the paint. Her skin had to be physically, gently touched and caressed with long brushes.

One morning in 2009, I descended stairs from the Champ de Mars, the vast lawn abutting the Eiffel Tower, into a bunker that had been used by the French military for telegraph and radio transmissions during World War I. It now serves as the tower's engineering headquarters. Dos Santos Baptista, the painter, was my guide. He had lined up a series of small metal Eiffel Towers to show her different colors. She has been painted every seven years or so. In 1889 she was clad with Venetian red rust-proofing, in 1892 with bright yellow, in 1899 with beige, in 1907 with five shades of brown. In 1954 she turned reddish brown, and in 1968 she went darker.

This time, she was being painted with sixty tons of semigloss in three colors: Brown 1, Brown 2, and Brown 3. The formulas are kept secret so they cannot be duplicated and marketed. There is a creamy tan on the bottom, a darker brown tinted with gray for the middle, and a denser chocolate for the top. Together, they create an optical illusion that gives a uniform look to her complex structure, with its different densities of metal. The color variations remind me of shades of foundation and highlighter that a woman might use to cover freckles and blotches on her cheeks and dark circles under her eyes.

"The higher up you go, the darker she has to become," said Dos Santos Baptista. "She moves from light to shade. She will always be a young maiden for me. I've spent thirty years in love with her. She still has hidden corners and keeps secrets from me. And discovering them gives me so much pleasure."

The Eiffel Tower astounds with her stature and looks. Yet she is only one example among many that embody the importance of cultivated beauty in France. Once the French had transformed seduction into a positive force, and delighting the senses became a national value, it was only natural that cityscapes would be refined along with food, fashion, furnishings, and scent. All of the senses, after all, are ripe for gratification. The beauty of Paris, France's defining cityscape, did not develop spontaneously. To sustain it requires coordinated effort, just as the beauty of an elegant French woman is far from a reflection of pure nature. The Paris that lures outsiders is the product of elaborate city planning, with little left to chance.

Pleasing the eye is more important in France than in the United States, in cities and in monuments to be sure, and also in the activities of everyday life—in the presentation of a meal, for example, or a landscape. The Germans and the English tend to enjoy nature as it is; the French like to enhance it. Just look at their gardens, all neatly organized like a geometry project. Even the wild-looking ones are often artificially constructed.

The Jardin de la Vallée Suisse is a case in point. Hidden beneath a flight of stairs near the Champs-Élysées in Paris, it is a lovely illusion, where nothing is quite what it appears at first sight. The rocks forming the pond and waterfall are sculpted from cement; so is the "wooden" footbridge. A visitor can sit on a certain bench and be enveloped by evergreens, maples, bamboo, lilacs, and ivy. There are lemon and orange trees, a bush called a wavyleaf silktassel that belongs in an Art Nouveau painting, and another whose leaves smell of caramel in the fall. Its gardener told me that despite the look of wild abandon, the garden is meticulously landscaped, planted, and pruned—and is much harder to maintain than classic celebrations of symmetry.

In the countryside, vistas must be carefully tended. Bordering roadways, especially in the south, are long *allées* of plane trees. Napoléon III ordered them to be planted, not only for their beauty but also as protection for his soldiers. The branches keep snow off the roads in winter; the leaves provide shade in summer. They are functional, but also pleasing to the eye.

Even fortifications may be dressed up. In *The Sorrow and the Pity*, Marcel Ophüls's four-hour film masterpiece about French collaboration with the Nazis during World War II, the former prime minister Pierre Mendès-France, who had been an air force lieutenant with the Free French, spoke with irony about the beautification of the Maginot Line. "Some self-righteous women from the Parisian bourgeoisie had organized a small club to . . . make the landscape . . . more pleasant," he said. "The idea was to plant rose bushes along the Maginot Line, to make it prettier, nicer, more attractive. And there were some people who gave contributions, who would write checks to plant rose bushes, so that our soldiers would not have to look at those inhumane and unpleasant cement walls, to allow them to live in a flowery context."

The preservation of rustic beauty is directly tied to an idealized view of French history. A website dedicated to the 150 "most beautiful villages of France" explains their history and heritage and entices visitors to share "an art of living, charm, and authenticity" in these places "charged with emotion." When François Mitterrand was the mayor of Château-Chinon in central France, he decreed that, despite the high cost, all roofs in his town be covered in genuine Anjou slate. It was, he wrote, "a question of attunement to the setting, of harmony with the texture of the surroundings."

In an effort to retain costly farm subsidies from the European Union, France often argues that the payments help preserve the beauty of the landscapes around the French country homes owned by citizens of many EU nations. Jacques Chirac spoke forcefully about preserving French farms and the surrounding countryside, arguing that they are national treasures. "The beauty of our landscapes is, quite evidently, part of the quality of our lives . . . ," he said. "It is unacceptable that all types of pylon forests distort our countryside, and even our most beautiful sites. . . . We have to begin reconquering our territories as soon as possible."

The love of elegant presentation leads to a concern for detail that borders on the fanatical, and this fastidiousness is taught from childhood. In many schools, students are required to write with a fountain pen and to demonstrate beautiful handwriting during exams. Neatness and penmanship can affect the grade by as much as 10 percent. Form is equally important in oral presentations. Students who deliver them with a sense of timing and a dose of panache can earn a perfect score even if content is deficient.

Elements of daily life must also adhere to a precise aesthetic standard. The French claim to have invented the sugar cube, and they take great pride in it. In 2009, they celebrated the sixtieth anniversary of the *morceau de sucre*, "the sugar piece" that is not really a cube but a rectangle in either white or brown. The sugar cube celebrates so much that is French—national pride, beauty that is ordered and constructed, and a craving for pleasure. In a news release marking the happy event, an industry group with the unwieldy name of the Center for Studies and Documentation of Sugar noted that with his invention in 1949, a French engineer used casting by compression to give sugar a domino form that was "smooth and calibrated," easily transportable, and adapted to daily meals. It ascribed "legendary gaiety" to this "famous domino" and called it "a national emblem, a cultural curiosity, and an illustration of the culinary 'French touch.'"

There seems to be universal agreement that cubes are superior to granules. My French friends never use granulated sugar for their coffee or tea; they tell me it is messy and imprecise. "How else would you get the right dose?" they ask. It goes without saying that individual choice plays no part in deciding what the "right dose" is. Even when granulated sugar is served, it never comes loose in a bowl but is packaged in slim paper packets that allow a precise quantity of the granules to flow evenly into the cup.

The positive side of this preoccupation is the French ability to make the most banal things beautiful. There is nothing unusual in baking a beautiful cake, but no one can top the French flights of fantasy in the *bûche de Noël*. Traditionally, this is a chocolate buttercream-filled sponge cake made to look like a Yule log. Not so for the fancy Parisian pastry and chocolate shops. Over the years, Lenôtre has hired fashion designers Nathalie Rykiel, Karl Lagerfeld, and Hubert de Givenchy, among others, to create *bûches de Noël*.

One year the chocolatier Jean-Paul Hévin produced a log called "Cinderella," a woman's stiletto in chocolate, with a scuff mark at the heel, filled with chocolate Christmas tree ornaments in red and gold. The Plaza Athénée produced the limited-edition "Red Carpet" *bûche* inspired by the hotel's architecture. The curved staircase was made of milk chocolate mousse and almond paste with a touch of a Japanese citrus fruit called *yuzu*, covered in white chocolate and a marzipan red carpet, with an ornate chocolate wrought-iron and gold banister. The price of a cake for six to eight people: eighty-nine euros, or more than one hundred dollars.

One of the negatives of the love of show is that aesthetics can trump practicality. A famous historical example is the uniform worn by French soldiers until early into World War I. It was important for the French to confront the enemy not with stealth but with dignity. They wore bright red trousers and blue coats and caps to announce their presence long after the British, Americans, Italians, and Russians had adopted neutral drab to blend in with their surroundings. It took carnage in the early World War I battles to get the generals to drop this line of thinking.

I learned firsthand how even the ordinary can be made exceptional when I met François Jousse, the lighting engineer for the city of Paris. For more than twenty-five years, Jousse, now in his sixties, was responsible for illuminating more than three hundred monuments, buildings, bridges, and boulevards.

His job was to adorn Paris to make it as beautiful as it could be. In the French way of thinking, the structures had to seduce, not only in the day but especially at night. Even the ugly ones were worthy of dressing up.

Working with a staff of thirty decorative lighting specialists, Jousse had Paris as the object of his passion, and the city succumbed to his charms. Unremarkable buildings glowed, like ordinary-looking women who turn beautiful in candlelight. Architectural details that were lost by day suddenly proclaimed themselves.

In some cities, lampposts are designed to light only the sidewalks and streets, with the surrounding buildings receding into darkness. In much of Paris, however, streetlights are attached to the sides of buildings, highlighting the curves and angles of the structures themselves.

When I met Jousse for the first time, in a café on the Île de la Cité, I expected a buttoned-up bureaucrat in a rumpled suit. Instead, he arrived in baggy corduroy pants and a worn leather jacket spattered with paint. His gray and yellow beard was long and bushy. His skin had the leathery look of someone who had spent too much time outdoors without a hat. He did not remember the last time he had worn a tie. He ordered a big glass of dark beer and chain-smoked foul-smelling Fleur de Savane cigarillos. So began my first lesson on the use of light to make any edifice beautiful.

When Jousse began to devote himself to light in 1981, most of the

Paris monuments were either unlighted or illuminated crudely with big spotlights that shone directly onto the facades. Jousse sought wisdom from urban architects and theatrical lighting experts. At a research laboratory, he and a team created fixtures and experimented with the color and intensity of light.

Jousse and I drove around Paris one day in his white Renault compact. He rattled off details about lighting history: in the fourteenth century King Philip V ordered candles to be lighted in three sites in Paris every night; in 1900 Paris earned the nickname "City of Light" with its electrical light displays at the Paris Exposition.

He recalled the time several years earlier when he and a team had been experimenting with light on the Sacré Coeur Basilica in Montmartre. They had colored it mauve. "The priest came running out and ordered us to turn it off," Jousse said, laughing between puffs on his cigarillo. "We just wanted to have some fun. Sacré Coeur is like an enormous cake with lots of whipped cream. But Paris is a very serious city."

As the afternoon light began to fade, Jousse drove straight onto the cobblestone walkway at Notre Dame, pushing tourists aside. He wanted to show me the redesigned lighting of the cathedral's south facade. He pointed out tiny fiber-optic electrical wires tucked into corners and crevices. We entered the cathedral, climbed a private stone staircase to the south roof, then waited for darkness to fall.

For half a century, the only hint of light on the south facade had come from spotlights hidden in phony booksellers' storage cabinets on the far side of the Seine River. The new lighting scheme allowed spectators to discover the cathedral's facade slowly, through the power and drama of detail. We did not have to wait long for the southern facade of the cathedral to light up, its pillars, gargoyles, and flying buttresses dressed in white. "Look, the light is stronger at the top, so you feel that you are moving closer to heaven," Jousse said. "This is not just a monument. It's a virgin floating above the city." Shortly afterward, in the distance, the Eiffel Tower began to glitter on the hour. "A visual clock," he called it, looking at his watch to make sure she was on time.

• • •

When the demand for beauty is applied to individuals, it can be oppressive. When a cover story in the magazine *Marianne* posed the question, "Do you have to be good-looking to succeed?" the answer of the experts interviewed was a resounding yes. The director of human resources at a luxury conglomerate said that despite fixed standards for hiring, the beautiful have an advantage. "Because we go so fast, we see so many CV's . . . in the end, the decision is based on criteria that are less rational," she said. "It has something to do with seduction. As though the brain had fallen asleep." A psychology professor quoted in the story determined that in France, grades can vary between 20 and 40 percent depending on a student's looks. The secretary-general of a French psychoanalytic and management institute said the pattern of favoritism of the beautiful begins in childhood. "When children are seen as seductive, they will be convinced of their ability to seduce," he said.

In the world at large, French men feel they have the right to comment publicly on a woman's looks. At a political meeting in Paron, a small town an hour from Paris, a young man stood up to ask a question of Rachida Dati, the former justice minister. Before he posed it, however, he said, "I find you very, very beautiful."

She neither ignored him nor told him he was out of line for commenting on her looks. Just the opposite. "Thank you for the compliment!" she said.

French tolerance of judgment and commentary about people's looks is bound up with the idea of personal attractiveness as a cultivated trait. Despite the emphasis on a seductive appearance, missing out on the gift of natural beauty is far from fatal in France. Like the Eiffel Tower's filigree of pig iron, a pleasing and stylish appearance—or at least a refined aesthetic sensibility—may be constructed by the plain, the elderly, the less fortunately born.

The sin is not the failure to meet a standard of perfection but the unwillingness to try. It is almost a civic duty to seduce—or if one cannot appear seductive, at least not to take a prominent spot on the public stage. By no means does everyone play along, but what is striking is how many people do. During the Clinton-Lewinsky scandal in the United States, both men and women in France questioned Bill Clinton's judgment. That he was sexually aroused by a woman other than his wife was less of a shock than the fact that Monica Lewinsky was not especially attractive—and seemed to lack style and elegance.

Men in public life, too, may be judged on their physical appearance. One reason that Barack Obama appeals to the French is his beauty. I was surprised that men—straight and gay alike—appreciate his good looks even more than women do.

The election of Obama gave the French a new hero. His intelligence and style charmed the elite; his blackness seduced those of Arab and African origin who so often feel invisible. Obama doesn't even have to work at being attractive. The French like Obama not because he's hot, but because he's cool. He is a leader more mysterious than confessional, a fierce guardian of his privacy, the guy who plays hard to get. Even though smoking is politically and culturally incorrect in America, he smokes. In secret.

Jean d'Ormesson, whose reputation as a *grand séducteur* accompanies him into his eighties, contrasted Obama's seductive power to that of the late president François Mitterrand. Mitterrand, he said, was less naturally seductive than the president of the United States and had to work at it, playing sophisticated games to win over others. By contrast, Obama's seduction is so immediately obvious that it requires no effort. "Obama is the image of American seduction," d'Ormesson told me. "He is elegant, he is handsome, he is intelligent." Whether he is black or white doesn't even count: "Accidentally, he is black. He is seduction itself. . . . Very handsome. He is very handsome."

Jacques Séguéla, the advertising executive, said much the same thing: "Obama—this is the triumph of seduction since his *beauté* makes you forget that he is black. You must not take me for a racist. But this is what is fantastic. His race has been transcended by his *beauté*."

"What do you mean by his *beauté*?" I asked Séguéla.

"*Beauté*, Obama's *beauté*, it's first of all one of gesture," he said. "His movement is seductive, his way of advancing, the way he looks at you, the extremely discreet play of the hand which is a game of fingers. The way you dress counts in seduction, and he is dressed like Americans of the belle epoque in films of the fifties or sixties . . . the same cut, the tie that falls a little bit longer, the black shoes. And the real seduction, in the end, is in words."

The French insistence on seductive appearance also helps to explain the culture clash involving the Muslim veil. In recent years France has been embroiled in an emotional political debate about whether to ban the "total veil," the all-encompassing garment that covers all but the eyes and is referred to universally as the *burqa* (even though the garment is technically not a *burqa*, which leaves a narrow gauze over the eyes, but a *niqab*, which leaves the eyes uncovered). No more than a few hundred to a few thousand women in all of France wear the garment. But just about every politician in the country seems to have an opinion on it.

In an interview on France Inter radio, François Hollande, the former head of the Socialist Party, trotted out the standard arguments about Islamic dress. First, he said, for a woman to cover herself, especially her entire body and even her face, is un-French because it violates the country's strict adherence to secular, republican values. Second, such coverage is an affront to a woman's dignity. Third, for anyone—man or woman—to hide behind a mask poses a security risk.

But then Hollande offered a fourth argument against the total veil, one that evoked aesthetics. No woman, he said, should have to feel herself "assaulted by the sight of another woman being imprisoned in a *burqa*." And not only women. Men, he added, "must also have the same attitude of revolt."

In other words, the veil is not pleasing to the eye. Hollande made no mention of the fact that a woman might wear the veil for her own reasons, as a declaration of identity, an expression of religious values, or a refusal to be viewed as a sex object.

I am convinced that Hollande's objection, which mirrors the larger French opposition to the head scarf, was not motivated solely by concern for the welfare of women but was connected to their appearance. Just as you would not want buildings to be badly lit, you would not want public spaces to be stained with ugliness. The female body should be seen and shown in its best light.

Women and men walking on the street belong to the cityscape. So they should be beautiful, or at least pleasant to look at. That's why the head scarf and the veil evoke such an emotional response from the French. Claude Habib, a specialist in eighteenth-century literature, argued that the French tradition of gallantry demanded an encounter with the female face, which the veil denies. "The tradition of gallantry presupposes a visibility of the feminine and more precisely a happy visibility, a joy of being visible—the very one that certain young Muslim girls cannot or do not want to show," she wrote. "The veil interrupts the circulation of coquetry."

No discussion of beauty and seduction in France is complete without mentioning the woman who has held the status of the most seductive woman in France for more than half a century: Brigitte Bardot. Not the Bardot of today, mind you, but the Bardot of the past, the sex-goddess actress who shocked and enthralled with her performance in Roger Vadim's film *Et Dieu . . . créa la femme* (*And God Created Woman*) in 1956, the film that made her an overnight star. Bardot today is in her seventies, overweight, gray-haired, her face sagging and lined from the cruelty of aging and too many summers in the unforgiving sun of southern France. Her twin obsessions are the protection of animals and a hatred of immigrants and Muslims. For an American parallel, imagine James Dean still alive, solitary, wizened, and a gun-toting member of the Tea Party.

Bardot's power rests in a permanent image that continues to grip the French imagination: the carefree child-woman and symbol of sexual liberation. She introduced a brand of aggressive, sexually supercharged beauty to the world, styled and perfected under Vadim's management but playing into her own natural inclinations.

I consider myself a faithful, fervent feminist *à l'américaine*. And yet Bardot has always intrigued more than repelled me, even with her pouting, ass wiggling, breast baring, and blatant use of sex in her films to get what she wanted. It took a while to figure out why. Bardot was the product of a comfortable upbringing in the wealthy sixteenth arrondissement of Paris. But instead of conforming, she became the most powerful liberated woman of postwar France. She burst onto the scene as a free spirit with the same sexual urges as men at a time when France was still recovering from World War II and the Nazi Occupation. She had affairs, married four times, and said openly that she hated being a mother. Even Simone de Beauvoir, the early French feminist, fell under her spell. "Brigitte Bardot couldn't care less about what other people think," de Beauvoir wrote in 1959. "She eats when she's hungry. She falls in love with the same simplicity. . . . She does what she wants and that's what's so disturbing." De Beauvoir was enthralled by the delicious contradictions of Bardot's beauty. She wore elegant clothing, corsets, perfume, makeup, and other artifices but often went barefoot. As for her way of moving, it was so sensual that, in de Beauvoir's words, "a saint would sell his soul to the devil for nothing more than to see her dance."

Bardot's style endures as the most persistent source of female sensual inspiration both inside and outside of France. The actress Drew Barrymore and the supermodel Kate Moss have imitated her poses. In 2009 you could buy a Louis XV–style silver vinyl armchair with a close-up photo of Bardot's face serigraphed on its back for 814 euros. For his May 2010 collection for Chanel in Saint-Tropez, Karl Lagerfeld, the reigning king of French fashion, paid tribute to Bardot by casting Mick Jagger's model-daughter Georgia May as a modern-day, mambo-dancing Juliette, the free spirit of *And God Created Woman*. The leather goods firm Lancel, meanwhile, turned Bardot into a handbag with curves.

In the 2008 promotion of the perfume Miss Dior Chérie, Bardot's red-hot sexuality was cooled down for the mainstream and filled with pleasurable clichés. It was the first-ever television commercial directed by the American film director Sofia Coppola, who set it to a classic Bardot song in picture-perfect Paris. Dressed in pale pink, the model rides a bike, strolls across the Seine, is fitted in a Dior dress, admires roses at a florist, nibbles on pastries, kisses her boyfriend, and is swept into the sky while holding a bouquet of balloons.

All the while, Bardot is singing "Moi je joue" ("I Play"). The song is of a love game in which the woman forces her lover into submission. "I won, too bad / it's what you deserved / you are my toy," goes one verse.

Coppola described the song as a "a charming, catchy melody, a little 'bubble gum.'" "Bubble-gum" sweet is the last thing the lyrics would have been called in the 1960s. The commercial ends with "*Oh! Oui, oui!*" It leaves out Bardot's orgasmic cry at the end.

The ultimate tribute—or perhaps insult—to Bardot came in a six-euro, limited-edition chocolate éclair created by Fauchon, the luxury food purveyor. Fauchon prides itself on its outrageous éclairs. The Bardot éclair was filled with rose-perfumed almond cream. It was covered with a firm curve of white chocolate on which had been printed in edible ink a 1959 photo of Bardot, her lips parted, holding a coral-colored towel loosely over her naked body.

According to Fauchon, the main customers for the Bardot éclair were men. In describing it, the Gogoparis travel website was too graphically sexual to be seductive. "How perfect to be able to eat her," it wrote. Fauchon took a more refined approach, calling the Bardot éclair full of "sensuality."

This was manipulated beauty, artifice at work, Fauchon's way of enhancing the appeal of a ubiquitous French cream pastry, altering it to create a lovely illusion that pleased the eye. It was not unlike painting the Eiffel Tower in three colors or shaping sugar into cubes. The humble éclair became a vehicle to promote a national symbol of French beauty, as she is lovingly and lustfully remembered. I wondered whether customers would eat the éclair more slowly, with more gusto or more delicacy, because of Bardot's presence. As for the taste, I preferred Fauchon's chocolate-almond éclair decorated with the eyes of Leonardo's Mona Lisa.

5

Intellectual Foreplay

. . .

> Language is a skin: I rub my language against the other. . . . I enwrap the other with my words, I caress, brush against, talk up this contact.
>
> —Roland Barthes, *A Lover's Discourse: Fragments*

> Women have orgasms first of all with their ears!
>
> —The actor Fabrice Luchini, paraphrasing the writer Marguerite Duras

Christine Lagarde, the finance minister, announced in a speech to the National Assembly one day that the French needed to abandon what she called an "old national habit." That habit was thinking.

"France is a country that thinks," she told the deputies. "There is hardly an ideology that we haven't turned into a theory. In our libraries we have enough to talk about for centuries to come. That is why I would like to say: Enough thinking, already! Enough hesitation! Roll up your sleeves."

She praised Alexis de Tocqueville for his revolutionary idea that making money is honorable, citing his book *Democracy in America*, an account of his nineteenth-century travels throughout the United States. She told the French to work harder and earn more, and expect to pay lower taxes if they get rich. The message was consistent with the policies of her boss, Nicolas Sarkozy, who won the presidency of France in 2007 on a platform of dynamism and change based on France's integration into the productivity-driven global economy. His mantra on the campaign trail was "Work more to earn more."

What neither Sarkozy nor Lagarde had factored in, however, was the deep national attachment to a particular form of seductive dalliance that I call intellectual foreplay.

For the French, life is rarely about simply reaching the goal. It is also about the leisurely art of pursuing it and persuading others to join in. How much fun would the sex act be without the flirtation, or the dinner without the bouquet of the wine? What joy is there in words without wordplay, or in ideas without fencing and parrying? And in the mundane arena of daily work, why rush to construct an action plan while skipping the nonlinear, often slower, more laborious, less efficient but perhaps pleasant step of theorizing about it? In other words, why focus only on the goal when there are so many other luscious things to distract? If something is too straightforward, direct, or easy, it feels incomplete.

Training begins early. In school, answering a math question is useless without an account of how the student arrived there, because the process, the demonstration, is more important than accuracy. The method for solving a problem might be worth nine out of ten points, the correct answer only one. The process requires such intellectual rigor that when it works, the pleasure that results is enormous.

Lagarde knows about the deep-rooted intellectual culture of her country. She looks like the pinup girl for the perfect French woman of a certain age. Tall, slim, tanned, silver-haired, she knows how to pose with the air of refinement that comes from good breeding.

But she is the most American of the ministers in Sarkozy's cabinet. She speaks such elegant English that she sometimes prefers it over French. She looked west to make her fortune, spending much of her career as a lawyer at the Chicago-based law firm Baker & McKenzie. She rose to become the first woman to head the firm's executive committee and was named one of the world's most powerful women by *Forbes* magazine. Returning to France, she became minister of foreign trade under President Jacques Chirac before joining Sarkozy's cabinet.

As soon as she uttered her offhand line in the National Assembly, deputies in the chamber—even some from her own party—erupted in howls of protest. "They were screaming at her; they were shouting," said her speechwriter, Gaspard Koenig.

It didn't take much prodding to get France's intellectual class—or at least its male members—to strike back with full force. Most female intellectuals didn't bother to comment. Perhaps they were too busy balancing the demands of work and family to consider whether they were thinking too much. Perhaps they agreed with Lagarde's practical approach. But for the men, here was a French woman brainwashed by too many years in America who was trying to castrate the intellectuals of France!

"How absurd to say we should think less," said Alain Finkielkraut, the philosopher, writer, professor, and radio show host. "If you have the chance to consecrate your life to thinking, you work all the time, even in your sleep. Thinking requires setbacks, suffering, a lot of sweat. Before discovering the truth, how many false starts must you endure!"

Bernard-Henri Lévy, the splashier philosopher-journalist who wrote a book retracing Tocqueville's American travels, claimed to have been even more shocked, shocked! "This is the sort of thing you can hear in café conversations from morons who drink too much," he said. For maximum effect, he spoke in sweeping historical superlatives. "To my knowledge this is the first time in modern French history that a minister has dared to utter such phrases."

Lévy found Lagarde too selective in quoting Tocqueville and suggested she read his complete works. "In her leisure time," he said.

The satirical weekly *Le Canard Enchaîné*, meanwhile, mocked Lagarde for praising the sheer joy of work and for quoting an oft-cited line from Confucius: "Choose a work you love and you won't have to work another day." Such "subtleties have escaped the cleaning lady or the supermarket checkout clerk," the newspaper wrote.

One reason the speech was so savagely criticized is that it was brutally direct and certain. It was delivered straight, American-style, like a double shot of Jack Daniel's. Had it been sweetened with humor, understatement, or irony, it might have gone down easier. Simply put, it lacked seduction.

Lagarde's salvo fits perfectly into the image we Americans have of France as a static country, stuck in the past, paralyzed by a thirty-five-hour workweek, a perpetual chain of workers' strikes, and an inefficient and bloated bureaucracy. We picture brooding, cigarette-smoking, espresso-drinking French intellectuals who seem to do nothing in particular for a living and have all the time in the world to ponder deep philosophical conundrums in Left Bank cafés.

The reality is more subtle. Thinking and verbalizing thoughts is a ritual the French use to decide whether they have found a shared basis on which to function. It is not a business transaction. "Seduction is saying, 'I want to create something in common with the other,'" said Stéphane Rozès, one of France's top political scientists. "To seduce someone you have to know what you share. It's not, 'Are you with me or against me?' It has to be a conversation, not an imposition."

France's history and literature reflect centuries of crafting ideas and intellectual concepts. The French have long pushed to persuade the rest of the world to consider and even adopt them. Modern philosophy originated in France, with Descartes. The eighteenth-century French *philosophes*—Voltaire, Montesquieu, Rousseau, Diderot—forged a set of values for society that gave preeminence to reason, democracy, and freedom. In the twentieth century, existentialism bloomed with Jean-Paul Sartre, Albert Camus, and Simone de Beauvoir.

The clash of ideas is part of French national identity, from the corridors of power in Paris to the central square in a remote village. Everyone is a philosopher. Madame de Staël, the renowned novelist and *salonnière*, observed in 1810, "In all the classes in France, one senses the need to talk; speech is not only, as elsewhere, a means of communicating ideas, sentiments, and business matters, but it is an instrument that one likes to play." During the global oil crisis of 1973, when petroleum-producing Arab countries threatened to cut off France's supply, the French government encouraged consumers to conserve electricity, launched a major campaign to develop nuclear energy, and touted the country's creativity. France's state-run television station ran an advertisement with the slogan "*En France, on n'a pas de pétrole, mais on a des idées*"—"In France, we don't have oil, but we have ideas."

Americans tend to value pragmatism in everyday life: "Great prices so buy now," or "New strategies for better health." In France, people often talk for the sake of talking, not with the purpose of resolution. "We're taught to believe in the beauty of the coherence of the argument," said Philippe Errera, a senior Foreign Ministry official. "We're taught to prevail not by convincing but with beauty."

Talking is a way to deepen emotions and spread France's "civilizing mission" around the world. Words are put on everything. One reason why Nicolas Sarkozy has been so often criticized as uncivilized is that he has boasted of being a nonintellectual. "I am not a theoretician," he once told a television interviewer. "I am not an ideologue. Oh, I am not an intellectual! I am someone concrete!" In the eyes of a Parisian intellectual, he might as well have said he wasn't French.

Intellectual foreplay at its best is strategically and cunningly played. It has an old-Europe, self-confident quality: knowing but not revealing all, reveling in the ability to keep secrets, being indirect. At times, the verbal play is a lot of fun; at times, it is nothing more than circle-spinning using irony or understatement to give your interlocutor a laugh when it works and a feeling of inadequacy when it doesn't.

For those who master this art, life can be more interesting, more rewarding, and more pleasurable, although often less efficient than going directly to the goal. Until you learn the rules—or at least how to fake them credibly—you can never be seductive enough to fit in.

When the verbal seduction is complete, the playful game is over. There is a victor and a vanquished. If you try to continue the game after that, it becomes boring. So the goal is to enter into a conversation and keep it so enticing that it never ends.

The 1996 film *Ridicule*, about surviving at the royal court of Versailles, offers important clues for navigating this verbal minefield. An experienced hand gives advice about verbal sparring to a young man seeking a favor from the court: "Be witty, sharp, and malicious . . . and you'll succeed. No puns! At Versailles, we call puns 'the death of wit.' . . . One last thing: Never laugh at your own jokes." One of the hardest conversational maneuvers is to make a pun subtle enough to allow the game to continue without breaking its rhythm. Otherwise, the pun becomes a verbal orgasm that brings the conversation to an end. It is even worse if the punster seals it with a laugh.

Among the refined tools of a French conversationalist is *le second degré*. Sophie-Caroline de Margerie, the writer and jurist, explained it to me.

"*Second degré* is when you say something and you can take it for exactly what it is, but there's a second sense which is the real sense," she said. "You say something and you don't take it literally. It's tongue in cheek; it's between the lines. You have very little of this with Americans and none at all with Germans. When you say something to a German, you mean it one hundred percent or else you don't say it. With *second degré*, you have to be intelligent. That doesn't mean you have to be droll all the time. But you have to feel the formulas to have a brilliant conversation with depth."

Second degré creates a dangerous climate because you can't always be sure when you are crossing the line into another meaning.

On the most primitive level, *second degré* can be racist, sexist, cutting, and cruel, the kind of bad-taste joking that went out of style in the United States decades ago. Alexandre Deschamps, my physical therapist, told me he learned the hard way never to use *second degré* with Americans. He found they were thin-skinned and didn't appreciate the humor.

Alexandre is an amateur jazz musician. Once he was playing bass in a French group that included an American drummer. "The French musicians started criticizing the United States, and the drummer got really upset," Alexandre recalled. "The drummer said that America had liberated the French in World War II and that we should be grateful. One of our group said, 'Oh, but we had it much better under the Nazis!' It was a joke, of course. It was irony. It was classic *second degré*. But the American got so angry he walked out."

Alexandre's story helps explain why *second degré* is a step beyond irony. An American would be unlikely to make this joke for fear of being taken too seriously; the French expect the double meaning to be understood.

Second degré can be used for even more cunning verbal jousts. Raphaël Enthoven, the philosopher, told me his version of a famous anecdote: The writer and humorist Sacha Guitry and his second wife, Yvonne Printemps, were in a courtroom getting divorced. "In front of the judge, Guitry turned to his wife, who was 'hot,' and said, 'You know, Yvonne, I just had an idea for what they can write on your grave: FINALLY COLD.' She looked at him, didn't move, and said, 'Point taken. And I have an idea of what they can write on your grave: FINALLY STIFF.' Not bad, no? You get it? It's beautiful!" he said.

"But it's cruel," I said.

"No, it's fun," he countered. "You don't like it? I love it." What Enthoven particularly liked was that for once, Guitry's sarcasm had been trumped.

Conversation works best when it appears effortless. "The real seducer is one who isn't seen," the writer Pierre Assouline told me. "For me, a man or a woman gifted in conversation is one who knows how to keep quiet, not someone who knows how to talk. A real conversationalist is someone who knows how to keep quiet in three languages."

"I don't get it," I said.

"It's a paradox, to know how to keep quiet in three languages," he explained.

"I don't at all understand the *second degré*," I said.

"This is the *troisième degré*" (third degree), he said.

Great, I thought to myself. This is what keeps outsiders out.

"To know how to keep quiet in three languages, it is to keep your place in society, whether it is with Americans or Italians or English," he continued. "There are codes to respect. It's to know how to be in a conversation but not to monopolize it, not to cut off the others. Sometimes in a conversation you say negative things about a person who is not there. But if someone else says, 'He's my friend,' you change the subject."

For Assouline, conversations give meaning to life and work. "You bring something to the other," he said. "I adore conversation, because I leave richer than when I came. I have given something as well."

A basic element of the French art of conversation is argument, intricate word games of one-upmanship played with grace and finesse. Whether at a dinner party or in the press, no subject is too trivial for profound and lengthy debate. The arguments are called *polémiques*, and the topics can be both erudite and banal—the real truth about Joan of Arc, the wisdom of allowing pedophilia in French novels, the validity of corporal punishment to discipline young children.

Prime-time television on Saturday night features roundtables in which groups of people sit around and talk. Sometimes newspapers and magazines choose two eminent figures to debate each other, with their photographs on opposite pages, pitting them against one another on topics like "Did the sexual liberation movement really liberate us?" "Does discreet charm exist?" and "Does liberalism govern our sexuality?" To an outsider, some of the most serious also seem the most self-indulgent, like this one in *Le Figaro* magazine: "What's the use of intellectuals?"

One holiday weekend, Andy and I were invited along with sixteen other people for a four-day sleepover at the château of French friends in southwest France. The first morning we covered the following subjects: the exit strategy from Iraq, the health care crisis in the United States, the pitiful state of print journalism in France, Tibetan scarf making from goats' beards, discrimination in the French educational system, and the wisdom of legislating a ban on face-covering veils for women. And that was before we finished breakfast.

Talking has long been a hallmark of French films. A main reason why the French have always loved Woody Allen movies—even the bad ones—is that there is so much talking and so little action. Allen is said to have been inspired by Eric Rohmer, who explored the pleasures of talking rather than copulating in his films. In *My Night at Maud's*, which had a cult following in the United States, Maud and Jean-Louis spend the night together. In a scene charged with promise and erotic tension, they end up in the same bed, but they never have sex—they are too busy talking. My all-time favorite line in a Rohmer film comes from *Les nuits de la pleine lune*. The actor Fabrice Luchini tells the young woman who is the object of his affection, "I love seduction for the seduction. It doesn't matter if it succeeds. Physically, I mean."

To some degree, this is a reflection of real life. "There is an intellectual flirtation that is very French," Laure de Gramont, a writer and editor, explained to me. "You can have a two-hour lunch with a man who is not your husband and never want to sleep with him. There's a bit of flirtation, of course. You will have made love with words. It's much nicer than playing footsie."

Gramont cautioned that this kind of play has a potential downside if it is done with too much enthusiasm. "Sometimes, after about ten minutes, the man feels guilty because his wife is watching," she said.

More generally, Gramont explained her definition of the witty French person: "You have a superior intellect and have the ability to utter the last word on any subject. You don't repeat what was in the newspaper that morning."

To navigate as an American in a culture of verbal seduction, I came up with my own set of rules. First, if your conversational partner tries to speak English, compliment him on his charming accent. Second, kill him with kindness and exaggerated politesse. Third, compliment a woman on her beautiful complexion. Fourth, make a man feel important. Fifth, make sure all this is done so cleverly that it doesn't come across as flattery and, even better, isn't noticed at all.

Along the way, learn banter, even for the most banal telephone conversation. One way to overcome the brusque initial response of the person who answers the phone at a business or office is to engage in light but respectful conversation. It draws the other party into the process, establishes her importance (it is most always a she), and can become an innocent game of momentary, fleeting pleasure.

An example:

SECRETARY IN THE MINISTRY OF CULTURE: Yes, Madame Sciolino, we received your messages. But this is a very busy time.

ME: Oh, how lovely it is to hear my Italian name pronounced so well!

SECRETARY: Ah, yes, it's important to preserve one's roots!

ME: Do you have as charming an accent when you speak English?

SECRETARY: (Giggles.) Perhaps. I don't know. . . .

ME: I hope it's not like the actor Fabrice Luchini. When he speaks English, he tries to talk like the American singer James Brown.

SECRETARY: Yes! He talks in English as if he's chewing gum!

I was brutally outmatched, however, in an encounter with Marc Fumaroli, a member of the august Académie Française. Fumaroli is nearing eighty and is perhaps the country's most learned expert on the art of conversation in seventeenth- and eighteenth-century France. When I called on him at the Collège de France in the heart of the Latin Quarter, he swatted my questions as if they were flies that wouldn't go away. At first I assumed it was part of a game of teasing and testing.

"What more do you want me to say?" Fumaroli asked at one point. He tapped his fingers on his desk. "I don't understand journalists who come and say, 'You have written a book. Explain to me what's in it.' My book explains everything in itself, Madame! No? The questions you ask me prove that you haven't understood what I mean, you see? That's what disturbs me. If you don't get it, I can't set you straight!"

"*Je voudrais m'exprimer en anglais*" (I'd like to express myself in English), I said. I knew he could read English. I didn't really care whether he spoke it or not. I wanted to set up a barrier.

"I'm really sorry I'm wasting your time," I said. "I came with *gentillesse*, *politesse* to start a conversation. . . . I don't want to waste your time, sir."

"No! Let's speak in French!" Fumaroli commanded, returning to French. "Speak in French, because if you speak in English, you spoil everything."

That was it. It *had* been a game for him but one that ended badly.

As I went to shake his hand to say good-bye, I looked closely at his face. It had a pasty matte finish, as if he were wearing makeup. Perhaps he felt he had to keep himself hidden.

Sometimes the *polémiques* take the form of a seamless and seemingly endless conversation. It is not unusual to have an entire book devoted to a conversation between two important figures. A classic is the 232-page dialogue between the philosopher Bernard-Henri Lévy and the late Françoise Giroud, the cofounder of the weekly magazine *L'Express* and the first minister of women's affairs.

The book, *Women and Men: A Philosophical Conversation*, was published in 1993, and it recorded their conversations while sitting under a fig tree in Paris one summer. As the title suggests, the core subject was male-female interaction. But the book was full of intellectual spin. The duo used Stendhal, Proust, Baudelaire, Freud, Valéry, Gide, Zola, Laclos, Sartre, and an army of other literary giants to make their points.

In the chapter "Seduction and Its Games," Giroud quoted the turn-of-the-twentieth-century writer Jules Renard, who said, "One experiences no pleasure in conversing with a woman who could not possibly become one's mistress." She asked Lévy whether this was true for him.

Lévy replied, "It's true that I do not believe in friendship between men and women, and when that touch of ambiguity is lacking, the relationship seems to me to be—what word do I want?—futile, sterile, useless."

In the chapter "On Ugliness as a Basic Injustice," Lévy made the surprising statement that it was harder to seduce an ugly woman than a beautiful one.

"The beautiful woman is used to it," he said. "She's experienced and clever. . . . She knows both the tricks of seduction and the rituals of seduction. You always know quickly whether it's going to happen or not. . . . The ugly woman is so flustered, she's so surprised at what's happening to her, she begins by being suspicious, incredulous, by telling herself there's something going on she doesn't understand, that someone's setting her up."

Giroud finished the thought. "The true libertine action today, the prime libertine adventure, would be to seduce an unattractive woman," she said.

It was inevitable that the two would seduce each other, at least spiritually. Lévy reminded Giroud about the first time he met her, at a dinner party twenty years before, and said she had been an "archetypal seductress." "It was all there in the smile, the look, a great attention to gestures—your own and others'—flirtatiousness, an endless fund of coquetry, and little ways of suddenly reassuring your partner."

Giroud replied that flirting gave her pleasure. "Did I really set out to do my best to charm you? . . . I'm sure I did it spontaneously, because you were a good-looking, dynamic young man and it amused me to get your attention. But for what purpose? . . . For a moment of pleasure. . . . I must confess that I've enjoyed that pleasure all my life."

She said there was a difference between being a "tease" and a "charmer." The charmer was engaged in "offering oneself and holding back, giving in and remaining aloof, an odd mix of playfulness and reticence."

Sounded like a tease to me.

In the fall of 2009, I went to see Lévy in the grand apartment he shared with Arielle Dombasle on the boulevard Saint-Germain. A thin, efficient-looking female assistant ushered me into a vast formal living room, where I sat on a taupe-colored couch and sank into red velvet accent cushions. The walls were lined in silk damask; the room smelled of incense. There was too much to look at: collections of boxes, old glass bottles, bronze Buddhas, stacks of leather-bound books, antique swords, daggers, stone eggs, gilt-framed mirrors, a stuffed bird.

Lévy made his entrance fifteen minutes later. He invited me into his office, a less formal space whose walls, carpets, drapery, and couches were swathed in comforting shades of sand that blended with the bleached oak-paneled walls. His desk was piled with books, magazines, and newspapers.

An Indian manservant in a white Nehru jacket with gold buttons brought me a small bottle of mineral water called Rosée de la Reine (The Dewdrops of the Queen). He served Lévy tea from a sterling silver pot set on a silver tray. I asked if seduction was a driving force of French life.

"It's more than a driving force," said Lévy. He leaned back on the couch, put his hand inside his trademark half-unbuttoned white shirt and rubbed his chest. "Life . . . is seduction. Civilization is seduction. What distinguishes men from animals is seduction."

The French understand seduction better than Americans for two reasons. "First, they have thought about it more and explored it in their literature; second, they repress it less than Americans do."

I can't say that I found Lévy seductive, but he knows how to think.

He had spent months traveling throughout the United States for his book inspired by Tocqueville's journeys, so I considered him an experienced observer of the differences between the Americans and the French. I asked him why he had called America a great mistress in his book.

"America is like a mistress with whom you spend great weekends, and you want to know if you can go further, if you can live with her, and you give it a shot," he told me. "Because a mistress on the weekend, it's easy; everything's beautiful. But can we wake up together, go to bed together, have problems together, have a daily life together? That's the question."

Americans, he said, are afraid of being seduced. "What struck me in America was this obsession to not let yourself be taken in," he said. "Even skillful seduction doesn't work in America because it scares everyone. In France, there is truly a desire to eroticize relationships to the maximum. All relations, human, political, professional—it doesn't matter—are eroticized, subtly eroticized. It doesn't trouble anyone."

"So in America, if you find a woman beautiful, you wouldn't tell her?" I asked.

"A hundred times no!" he exclaimed. "When I find a woman beautiful and if we know each other, I have a tendency to tell her. If I don't know her, she can't help but see it in my eyes. I realized that in the U.S., I had to force myself to avoid showing a woman that I found her seductive, because I knew that instead of creating complicity between us, it would create a barrier."

He told about trying to compliment the assistant of a newspaper executive friend. "I saw the girl in question arriving, and I told her: 'This morning you look like a bimbo!' "

I burst out laughing.

"I really thought she was going to slap me," he said. "I knew I had made an enormous mistake. I apologized. I said: 'But wait, no, I believed this was a compliment!' Even if it had been flattering, I had the impression her reaction would have been the same."

"Exactly," I said. "Even if you had said, 'You're such a beauty,' you could have gotten the same reaction."

"But if I had said, 'You are a baby doll,' that would have been . . ."

"No, Bernard-Henri, 'baby doll' is also pejorative!" I replied. "In the United States, even if you said, 'You look like a beautiful Greek goddess,' you could have been in trouble."

"Terrible," he said. "For a French man, that's a real problem!"

The game of linguistic seduction is played every day, in every social class and in every corner of France, with two little words: *tu* and *vous*. Anyone who speaks even a hundred words of French knows that *vous* is the formal, polite form of "you" and *tu* the familiar, warmer form.

Moving to the familiar is a way to offer yourself, to make yourself available to the other. "Why don't we say *tu* to each other?" suddenly moves the relationship to a deeper level of intimacy. Because the transition is so loaded with significance, knowing how and when to switch simultaneously pleases and shows respect. It must never, ever be crass.

For some situations, there are rules to rely on. *Tu* is safe to use with family, friends, and children, and usually with colleagues of the same but not higher or lower hierarchical level at work. Beyond that, things get tricky. In Spain or Italy, moving to the familiar form comes quickly in a new acquaintance, but in France it is better to wait. In a romantic relationship, where both parties know that intimacy is the goal, the right approach is supposed to be clear. A couple is expected to use *tu* once the relationship becomes intimate. As Léon Blum, the twentieth-century Socialist leader, wrote in his literary essay *Du mariage*, the switch to *tutoiement* "follows sexual penetration almost immediately. And this is true for young brides as well as for easy women."

The *tu* brings with it a dangerous point of no return. Going back to the *vous* is like telling someone you only want to be friends after you've slept together. But for some couples, the *vous* can signal increased intimacy, a complicity only the two of you understand. "The most beautiful friendship is one in which, in the end, you are rid of all familiarity," Raphaël Enthoven told me.

My problem with *tu* and *vous* is that I sometimes forget whom I've agreed to *tutoyer.* There are moments when I find myself in midsentence awkwardly changing course.

The etiquette of *tu* and *vous* is so subtle and fluid that even the French are permanently kept on edge. Some businesses use *tu* to foster team spirit and dynamism. *Tutoiement* is often mandatory in high-tech, communication, publicity, culture, press, design, and architectural offices, but banks stick to *vous*. When a subordinate uses *tu* to address the boss in a meeting, it usually is a coded message of a more personal relationship.

In his French law office, Andy uses *tu* with his two closest French male colleagues. One is older and more senior than Andy in the hierarchy; the other is younger. The younger colleague uses *tu* with my husband but *vous* with the older colleague.

On popular television, just about everyone uses *tu*, perhaps a way to keep the issue from distracting the audience.

Even within the family, *tu* and *vous* may have complex meanings. Bruno Racine, the president of the Bibliothèque Nationale, told me that his parents use *vous* with each other in front of other people but switch to *tu* when they are alone. They address their middle-aged children with *tu*, and the children reply with *vous*. As a child, Bruno was allowed to use *tu* with his mother. "It was the privilege of the *petit dernier*," the youngest child, he said. When his mother got angry with him, she reverted to *vous*. Then when he turned eighteen, he was required to address her with *vous*. "As you see," he said, "nothing is simple."

Arielle Dombasle used the formal *vous* with Bernard-Henri Lévy (but in front of me she called him "*mon ange*" and kissed him on his lips). The *vous*, even between spouses, is a lingering habit of the French titled and upper classes; Jacques Chirac and his wife, Bernadette, are said to use it with each other. But Arielle's reason was different. It keeps the excitement alive, she told me. "Le *vous*, this is a caress."

Laure de Gramont told me that, years ago, she had used *vous* with Woody Allen in French, and he told her to use the *tu* form. "I told him, 'You are a genius, and I can never use *tu* with a genius,'" she said.

Nicolas Sarkozy tends to use the informal *tu* instead of the formal *vous* with his foreign counterparts, his colleagues, and journalists.

When he used *tu* in addressing Barack Obama at their first joint news conference and at a public event with Chirac, his predecessor, he was criticized for irreverence. Indeed, not everyone appreciates the closeness he imposes on them. In his memoirs, Jean Daniel, the director of the weekly magazine *Le Nouvel Observateur*, criticized Sarkozy's everyday behavior as too familiar. "He addressed me as '*tu*,' that irritated me!" Daniel wrote. That struck a chord with me as well. I personally don't like it when someone I hardly know says, "Let's use *tu*." What if I don't want to?

Shéhérazade Semsar de Boisséson, who is Iranian-born, American-educated, married to a Frenchman, and the head of her own company, has devised her own strategy. She hangs tough. She never uses *tu* in business dealings. When the other side moves to *tu*, she fights back with *vous*, even if the verbal warfare lasts for an hour. Eventually, the other side gives in.

I learned early on that reporters tend to *tutoyer* each other quickly, especially if they are traveling together. But I tend to use *vous* because I know the French complain that Americans are much too friendly in the beginning of a relationship.

Still, I have always known that *Le Nouvel Observateur* is exceptionally *décontracté*—informal—so when François Armanet, one of its editors, called one day, I immediately launched into *tu*. We continued talking for several minutes, but it was too much for him. "I'm still using *vous* and you've moved to *tu* and we never talked about whether we would do it," he said. "It's charming."

Oh God, I thought, he thinks I'm *dragué*-ing him. (If you say of a woman, "*Quelle dragueuse*," it means, "What a flirt!")

I decided to keep the conversation light. I laughed and told François the story about how I had apparently insulted one of his colleagues by using *vous* when she had moved to *tu* and that I wanted to avoid insulting him as well. That led to a discussion about intimacy.

"The move from *vous* to *tu* is a fragile moment," François said. "It's a radical change. It implies certain complicity. It can be a great privilege."

I suggested we move back to *vous*. He resisted. I suggested we start over but leave open possibilities. We could go back to the *vous*, then meet one day, perhaps for a coffee or lunch. Then, at some point, maybe we would look at each other and decide to go all the way to *tu*.

He thought that was a swell idea. Then he got around to the real reason for his call: a bit of journalistic business. We resolved it with efficiency, elegance, and *vous*.

The French find beauty in the French language itself. Their very identity is wrapped up in it.

"France is the French language," the great twentieth-century social historian Fernand Braudel proclaimed. In the 1990s, Prime Minister Édouard Balladur created a High Council of the French Language. He told its twenty-nine members (seriously) that defending their tongue was "an act of faith in the future of our country."

Then, in 2007, Maurice Druon, a hero of the French Resistance in World War II and a writer who became the defender-in-chief of French, led a fruitless campaign to persuade the European Union to adopt French as its chief language. "Italian is the language of song, German is good for philosophy and English for poetry; French is best at precision," he said.

Yes and no.

Centuries ago, French was chosen as the primary language of diplomacy in part because it offered negotiators both precision and maximum flexibility. The indirect approach survives in French today. It adds to the mystery. In her 1986 book on language, *L'implicite*, Catherine Kerbrat-Orecchioni observed that " 'It's warm in here' never means that 'It's warm here,' but, at some point, 'Open the window,' 'Turn off the radiator,' 'Can I take off my jacket?' 'It is cool elsewhere,' 'I have nothing more interesting to say.' "

Then there are double negatives like "There's no reason to think the contrary" that drove me nuts when I was first learning French. One day at lunch I asked my researcher, Florence, if she'd like a piece of cake from a new bakery nearby that was so fancy it put individual pastries under bell jars as if they were jewels. She didn't say, "Yes, please," but "This is not the kind of question that can be answered with a 'no'!"

Then there is *pas mal*. Literally, *pas mal* means "not bad," which in English can mean "so-so." But in French, it can mean "Wow, you look fabulous!" or "Absolutely fantastic." Saying it with a flat and serious tone makes it even more powerful than if it is uttered with enthusiasm. On the day Andy and I moved to a new apartment, I realized that our big but very old American General Electric refrigerator would have to be replaced. The mover rattled off brand names he said were "*pas terrible*." Knowing that *pas mal* could mean "terrific," I figured *pas terrible* must be even better. I was wrong. It means "pretty bad" and definitely to be avoided.

In both everyday and formal language, expressions that sound pretentious or effeminate to American ears are considered elegant and appropriate in French. The tradition has its roots in the seventeenth-century literary movement called *préciosité*, based on gallantry and characterized by an ideal of manners and behavior.

In a business letter, "I appreciate your delicate attention" is not obsequious, but proper. In polite society, circumlocutions, hyperbole, and superlatives are to be embraced. Adhering to standards is a sign of gentility. Even grim news can be delivered with a frisson of the poetic. I needed an MRI at one point for a severed hamstring. Perhaps the radiologist thought it would have been too direct to say, "You have destroyed your hamstring forever." Instead, he told me, "You really did this beautifully, madame." Pausing for effect, he added, "The tendon. It floats. In a sea of blood."

The French give themselves the right to be intellectuals, even if their professions say they do something else. If they play the role badly or to excess, they might be guilty of *touche-à-tout*, or "dabbling." But if they do it well, they are admired. In France, it is a compliment to be called a "generalist," a concept originating in the seventeenth-century ideal of the *honnête homme*, a kind of Renaissance man who has mastered both the humanities and mathematics. In the French law firm where my husband works, at least two of the partners are published, well-reviewed novelists.

For me, the model is Bruno Racine. I first met him in the 1990s when he was the Foreign Ministry official responsible for policy in the Balkans.

I caught up with him later when he was working on France's possible reintegration into the military wing of NATO. After that, he went to Rome as director of the French Academy, then back to Paris as president, first of the Pompidou Center and then of the Bibliothèque Nationale. He represents the French government in international forums on nuclear disarmament, collects nineteenth-century French paintings, lectures on Petronius, writes novels, and fences. (He specializes in the saber.) He insists he is not an American-style workaholic. "I'm not someone who leads a monastic life," he said. "I don't get up at six in the morning to write."

A more practical intellectual is Alain Minc, a financial adviser and former chairman of *Le Monde* who has written thirty books ranging from the history of economic thought to a novel about Spinoza. He now runs a consulting company out of swank offices on avenue George V. He is also an informal but trusted adviser to his close friend Nicolas Sarkozy.

"Nothing is more pleasurable for a previously published author than to frolic in a discipline that is not his: the feeling of intellectual freedom . . . is unmatched," he wrote in a 483-page tome on the history of France, from the Gauls to Sarkozy.

"What do the French mean by the word *intellectuel*?" he asked himself during one of our conversations. "It's someone who gives himself permission to speak about things he does not know but is able to master through cleverness or culture. Our culture is less deep but much broader than yours."

He gave the phenomenon a name: "Profound superficiality, to know about a lot of things, to have much partial knowledge."

By contrast, he explained, Americans tend to be specialists in only one field. "Your entrepreneurs have no education. They may be geniuses but they have no education—in philosophy, history, sociology, literature. They don't seem to read anything."

Yet Americans have learned to navigate in France. It was the art of good conversation that attracted the American novelist Edith Wharton to the French. She felt as if she could compete in the salon and at the dinner table with the wittiest and most elegant of partners and adversaries, her intellect trumping the handicap of her gender.

The Americans who have most successfully endeared themselves to the French are those who know how to play the game of profound superficiality with ease and elegance. To move effortlessly in a conversation *du coq à l'âne*, from the rooster to the donkey, from one subject to another—is considered a valued asset.

Benjamin Franklin knew how to do it, and used the skill in a life-and-death campaign of seduction on behalf of his infant country. When he was the American minister to France during the Revolutionary War, he continued to pursue his love of science, philosophy, and printing. He did more than just learn French—he played at it, writing love letters to women and essays to Parisian friends. Charmed, they corrected his grammar. Ellen Cohn, the editor of *The Papers of Benjamin Franklin*, called the process "a big parlor game." In an age when laughter and lightness were important, Franklin sought to sow happiness and get the French to like him, not just for purely intellectual or frivolous reasons, but because America needed French soldiers, French ships, and French money.

As Franklin's papers show, he immersed himself in the oddities of French culture, like papermaking and hot air balloons. He investigated how to improve insane asylums and how to make a better bread-making oven for prison bakeries.

The antithesis of this approach is personified by Franklin's fellow diplomat John Adams, who considered his colleague's joie de vivre a sign of laziness and his politesse and errant interests a waste of time. Adams rose at five a.m., Franklin at ten. Adams was a straight talker; Franklin had embraced the French habit of indirection and the avoidance of overt conflict. Adams looked at the relationship with France through the prisms of power and profit: if America won its independence, France would enhance its influence in Europe at Britain's expense and capitalize on a favorable trade relationship with the United States. The French hated John Adams.

Franklin's Frenchness continued to serve him well in negotiating a peace treaty with the British after the American victory at Yorktown in 1781. "Great Affairs sometimes take their Rise from small Circumstances," Franklin wrote in his journal about the negotiations. Take the example of his letter to a longtime acquaintance, the Earl of Shelburne. In addition to expressing hope for a general peace, Franklin made detailed reference to gooseberry bushes the earl had sent to one of Franklin's neighbors. The letter was the catalyst for peace negotiations.

I do not know whether Christine Lagarde would consider Franklin a man who thought too much, particularly about trivial subjects. But when he died, France went into mourning for three days. He loved France, and France loved him back.

6

You Never Know

. . .

> [The Frenchwoman] is, in nearly all respects, as different as possible from the average American woman. . . . Is it because she dresses better, or knows more about cooking, or is more "coquettish," or more "feminine," or more excitable, or more emotional, or more immoral? . . . The real reason is . . . simply that, like the men of her race, the Frenchwoman is *grown-up*.
>
> —Edith Wharton,
> *French Ways and Their Meaning*

> You know what charm is: a way of getting the answer "yes" without having asked any clear question.
>
> —Albert Camus, *The Fall*

Sophie-Caroline de Margerie speaks English with bell-like tones and an upper-class accent that's a bit too perfect, like the one Henry Higgins's reinvented flower seller acquires in *My Fair Lady*. Eliza Doolittle was judged by a linguistic scholar to be "born Hungarian" and a princess; Sophie-Caroline is the daughter of a Polish count. The British journalist friend who brought us together told me that only a sensitive British ear can detect the mysterious foreignness in her voice.

Her address on rue Bonaparte near the Seine in the sixth arrondissement is one of the best in Paris: her apartment is understated and dressed in shades of soft taupe and gray. The paintings are the fruit of decades of collecting by someone who knows good art. They are hung so discreetly that it is difficult to study them without appearing to stare.

I met Sophie-Caroline for the first time when she invited me to lunch. A member of the Conseil d'État, the highest administrative and public law court in France, she appeared at the door of her apartment perfectly done up. She wore a cashmere sweater that did not hide her cleavage, a pencil skirt, matching gray hose, and high-heeled black pumps. Her hair was styled in loose curls that framed her face; her cheeks were slightly rouged, her large eyes made larger with shadow and liner. She was almost too beautiful.

A maid served us a three-course meal at a long, damask-covered table. Like me, Sophie-Caroline was on leave from her day job and writing a book at home. I was curious why she'd put herself into such elegant but restrictive clothing when she didn't have to.

"My working days are for me and myself, and yet, I'm well turned out," she explained. "This is my work uniform. It gives me discipline. It defines the moment when I start working. If I go to work in my dressing gown, I'm not a hundred percent at work."

I asked her if she, like so many French women I know, dressed up to buy a baguette.

"Of course," she said, moving into French. "*On ne sait jamais*"—One never knows.

"One never knows what?" I asked.

"*On ne sait jamais* is the impulse to look one's best all the time," she replied. "Maybe not one's best, but to look . . ."—she struggled for a word—". . . okay."

Okay? I thought. Either she was being modest or she was clueless about the effect she had on people, or she knew and was pretending she didn't.

"Why do I dress up a bit when I go and buy the newspaper?" she went on. "Well, because there is the odd chance that the window cleaner might whistle, and if he does, my day will be sunnier!"

"No!"

"That's the bigger part of *on ne sait jamais*. Then, of course, there's the odd chance that I might bump into an old friend or school chum, and I don't want him or her to think, 'Ooooo, she looks old,' which he or she might do anyway, but in any case a bit less. Voilà. There you have it."

"So it's a connection with the other?" I asked.

"Yes. It's a connection with the other."

"In the United States, if a window cleaner whistles at you on the street, he's invading your space, and as a good feminist, you'll be insulted," I said.

She saw it differently. "On the contrary, I walk away with a springier step," she said. "I might even text somebody with a message of 'Guess what happened today?' Not that it happens that often. But when it does, it makes my day. It certainly does. Like a macaroon."

Afterward, I asked Florence about *on ne sait jamais* and whether she feels flattered or insulted when an unknown man on the street comments on her appearance. She said she enjoys the game, and she explained the rules.

"Men's compliments on the street? Of course, I love that," she said. "As long as it remains light, and as long as it doesn't demand anything from me. Ideally, I pretend I don't hear or see anything."

A certain distance has to be maintained, she said. "If a man yells at you because you don't respond to his compliment, or starts being rude, it becomes disagreeable," she said. "Absolutely."

The same compliment that is acceptable on the street, where the encounter is brief and fleeting, would be off-limits in a confined space like a bus or the Métro. "You don't want to engage with someone and then have to face the consequences," she said.

Florence told me the story of her trip to work one morning on one of Paris's bikes-for-rent. It was a sunny day, and she was wearing a short skirt. ("Neither vulgar nor provocative," she said.)

"I was perfectly aware I was doing my 'girl who rides a bike in a skirt' act," she said. "One man gave me a look of approval. I smiled at him. No risk at all! I was on my bike and by the time I smiled, I was gone. Another one told me I was 'charming.' I said, 'Oh, thank you!' and kept going.

"Along the way, while I was crossing the Alexandre III bridge, there was a car with two or three men in it. They were looking at me. We were blocked at a stoplight. I didn't 'answer' at all and was looking as indifferent as possible. But when the light turned green, I looked at them and gave them a bright smile as I rode away. I heard them exclaiming, 'Wow.' And that felt good!"

Sometimes the line can be crossed. An Australian dancer at the Lido cabaret club told me about the time she was coming out of a butcher shop at three in the afternoon wearing normal street clothes and little makeup. A young man on a motorcycle pulled over and asked, in all seriousness, "Excuse me, would you be interested in being part of a threesome?"

As for my own style on the street, it is as relaxed as possible unless I have to dress up, even in the upscale neighborhood where I used to live. Take the Saturday afternoon I was making cookies with my daughters and ran out of butter. Dusted with flour, still in my jogging clothes from a morning run, I dashed out to the convenience store up the street.

But this was not just any street. It was the rue du Bac, a chic place to see and be seen on Saturdays. I heard my name called and turned to face Gérard Araud, a senior Foreign Ministry official. He was wearing pressed jeans, a soft-as-butter leather jacket, caramel-colored tie shoes, and an amused look. In his hand was a small shopping bag containing his purchase of the morning.

Gérard invited me for coffee. We sat outdoors at a café on the corner of the rue de Varenne. In retrospect, I should have known better and invited him into my kitchen. This was one of the premier people-watching intersections in all of Paris. I was inappropriately dressed for the curbside chitchat that followed.

The Swedish ambassador and his wife rode up on their bikes and stopped to say hello. Both were in tailored tweed blazers, slim pants, and expensive loafers. Then Robert M. Kimmitt, the American deputy treasury secretary at the time, who happened to be visiting Paris, walked by. He accepted Gérard's invitation to join us.

"I see that Paris hasn't done much for your style," Kimmitt joked.

"At least I'm wearing black," I replied.

When he left, Gérard made what he considered an important point with as much seriousness as if he were delivering a diplomatic démarche to a recalcitrant ally. "The rue du Bac is not the Upper West Side," he said.

"All right, all right," I conceded. I knew the rules: jogging clothes (shoes included) are to be removed as soon as one's exercise is over if you don't want to look like a rube or an American or both.

Then I got a bit defensive. "This is my neighborhood," I said. "I belong here. So I can dress however I want!"

"You can," he said, with the sangfroid that makes him such a good diplomat. "But you shouldn't."

I'm convinced that American-style feminism has prevented me from easily absorbing the reality of the playground of the streets.

It took years—and two tours as a foreign correspondent living in Paris—before I fully understood the *on ne sait jamais* of public space. I found it both sexist and offensive that strange men felt entitled to comment on what I wore or how I looked. Maybe I never got over an episode during my first stint in Paris in the late 1970s, in the days when joggers were as rare as bicycle helmets. I used to jog several mornings a week in the Champ de Mars, under the shadow of the Eiffel Tower. One morning a young guy walking with his buddies yelled out, "*Allez, vieille sportive*!"—"You go, old gal!" I was approaching my thirtieth birthday.

In Paris, women and men are supposed to please each other on the street. You never walk alone but are in a perpetual visual conversation with others, even perfect strangers. Mona Ozouf, the historian and writer, described men's compliments to women on the street as "benedictions, and not at all aggressions." She was eager to elaborate. "If a mason standing above on scaffolding whistled at me—it hasn't happened in years—it was marvelous! It was absolutely marvelous!" she said. "And this kind of thing, this gesture of homage, is very rarely taken in France as harassment. It is interpreted more as approved gallantry: the elementary politeness of the relations between men and women consists in the expression of tributes."

One summer, when my daughter Gabriela, a college student, was working in Paris, she told me that in a single day, she was called "*superbe*," "*magnifique*," and "*belle blonde*" by older men as she maneuvered the streets. "Men don't have the right to say these things," she said, "especially when they're old. But the vocabulary is much more elegant here than in the U.S. So they can get away with being sleazy."

A French woman I know felt out of place when she lived in the Chicago suburbs because she got dressed up every day and no one seemed to notice. "In France, men look at you," she said. "It brings pleasure. Even women look at you. It's not always positive, but it's an acknowledgment that you exist. You walk differently when you know someone is looking at you. It's the one thing I missed in the States. The 'look' is missing. I think it's why American women get fat."

A poll by the respected polling organization CSA for the magazine *Figaro Madame* stated that, on average, 21 percent of French men say they turn around to look at a woman once or twice a day, 32 percent between three and five times a day, and 5 percent at least twenty times a day. Head turning occurs whether the man is married, involved with a woman, or unattached.

"It is not politically correct to admit it," said Jean-Daniel Lévy, CSA's political director. He added that "the candor of the poll respondents to this question" made the results credible. In the same article, an anthropologist argued that the practice of head turning could be the result of society's "patriarchal validation of the man who knows how to appreciate beautiful women." A psychiatrist urged women to see men's stares as a positive way "to start communicating," and not just "a hormonal response."

I asked several French men how many times a day they turn their heads to look at a woman. Philippe Labro, the author, journalist, and television host, who is in his midseventies, e-mailed me the following answer: "A thousand times, but 900 times it's to look at my wife! Is that enough of a good French answer?"

"Who are the other 100?" I asked.

"The other 100 are the marvelously gracious and unknown Parisian or French beauties whom one can cross in the streets, in restaurants, public places, on the terraces of bistros the minute the sun comes out," he wrote back. "These mysteriously serene or inhabited-by-their-intimate-stories women without whom the urban scenery would be dreary and sadly grayish."

Then I asked a physical therapist whether any of his male patients had suffered a car or bicycle accident from turning his head to ogle women. "Not that I can recall," he said. "But it's good for upper body mobility to turn your head around several times a day."

The game of the sexes also extends deep into the workplace. In the United States, the mildest playfulness during business hours and in a business setting is forbidden; in France, it is encouraged. In American corporations, men are told routinely that they cross the line when they compliment a female employee on the color of her dress or the style of her hair. In France, flirtation is part of the job.

My husband, Andy, is the only American in a French law firm. He took the French bar examinations a few years back and more recently gave advice to a young, female American lawyer who was doing the same. She had just completed a practice oral exam for a bar review course and had worked hard to come across as sober and serious. So she was stunned by the professor's comments.

"He told me I was too stiff," she told Andy. "He said I had to be more *séduisante*"—more seductive.

Andy tried not to laugh. "The French use the word *séduisant*, but they don't mean it the way we do in English," he told her. "I'm sure what he meant is that he wants you to try to be more . . . engaging."

I told the story to French friends one evening, and Bertrand Vannier, a senior executive at Radio France who had spent several years as a correspondent in Washington, said he could top that story. "I once had a young female reporter who couldn't have been more than twenty-six or twenty-seven years old, but she was so solemn and serious that she seemed double her age," he recalled. "She walked as if she had the weight of the world on her shoulders. She kept her head down. She wore long black skirts. Her reporting was good, serious—but boring.

"So I took her aside one day and gave her my 'miniskirt and makeup' lecture. I suggested to her, 'Why don't you work and write your stories as if you are wearing a miniskirt and makeup?'

"She didn't put on a miniskirt and makeup but she did something even better. She met a guy, fell in love, and had a baby. She was happy. She finally became what I wanted her to be: a good, serious, and not boring reporter."

I thought of Bertrand's story when I saw a cartoon entitled "It Doesn't Take Much" by Pénélope Bagieu, a young Parisian illustrator.

A young man and a sour-faced young woman are passing each other on the street. The woman is dressed in dark brown and carrying a duffel bag. Her shoulders are hunched, her long hair unkempt and falling into her eyes. The man, serious-looking in glasses and a trench coat, turns around as she passes and utters three words: "You are ravishing." Her eyes open wide, a small smile forms on her lips. She is transformed. Her hair flies in the wind, her lips form a big smile, her jacket opens to reveal full breasts under a tight pink shirt.

I discovered a variation of this cartoon in an illustration by Sempé, the artist made famous in the United States with his work in *The New Yorker.* It shows an elegant woman of an indeterminate age walking on a Paris street. She wears a ruffled skirt and a close-cropped jacket, high heels, earrings, a necklace, and a hat and has a confident walk. She is smiling. Seven men—a team working on a building renovation—whistle at her as she passes.

She could have been Sophie-Caroline.

Do professional women feel they are at a disadvantage and not taken seriously in a society that can seem so sexually charged?

I belong to a club of about two hundred high-powered women, among them corporate executives, judges, lawyers, elected officials, doctors, journalists, museum curators, academics, writers, fashion designers, and cultural figures. Founded in 1985, it is probably the most powerful private women's club in the country. It is also secretive and virtually unknown. It is not included in any of the books or articles on the influential private clubs of France. By choice.

Commercial and political self-promotion is forbidden. There is nothing specific about sisterhood or the promotion of women in our bylaws. To become a member, you must be sponsored by a "godmother" and undergo a "tryout," at which you give a three-minute presentation in French about yourself and your professional accomplishments, delivered with just the right balance of self-assuredness, humility, and humor. Only a handful of members are foreigners.

The club sometimes meets in a private upstairs dining room at Fouquet's, the glittery restaurant on the Champs-Élysées that has welcomed famous diners like Charlie Chaplin, Maurice Chevalier, Marlene Dietrich, Winston Churchill, and Jacqueline Onassis. Nicolas Sarkozy was there on the night he was elected president. The waiters (most of them men) regard us with a blend of humor and haughtiness.

Some of the women who come to the club for the first time express either discomfort or amazement. "It's a pleasure to say '*Bonsoir à toutes,*'" said one women invited as a guest, as she used the feminine *toutes* to refer to "everyone." "I have to confess that I like men," she went on, "and at first I resisted coming to an all-women's club."

Our gatherings are organized for serious conversation, much needed in a country where women's salaries are about 20 percent less than men's, where women hold only slightly more than 10 percent of board seats in the top 650 companies, and where only 18 percent of the deputies in Parliament are women. (French women received the vote only in 1944, so they have had a lot of catching up to do.) Each table has an assigned head whose role is to lead the discussion. Seat assignments for our dinners are strategically thought out to facilitate getting to know as many other members as possible.

But these encounters are also designed for fun. Most of the women get dressed up, in well-cut suits or dresses, high heels, and good jewelry. A money-saving suggestion to eliminate champagne during the cocktail period before dinner was resoundingly rejected. A number of women said they'd rather give up dessert.

Michèle Fitoussi of *Elle* suggested I poll members of the club on their views about seduction. Because of the club's strict rules about soliciting, I was permitted to send the poll only to part of the membership, and even then, on a personal basis. About three dozen responded. Most of them got into the spirit, saying they could never live without seduction. For some, the concept invoked the "smile," the "look," "elegance," "refinement," "charm," "culture," and even "gallantry." Others saw it first and foremost as a "game" associated with the ideas of "lightness," "pleasure," and "banter."

"It would almost be considered rude not to try a little seduction in all kinds of situations," said Nicole Bacharan, a political scientist who specializes in American politics. "But it should not be taken seriously. French seduction is often directed toward everybody, but nobody specifically. It doesn't need a purpose." A writer in our group said that seduction "is something instinctive, sort of like breathing."

The subtlety of the French language fueled the ability to seduce, they reported. "It's a game with language before being a strategy of conquest," said Nicole Gnesotto, a political scientist and one of France's leading experts on the European Union. "It is based on humor, irony, complicity, and what is left unsaid. Italians play even more with words than we do, but they have real intentions, whereas we play with seduction but don't try to bring it to a conclusion."

Despite her serious, high-level position, Gnesotto has a range of uses for seduction: "with my florist, to be offered an extra rose; with my regular shopkeepers with whom I perpetuate the same rituals of seduction, just for pleasure; with the bureaucracy to try to get a little favor—to get the bus driver to let me off where I want and not have to wait until the stop."

Only one member who replied, Florence Montreynaud, the strictest feminist in our group, rejected this exercise. "I'm troubled by the word and the idea of 'seduction' which is too sexual for me," she wrote in an e-mail. "It's to turn away from the right path, to try to be attractive in a disloyal way."

I asked the women whether they are outraged by the perpetual game of seduction in their professional lives. I found that if American women engage in a perpetual battle of the sexes, French women are more likely to collaborate with the opposite sex. In France, said Marie-France de Chabaneix, the founder and president of a dietary and cosmetics company, women use seduction "as a weapon to defend themselves against the machismo of men." A professor of rhetoric said that as a teacher,

"You have to play with seduction. Otherwise students don't listen to you."

Most of the women believe that the use of one's femininity is a convenient tool in nonsexual situations and everyday life. One government jurist found seduction helpful "to convince the garage owner to repair my car before anyone else's."

The most exasperating thing I heard was that there are no fixed rules. You just have to intuit them, as if you are feeling your way up a vertical rock formation. There has to be perpetual fine-tuning, deciding the border between "empathy, closeness, affection and ambiguity and too much intimacy that can get out of control," said an investment adviser.

It is quite easy to get it wrong. One woman in a senior government position told the story of inviting an older colleague to lunch one day. "I suggested we have lunch to talk about work," she said. "You can't imagine how surprised I was when he answered: 'I thought you were already in a relationship!'" The seductive professional woman, she added, has to watch out for another reason, jealousy: "Seduction is a tool for certain women, but dangerous, because it strongly displeases others."

Every woman polled said that when it comes to male-female relationships in the workplace, there is a cultural divide between France and the United States. Some called the American approach more straightforward and serious; others praised the American efficiency that avoids vapid speech and playacting. But some women found that this seriousness robs the work environment of creativity, instinct, and sensitivity. Nothing seems worse to these professionals than to be considered feminists in the American way. To avoid it, they advised, women should use humor, not anger, to get their points across. "The American executive woman, the entrepreneur, has to assume a distance, like putting on armor," said the investment adviser. "She needs to be harsher and more manly to be convincing. Her feminine attributes—sensitivity, softness, charm—have to be erased because they 'weaken' her and are not synonymous with efficiency, performance, excellence. What a serious business it is, work without seduction!"

What surprised me most was that a number of my women's club members do not favor uniform gender standards in the workplace. I responded that if they have to play the femininity game, they will always be treated as somehow inferior. Not so. Here's what one member said: "If you want to have equal opportunity and treatment in professional life, you should above all stick with seduction. It's the only way to avoid frightening men."

Most of the women in the club who had spent time in the United States consider the politics of American feminism divisive, brutal, and unnecessary. All have stories to tell about sexual harassment consciousness-raising.

For Fabienne Haas, a corporate lawyer and mother of two, it happened when she was a young intern at a white-shoe New York law firm. Fabienne is nearing fifty, but she wears V-necked lacy camisoles under her sober suit jackets. In New York in her midtwenties, she was buttoned up to the neck. A married male associate in the firm, four years older than she, had been inviting her regularly to lunch, a gesture she found endearing as she was on a tight budget. But one day a colleague spotted him touching her hand and reported the incident to management. She was ordered to show up at an emergency meeting at 8 a.m. the next day. There were six male lawyers in the room. She was terrified. "Did he try to abuse his power? Did he try to pressure you?" she was asked. "I tried to keep a straight face and convince them nothing wrong had happened."

Stéphanie Cardot, a mother of three in her midthirties who runs her own company, said she adored the American system, which rewards efficiency and hard work above all. She criticized the failure of the French corporate world to modernize its business strategies and eliminate cronyism. Stéphanie has impossibly big blue eyes and near-perfect English laced with colloquialisms acquired during her years living in New York. She wraps herself in her femininity, even though she is tough as nails in her decision making.

"In the U.S., you seduce by hard work and by being more professional than everyone else, which is all good, all very efficient," she said over breakfast one day. "You have great results. But relationships are really dry. What I can't accept is the lack of seduction in everyday life. In France, on the other hand, there is too much of it. Seduction is used as a way to be a little bit lazy. What I mean is French people—especially the elite—have always had this belief that work is ugly and that intelligence, pure intelligence, and seduction will get you anywhere."

That said, Stéphanie failed to understand the American obsession with political correctness. "All this sexual harassment business is just killing the reality of the man and the woman together in the workplace," she said. "How can you show real charm if you are afraid you are going to be sued for sexual harassment or whatever. It comes to a point where some men will not stay in an elevator with a woman. They will not open the door for you or light your cigarette."

Stéphanie told me about the time she failed the sexual harassment test needed for a work contract with an American corporation on Wall Street.

"So I sit down and the first question is: 'You're a woman. You walk into a room full of guys, and they're telling a dirty joke. They stop telling the joke. Is that sexual harassment?' I'm thinking to myself, 'No, it's not, and besides, I want to know the end of the joke!' But I say to myself, if I'm being asked the question in the first place, the right answer must be 'Yes.' So I click 'Yes.'

"And the next question is, 'You're a woman. You walk into a room full of men, and they're telling a dirty joke, and when you come in, they keep telling the joke. Is that sexual harassment?' So I think that if the previous answer is yes, this one must be 'No,' so I click 'No.' "

She was wrong both times. It was a no-win situation. "So I'm like, either I don't get to hear the end of the joke, or I get to hear it and I'm seen as the slut of the office," she said.

After she failed the test, the human resources department gave her sexual harassment training. "The trainer says to me, 'Okay, you walk into the office one morning after you've just cut your hair, and I say, 'Oh, Stéphanie, you're gorgeous this way!' What do you tell me?'

"So I say, 'Thank you!' He says, 'No! You report me to HR. I just sexually harassed you.'

"I say, 'I'm sorry. I just don't get it.' He gives up. He's like, 'You know what? Just get out of here.' "

• • •

There is something light and fun going on in the way French men and women relate to one another but also something very strategic and deliberate. There is nothing ad hoc about the French style of seduction. "It's as if we French constantly play with it," a French woman in her early twenties explained. "Look at French girls when they go abroad! They accentuate their French accents; they try to be more French. French seduction includes consciousness of what it is. It's the knowledge of codes that are universally recognized as French."

Much of the reason for playfulness in the workplace is that women in France are not used to gender segregation. They enjoy being with men. The historian Mona Ozouf told me about the six months that she spent at Princeton University in 1972 with her husband, when he was a history professor there. Ozouf was flabbergasted when she was invited to join a group called History Wives.

"For the French, this is an anomaly," she said. "That the 'history wives' got together and there was, after all, a kind of segregation, this is unimaginable in France. There is sensitivity in France that women are omnipresent."

The Tony Award–winning playwright and author Yasmina Reza followed Nicolas Sarkozy on the campaign trail for a year before the presidential election, and he gave her unusual access, allowing her entry into the most private of meetings. She turned the experience into a best seller. Soon after the book was published, a magazine interviewer from *Le Nouvel Observateur* asked her whether Sarkozy had ever tried to seduce her. "No," she replied. "He wanted to seduce France." Then, she added a line that could have worked well in one of her plays: "It is almost insulting to spend an entire year with a man without him trying to seduce you."

When the codes are understood and accepted by women, it encourages men to perpetuate the game. It doesn't seem to occur to men, even to some whose job is to deal with foreigners, that their words or gestures could be perceived as inappropriate. A male French diplomat told the story of being confined with a beautiful American woman in an elevator in a New York skyscraper one day. A trained observer, he caressed her body with his eyes. When the elevator reached its destination, she whipped around and asked bluntly, "Do you want the name of my lawyer?"

"I thought I was paying her a compliment," he told me. "She was too lovely a sight to ignore. She was ready to sue me."

I asked the British journalist Charles Bremner about the ease with which French men and women flirt. "There is a playfulness that has disappeared from northern European countries," he said, observing that even Michèle Alliot-Marie, who has headed a number of key ministries, including justice and defense, puts seduction into her style. "Here she is, a powerful, senior politician in her sixties, and when we appeared together on a television show, she was wearing a tight skirt and high heels and was flirting," Bremner recalled. "She showed her little girl side. It was not a conscious act."

The writer Pierre Assouline put it in starker terms. He explained why so many French men and women prefer a conversation with a member of the opposite sex. He said that a conversation with a flirtatious twist is always more intriguing and interesting than one that is straightforward.

"'There's a *pourquoi pas*" (why not), he said. "There's always a *pourquoi pas*." I took this to be a provocative variation of Sophie-Caroline's *on ne sait jamais*.

Finally, I wanted the viewpoint of a younger man, so I asked Alexandre Deschamps, my physical therapist. Alexandre has spent a lot of time in London. His girlfriend is Greek. Because he speaks English, many of his clients are foreigners. He is good with teenagers and had treated both of my daughters, one after a kayaking accident, the other after knee surgery.

"I would be in prison if I had to work in the United States," he said. "When I see a beautiful woman on the Métro in Paris, I might want to tell her, 'You know, you are really beautiful.'"

"But aren't you invading her space?" I asked.

"It depends on how you do it," he replied. "If you say it nicely and with respect, women really like it."

"Of course, you couldn't say that to a female colleague," I said. On the contrary, he said. He told me he could be much more relaxed with a colleague than with a stranger. "Do you know the woman therapist here?" he asked. "She's very young and pretty. We like to joke around. One day she asked me to give her a massage. So I said, 'Sure, but only if you're naked!' It was a normal joke."

"What about your female clients?" I asked. "Would you tell them they're beautiful and you adore their perfume?"

"Of course!" he replied. "And they would smile."

I tried to join in Alexandre's game.

"In that case, the woman who came in the same time as I did is so sour today that she looks like she swallowed a lemon," I said. "You would make her day if you tell her she looks beautiful."

"I could, but I won't," Alexandre said. It was a question of integrity, he explained. "There has to be some truth in what you say."

7

Make Friends with Your Butcher

. . .

> Here, nose to nose, face to face in the Métro.
> Here, glued, tight, skin almost against skin.
> Noise, but no smile. . . .
>
> —Louis Chedid, *Ici*

> To seduce in the French way is not the American way. It's a question of keeping the attention of the consumer, of having a lively relationship with her. It's not a question of seducing her to get her into bed. She has to open up to you. If she is suspicious, closed, not open to a dialogue, it is . . . difficult.
>
> —Maurice Lévy, president of Publicis

It is a drama I have seen played out hundreds of times. The scene is the Paris Métro—or maybe a street where the sidewalk is too small for two people walking in opposite directions to pass each other without some maneuvering.

Parisians are going about their daily business, commuting, shopping, running errands. All is quiet. If there is talking, tones are subdued. The subway car door opens—or the walking traffic reaches a corner—and a group of American tourists appears, talking and laughing in voices that shatter the calm. Suddenly they come so close to a Parisian that they are nearly touching. The Americans smile, reaching out with what they perceive as the most natural gesture of kindness. But the smile is not returned. It is greeted with a blank stare, or even worse, a scowl.

Taken aback, the Americans move on, convinced they have confronted, once again, the most puzzling paradox about France: Why, in this charming country where even the air feels like an invitation to enjoyment, are the natives so cold? What objection can these people possibly have, after all, to well-intentioned visitors with pockets full of cash?

What has happened is a disconnect in manners, not unusual in any foreign country, but a particular hazard for Americans in France. French rules regulating interpersonal behavior are a complex maze, intended, in part, to regulate the daily interplay of seduction. One wishes to seduce but not indiscriminately. There are matters of taste to consider. To be overly familiar is to invite revulsion and scorn. On top of this, there is the universal fear of the stranger, which penetrates deep into French soil. But when the encounter is kept at a safe distance, barriers can fall. Advertisements, for example, can be daring and even invasive because they do not involve direct personal interaction. Close up, barriers stay high.

One way to understand the tension in everyday public behavior is to consider the importance of the smile. Smiling is complicated in France. Americans are accustomed to smiling at strangers; the French—particularly the Parisians—are not. That helps explain why some Americans find Parisians rude. The reluctance to smile does not indicate the absence of kindness in the French character, but it does signal reserve. A French smile is fraught with too much meaning to be bestowed as a mere pleasantry. When a smile is shared, on the Métro, for example, complicity is created and the two smilers suddenly exist as a pair; even without a word, they are no longer separate individuals.

Perhaps the nonsmiling stems from French history—foreign invasions, revolution, and civil wars—that fueled suspicion and contributed to the construction of facades of politesse. Whatever the historical reason, a smile is weightier in France than in much of the world. And this is even truer in Paris. According to a February 2010 poll, 71 percent of French people living outside Paris believe Parisians smile less than the rest of the French.

I was having lunch in a bistro one day with two women friends when two elegantly dressed men, in their late twenties perhaps, were seated next to us. The tables were so close that we had to move ours to accommodate them. One gave me a smile that showed teeth and spoke openness. *He's dressed like a French man, but he's not French*, I thought to myself. *No French man would smile like that.*

I was right. He was German.

A smile can have a purpose. For Christine Lagarde, the finance minister and former national swimming champion, it is a symbol of power and strength. "Political life has hardened me," she once told an interviewer from French *Elle*. "When I was on the French synchronized swimming team, the coach hammered into us: 'Grit your teeth and smile.' So now, today, I grit my teeth and smile. And I do the job!"

When the smile is bestowed one-on-one, it is a gift. Or more. It is so powerful it can suggest sexual interest.

In the movie *Le Divorce*, Kate Hudson, who plays an American ingenue living in Paris, is advised by her young French lover to look more serious. "You were smiling too much," he tells her when she has an unpleasant encounter with the American husband of her brother-in-law's lover. "Don't do that. Smiling gets a girl in trouble."

Bernard-Henri Lévy, the writer, couldn't tolerate the smiles of strangers as he traveled across America. In his book *American Vertigo*, Lévy railed against "those affectless, emotionless smiles, smiles that seem to be there only to signify the pure will to smile."

When I asked Lévy about this observation, he told me that in France the smile is a deliberate sign. "We decide at what point we send it," he said. "And we don't send it right away. We send the signal when the process of seduction has begun. In America—it's nothing. It's like—" his voice filled with disgust as he uttered the next two words—"shaking hands!"

A French businessman I know who travels all over the world said that when he visits the United States, the most uncomfortable place for him is the elevator, because people smile and strike up conversations with him and he can't escape.

Whenever I'm baffled about French customs, I turn to the writer and television host Philippe Labro. I asked him about smiling, and he replied with a story from his time as an exchange student at Washington and Lee University in Virginia in the 1950s. Labro was shy, awkward, badly dressed, and only eighteen when he landed on the campus, with its Southern culture, coat-and-tie dress code, and strict rules. One was the "speaking rule."

"You had to say 'hello,' 'good morning,' 'good evening' to anyone you passed," Labro recalled. One day he was summoned by a student advisory council and told that he wasn't greeting people properly. "It wasn't a trial or anything like that, but I can remember the sentence. It's printed in my memory: 'Philippe, you don't quite understand the spirit of the speaking rule.' "

Labro replied, "Of course I do. I say 'hello' and 'good-bye' and 'good morning' and 'good evening' to everyone."

"Yes," the student representative said. "But you don't smile."

"For me," Labro continued, "It was a good moment, because I thought: 'Okay, I'll get you guys. I'll smile, don't worry. I'll play your game.' And I played the game."

"So was it hard?" I asked.

"No, because it's not hard to play a role in a comedy," he said. "Yes, a comedy. I mean, it was forced. Why should I smile at someone I don't know, and maybe I don't like? It's completely hypocritical to smile all the time!"

The French reticence to smile immediately and indiscriminately, he said, "comes from what is taught from childhood: a rather strong dose of skepticism, of reflection. We are a critical people. We are a literary people. We have to question everything. It's so we will never be duped." For Labro, *le regard*—the look—is much more important than the smile. "You can see more in the eyes than the lips," he said. "The eyes are total life, the absolute personality of someone. There can be magnetism. There can be light. Boredom. Stupidity. Yes, stupidity, the emptiness of the look."

There it was again, *le regard*. I told him I had a stupid question. "In

America, we're taught to stress our good points," I said. "So, if you have a great smile, to use your smile, et cetera. What if you have terrible eyes? How do you do *le regard*? I'm nearsighted. So how do you talk with your eyes if you can't see? And what about when you get older and your face droops and you smile more to look younger?"

"You compensate," Labro said. "Your body has many, many weapons. You use the rest of your body. You play with your hands. Your voice. Voice is a fantastic weapon of seduction. And you use humor and make people laugh. Any man who can make a woman laugh can have that woman. *Bien sûr.*"

On that point, he was right. *Bien sûr.* But that talent is universal.

My former neighborhood in the seventh arrondissement is a place of refinement and politesse. If you look as if you belong and are not just an itinerant shopper, people you don't know will give you a ritual *bonjour* when they pass you on the street.

In its commercial guise, it is upscale: its sidewalks lined with specialty shops selling narrow categories of goods from fine and overpriced stationery to fine and overpriced hosiery. I could have paid eighty-seven euros for a fine and overpriced key at the local locksmith that ended up costing just eighteen euros at the department store BHV.

It is the same with food. To furnish the table for the evening dinner, the shopper can pay a lot of money at one high-quality shop after another, for produce, for cheese, for bread. Even in Paris, supermarkets and big-box stores are pushing aside shops like these, but many of them manage to hang on.

There are two shopkeepers in the neighborhood who taught me very different strategies in seduction. Both run small, expensive shops and have been in business for decades. Both know their customers' tastes. Both deliver correct service and gastronomic excellence. Both display their wares artfully. But there the similarity ends.

La Boucherie de Varenne is a butcher shop dedicated to the art of conversation. Roger Yvon, its owner, is more than a cutter of meat. He is a playful spirit, the soul of the rue de Varenne. This is the street where the writer Rainer Maria Rilke and the sculptor Auguste Rodin lived and worked while Edith Wharton was writing in her grand apartment a few doors down. Roger is an available and faithful suitor who entertains his clients by telling stories, sharing recipes, and making introductions as if his business were a modern-day salon. The gratification is instant.

Roger is the exception to what I call the customer-is-always-wrong rule too often adhered to in France, and especially in Paris. I once watched him spend five minutes as he lovingly chose two center-cut lamb chops for a female client. Were they to be cooked today or tomorrow? Were they to be grilled or sautéed? What were the side dishes? What was the sauce?

Around the corner and down the street from Roger's butcher shop is a seafood shop, La Poissonnerie du Bac, which prides itself on honesty, efficiency, and brusqueness. Sure, it beckons with luminous oysters displayed on ice-lined racks that spill out onto the sidewalk. But as is customary with many French fish stores, the shop has no front door or even protective curtain, so in winter it is cold and damp. The low temperature may suit the fish just fine, but it does little to enhance the personalities of the people who work there.

Here, the customer must court management, a process that is glacially slow. The manager-cashier, an older, full-figured woman whose wardrobe changes very little, plays so hard to get that at first I wondered whether she cared if I ever came back. Yet in a perverse way, her indifference made the chase more stimulating. Andy and I kept returning, hoping that one day the obligatory *bonjour* would be followed by a comment about the weather, an inquiry about our health and our children, and a smile.

France, a nation whose magnetism is so strong it is a cliché, is also the home of the surly shopkeeper and obdurate bureaucrat. What, I have often wondered, can explain this contradiction? In the worlds of commerce and officialdom, even French people must often battle to be treated with civility. For foreigners setting out to live in France, especially those who don't speak terrific French, the challenge can be daunting.

When Andy and I first moved to Paris, we were treated repeatedly like foreign invaders, outsiders who ruined the neighborhood with our American accents and itinerant ways. I well understood the suspicion of the outsider, so familiarly tribal and European, from seeing it in one of my Sicilian grandfathers. He cursed the *stranieri*, the foreigners, the outsiders. The only people who could be truly trusted were family members, and even some of them were unworthy. My grandfather saw the world as a series of concentric circles with himself as the center, then the family, then people who had emigrated from his hometown, then Sicilians, then other Italians, then everyone else. For a long time in Paris, Andy and I were "everyone else."

What I did not understand was how businesspeople could expect to attract and hold a clientele when they seemed so lacking in basic customer service skills. But I bonded with Roger the butcher, whose natural warmth made him easier than most, over the issue of Thanksgiving—after another butcher had given me the brush-off.

The French don't know much about our Thanksgiving. Almost all of their official holidays mark either military victories or major religious (that is, Christian) events; May 1 is the equivalent of our Labor Day, but it doesn't come with backyard barbecues, just workers' protests.

I have explained to French people that Thanksgiving is an American holiday that draws its inspiration from traditional harvest festivals in Europe. At the first Thanksgiving in 1621, the settlers at Plymouth Colony in what is now Massachusetts joined with Native Americans from the Wampanoag tribe to give thanks to God for the fall harvest. They ate venison, waterfowl, lobster, clams and other seafood, berries and other fruit, pumpkin, squash, and, of course, wild turkeys. I mention that no presents are exchanged, a fact that surprises those Frenchmen who believe that Americans care too much about material things. In addition, the holiday is all about the preparation and consumption of ritual foods, a concept the French fully understand.

Because the French don't celebrate Thanksgiving, finding a turkey can be challenging. French turkey farmers hoard their birds until

Christmas, the holiday when turkeys are served along with oysters, smoked salmon, foie gras, and champagne.

Our first year in Paris, I was determined to give a proper Thanksgiving to my children, still unhappy about being wrenched from their safe and predictable lives in America. I ordered a turkey from the butcher at the local fancy-food emporium, where just about everything is pint-sized and wrapped in elegant but environmentally incorrect layers of packaging. Bargains are nonexistent.

I told the butcher I wanted a five-and-a-half-kilo turkey, about twelve pounds. When it arrived a few weeks later, it weighed twice that. I would have cooked it, but it didn't fit into my oven. A British friend told me to cut it up, but I decided that a turkey coming out of the oven in pieces would symbolize for my daughters the brutal massacre of their American way of life.

I called the butcher, told him he had made a mistake, and demanded an exchange. He told me I was at fault and hung up. Then I called the store's customer service department; my calls were not returned. It took another day and a lot of complaining, negotiating, and sweet-talking to get a smaller bird.

It was the turkey experience that prompted me to make friends with Roger. He has become one of the most important men in my life.

Roger doesn't really belong on the rue de Varenne. The presence of the prime minister's office just a few doors down keeps the street quiet, boring, and guarded round the clock by police, who block it off at the faintest whiff of a demonstration. Roger is too outgoing, too familiar, too non-Parisian in his style of promoting his pâté of wild hare or his chicken sausages seasoned with lemon and parsley. He might fit in better in a more raucous neighborhood like Belleville on the eastern fringe of Paris or the area around Abbesses, where the movie *Amélie* was filmed. But he is an accident of the neighborhood. He quit school and started apprenticing as a butcher at the age of fourteen. He married Sylvie, the butcher's daughter, and took over the family business.

Roger enjoys breaking the codes of the quartier. He has posed for photographers with necklaces of thick homemade pork sausages around his neck. When the Beaujolais Nouveau arrives in the fall, he sets up a stand on the sidewalk and offers the young wine and thin-sliced charcuterie to passersby. At Christmas, he and his team of butchers put on elves' hats with blinking lights. For Valentine's Day, he fashions chopped meat into hearts. Eyes may roll, but most of his customers love him for this. He is so deeply trusted that when avian flu struck France, his poultry sales went up, not down.

The day he hired a ten-piece brass band to celebrate the thirtieth anniversary of his shop, a neighbor called the police, who ordered the musicians to stop; Roger told them to play on. He was slapped with a fine of thousands of euros. Two years later, he was still fighting in the courts.

I had already been a casual, if fickle, customer when I betrayed Roger by sneaking off to the fancy-food emporium for the turkey. I later confessed what I had done. But forgiveness of my infidelity did not come easily.

"How could you do that when I sell the best turkeys in all of France?" he asked. He told me the turkeys from the fancy-food place are ordinary fowl. His, by contrast, are a special race raised on the same farm since World War II. He shoved under my nose an eight-page color brochure that showed a lot of fat turkeys roaming free and lovingly fed with the finest cereals in the land. From then on, my Thanksgiving turkey came from Roger. He cooked it in his oven when it was too big for mine. One year, when I ordered a sixteen-pound turkey and got an eleven-pound bird instead, Roger gave me an explanation that sounded more like a tall tale.

"The turkey's way too small, Roger," I said.

"It was the foxes," he explained. It seemed that the electric fence surrounding the turkey pen at the special farm had shorted out. The foxes ran wild. "They were very smart," he said. "They only ate the big turkeys."

My experience with Roger illustrates a twist on the universal shopkeeper-customer relationship that seems particularly French. In a small, privately owned shop, seduction is a game both parties are expected to play. The shopkeeper selects his merchandise carefully and often presents it elegantly. He may feel that this should be enough to win your appreciation, which you should then find a way to express. It's almost as if the merchant is telling you, "You should come here for the quality and the beauty of what I offer. I shouldn't have to woo you further."

An American accustomed to the direct and forceful appeal of price specials and chirpy exhortations to have a nice day may find a wall of reserve instead. Breaking it requires the right degree of friendliness and a lot of time. But when the wall is breached, a relationship can take root. The pattern is a familiar one: once you get beneath the layer of the clever, performing intellectuals, there can be quite a bit of earnestness in the French character, and it has a lot of charm.

It took much longer for Andy and me to break the ice at the fish store. It finally happened over a platter. Andy was picking up a whole poached salmon for the office Christmas party we hosted every year.

"Where is your platter?" asked the manager-cashier, to whom I had privately given the nickname Madame la Poissonnière.

In years past, when we were asked for our fish platter, we had to confess we didn't have one, which always produced a loud sigh of frustration from Madame la Poissonnière, who then had to order the staff to secure the fish on a bed of Styrofoam. This time, however, Andy was ready. He dutifully produced a tin platter we had obtained. Alas, it was a tad too small. Suddenly, and without fanfare, the invisible barrier cracked and shattered. Madame la Poissonnière asked one of the fishmongers to find a proper platter. She smiled at Andy and told him to return it sometime after the party.

After that, we were treated not exactly like family but at least as if we were worthy of entering. Whenever I passed by the shop, Madame la Poissonnière and I would greet each other with a *bonjour.* One day when I was struggling with a bunch of green ferns from the florist up the street, Madame la Poissonnière insisted on tying them together. She was standing outside the shop, a cigarette dangling from the side of her mouth. She looked much younger than when she stood behind the cash box, and she was smiling. I told her she reminded me of the late and great actress Simone Signoret. She filled the street with deep, smoke-filled laughter.

• • •

Little by little, I began to make the rue du Bac and its arteries my own. First, I had to tell the longtime merchants that I was living in the neighborhood. Then I had to engage in long discussions about the merchandise, the way Julia Child might have done. The Italian *traiteur* turned talkative when I looked interested as he rattled off temperatures for grape growing in the south of Italy. The pinched-faced pharmacist smiled when I asked her to explain the medicinal benefits of the herbal teas, sprays, and oils.

Most important, Roger opened doors. He liked nothing better than to throw off his butcher's apron, leave the shop, and introduce me to his friends. I met a third-generation owner of the street's glove-and-hosiery shop, who uses a closet in the back as an archive and command central for the history of the rue du Bac. He, in turn, introduced me to the printer of fine stationery and calling cards. When, after several years, we decided to move to another neighborhood, Roger took me to meet Isabelle, the real estate agent across the street, who oozes elegance in her upswept hairdos and her swishing skirts. Soon, Isabelle was inviting me to tea in the attic above the office, where she keeps a pet turtle and vases stuffed with fresh flowers.

There was mourning every time an old business closed down: the pharmacy transformed into a women's clothing store, the milk-and-cheese shop turned into a hair salon, the *traiteur* turned into a Nespresso boutique. It was especially sad when Monsieur Renault, whose family had been running a hardware store for sixty years, shut down to make way for a Benetton.

Over the years, some of the merchants abandoned their reserve and tried to woo customers to come inside as if this were Main Street America. Christine, the seller of antiques and bric-a-brac, set boxes of used books on chairs on the street. The owner of the liquor store that displayed hundred-euro bottles of Armagnac in the window put bargain bottles of rosé at the open door at the entrance and offered free tastings of port. The lure of the bargain was coming.

Learning to feel comfortable did not, however, put me under an illusion that the manners and folkways of French consumer culture are easy to deal with or understand. There are too many obvious frustrations, too widely shared, and not just by foreigners.

There is, for example, the maddening reluctance to correct or apologize for missteps. Whether they run small businesses in residential neighborhoods or large ones that are far less personal, merchants find it hard to admit they are wrong, and harder still to apologize. Instead, the trick is to somehow get the offended party to feel that the mistake was his or her own. I'm convinced the practice was learned in the strict French educational system, in which teachers are allowed to tell pupils they are *nuls* (zeros) in front of the class. What outsiders do not understand is that the French can be rude even to their own.

Just about everyone I have ever met in France has suffered from the lack of a service mentality in Paris. A doctor I know told me he once bought a coat at a small men's boutique only to discover that it had a rip in the fabric. When he tried to return it, the shopkeeper gave him the address of a tailor who could repair it—for a fat fee. They argued. The doctor reminded the shopkeeper of the French saying, "The customer is king."

"Sir," the shopkeeper replied, "France no longer has a king."

Maybe rudeness is a perverse form of seduction. This is my theory: seduction is all about illusion and expectation, not the end result. That means there should be pleasure in the process of getting something done, whether it is being served a *steak frites* or buying a cell phone. The processes are to be obeyed; the master will have his pleasure.

France also lacks the other motivator that fills American commerce with smiles and false friendliness: the Protestant ethic. I asked the business consultant Alain Minc why. He blamed it on the abrogation of the Edict of Nantes. I hadn't thought about the Edict of Nantes since graduate school, but it is a sign of weakness to show ignorance, so I nodded solemnly and kept listening.

The Edict of Nantes, promulgated by King Henri IV in 1598, was a visionary act of reconciliation that gave France's one million Protestants freedom of worship and other rights. In 1685, his grandson, Louis XIV, revoked it in a campaign to purge France of Protestants, who for him challenged the order of things. Several hundred Protestant churches were destroyed. The property and possessions of Protestants were confiscated. Business and financial leaders left the country; others died in prison or were sent to the galleys. Most Protestants were pressured into converting to Catholicism. "It was a dramatic move for the French economy because the Protestants had been the best entrepreneurs," Minc said. "The absence of a Calvinist bourgeoisie explains much of the gap between the United Kingdom and France, industrially speaking. Aristocrats were not allowed to engage in trade. So there was nobody to engage in trade in France."

Moneymaking is still not talked about much. Even France's top business executives are loath to reveal or revel in their wealth. Money does seduce, but it is supposed to be used discreetly, quietly. This is one of the reasons French people of all classes disapproved of what they called Sarkozy's "bling-bling" style early in his presidency: his Ray-Bans, his Rolex, his gold necklace, his penchant for hanging out with French billionaires.

"In L.A., when you drive a red Ferrari, people look at your car with envy; in Paris it gets scratched," said Alain Baraton, the gardener at Versailles. "Money is still a taboo in France. People don't dare say how much they earn—except the *nouveaux riches*. Either they earn very little and they're ashamed of it, or they earn too much and they're ashamed of it. You Americans dream about getting the other guy's job; in France, you resent the guy who has the job and think he doesn't deserve it."

It's the difference between a young country looking forward and an old country looking back. Frenchmen who have spent long stretches of time in the United States come back and tend to complain about French inefficiency and an uneven work ethic. "In the U.S., you say to people, 'Okay, how can we go from A to B, the fastest way, where we can make the most money and have fun at the same time,'" said Andrée Deissenberg, the director of the Crazy Horse cabaret. "The French will go, 'First of all, define A, define B, and why should we go from A to B if we can go from A to C to B?' This is fabulous at the café but not necessarily in the business world."

She blamed it on Descartes—and on the French habit of seducing. "Seduction is not fast, it's not from A to B," she said. "There is a bridge somewhere between this very pseudo-intellectual deconstruction of everything and seduction. When you seduce, what's behind it is thinking, not gratification."

Conspicuous self-promotion is also suspect, and the French can be confused by Americans' insistence on "selling" themselves in the business world. When Bruno Racine was director of the Pompidou Center, one of his American assistants pushed him to promote the museum—and himself. "She told me, 'You have to sell yourself,'" he recalled. "I would answer, 'That's too arrogant. We need to be more subtle.'"

In a world of such complicated codes of manners and taste, consider the plight of the business that wants to seduce customers with advertising. French advertisers are freer than those in the United States to play with nudity and sexual seduction, which can feature in soaring billboards in public spaces. Secure in the knowledge that there is no face-to-face encounter with another person involved, French advertisers feel at liberty to promote fantasies, even those that dare to stretch the limits of taste. Since so many of the ads don't mention price, they can be used to sell dreams. But even here, there are red lines. What can be shown, and what said? What will give offense, and what will please? When used in an advertisement, nudity must be fun; to be too obvious would be "violent."

Ask French men and women of a certain age the advertisement they remember best and they are likely to say "Avenir," which is both the name of a billboard advertising company and the French word for "future." On Monday, August 31, 1981, an unidentified nineteen-year-old brunette with short hair, a big smile, and a wet body clad in a green bikini suddenly appeared on thousands of ten-foot-high billboards across France. Her message was both provocative and mysterious.

"On September 2," she proclaimed, "I'm taking off my top." Two days later, a new poster appeared. She had kept her promise. Not only that, but she made another that was even more daring: "On September 4, I'm taking off my bottom." Indeed, right on schedule, she appeared totally naked, but she was posed with her back to the camera. This time the ad announced, "Avenir, the billboard company that keeps its promises."

The ad both titillated and shocked. Newspapers took sides. The country's advertising watchdog agency condemned it. A women's group in Lille won a court order forcing the company to cover the model; a deputy in Parliament vowed to draft legislation for an advertising ban on "the abusive use of women's bodies."

In a way, though, it was the perfect French ad: it offered anticipation, amusement, and female nudity all for free. Because the actual target audience—potential buyers of space on billboards—was small, the great majority of viewers were not being asked to buy anything. The ad is so revered that in 2010, nearly thirty years later, the financial newspaper *Les Échos* touted it as a model advertisement.

To learn more, I went to two of the giants of French advertising, Maurice Lévy, the president of the Publicis group (the man who demonstrated to me the different styles of hand kissing), and Jacques Séguéla, the head of the competing firm Havas.

Lévy leaned forward in his chair and looked deep into my eyes when he spoke. We conversed in French, but when he moved briefly into English, he spoke with the old-style French accent of Yves Montand, not the flat, globalized, and Americanized accent of executives who have gone to business schools. He doesn't look much like Montand, but the role he was playing was not so different from Montand's character in the 1960 musical comedy *Let's Make Love*, a billionaire who falls in love with Marilyn Monroe. Lévy's only flaw is that he is aware of his power, so his seduction is not sufficiently hidden.

Lévy said that the French approach advertising in a radically different way from Americans. "Never forget that advertising in France is almost suspect," he observed. "The majority of French people used to think that when a product was good it didn't need advertising. That's why we had to be more subtle and use seduction more often. The French approach is based on 'seduction,' not with its sexual connotations but *à la française*, which means you create an emotional bond rather than convince with rationalization."

Sure, selling is the goal of advertising. But like any good seduction, the selling process can't be seen. The best advertising makes consumers complicit in a process in which their senses are awakened; only then can the notion of a transaction be introduced. There is little hard sell in France based on lower prices and greater volume. In most cases, criticizing competitors is against the law, as are ads that directly compare two brands.

While Lévy talked as if time had no limits, Séguéla was fast-moving and fast-talking. He could have been American. He reduced the aesthetics of advertising to a formula he has used for years: the British are intellectual and go from the head straight to the heart; the Americans are pragmatic and fact-based and go from the head to the wallet; the French are emotional and sensual and go from the heart to the head.

"I am the Casanova who has the task of seducing the 3.5 billion women who are on this earth!" he told me.

"Three point five billion, not bad," I said. "But it's only women you seduce?"

"Of course," he said. "Eighty percent of consumers are women. So the advertiser is a seducer of women."

It was Séguéla who created the ad campaign for Carte Noire coffee that called it "A coffee named desire." He explained, "In this coffee, we don't say the aroma is the sweetest, or it's the best, or it's the least expensive, or it's luxurious. We say simply it has imaginary value."

When the French talk about bargains and saving money in their ads, they tend to fill the ads with American imagery. During the global financial crisis of 2008 and 2009, Alain Némarq, the chairman of Mauboussin, the prestige jewelry firm, made waves in the luxury world by slashing prices and asking other luxury goods makers to do the same. One of his print ad campaigns was a two-page color spread that offered customers a cash rebate if they bought an expensive enough piece of jewelry. The backdrop was a waving American flag, with the caption in English, "Yes we can!"

It's more common to push products by evoking beauty, pleasure, and the promise of sex. Anne Saint Dreux, a writer and head of La Maison de la Pub, a research group that organizes events about the history of advertising, told an audience in Paris one evening how different American and French cultures are, citing the reaction to a presentation she had given in New York on French advertising style.

"Obviously, I had to show some footage in which the female body was a bit naked," she said. "I was showing ads for yogurt and cars, and then all of a sudden I felt silence. The Americans were really shocked because while you have to undress women to sell soap, to do it to sell yogurt is a mortal sin. So tonight—since we are French—we're not going to have the same discomfort."

She then showed French film ads over the years that were bolder and more brazen than anything one would see in America: bump-and-grind music for an ice cream; the sound of a woman sighing for a vegetable oil; a mistress and a wife together for a French beer; the orgasmic cries of a woman for a racing car.

Even more daring than the artful anticipation of seduction is the blatant manipulation of the sex act in advertising. Subtlety can sometimes elude the French, as happened some time ago in a campy television advertisement for Perrier water. The fingers of a woman's right hand, with nails painted red and a ring on her middle finger, slowly stroke the neck of a green, eight-ounce bottle of Perrier. Then both hands briefly caress the bottle, then just the right hand again. The neck of the bottle gets progressively longer until the cap turns and the fizzy water explodes into the air. Today, the ad campaign has its own web page at www.lamainperrier.com. *La main Perrier* means "the Perrier hand."

Commercially, the Perrier ad was a failure. "It was closer to pornography than eroticism, because there was an erection," said Séguéla. "Even though it was only a simulated erection, it was provocative. Female consumers had no desire to make a sacrilege of the erection. It was a marketing mistake to make this film. Publicity must astonish but not shock."

That helps explain why Bruno Aveillan's 1998 advertisement for the Paco Rabanne perfume XS is considered a classic. The opening seems straightforward: a couple bathed in golden light and embraced by a shiny flowing satin sheet is copulating in midair; her pearl necklace is torn from her neck; a bottle shatters. Their entwined bodies float as effortlessly as if they are weightless. The ad was a feat of engineering, filmed in a thirty-foot-deep basin of water with no bubbles in sight; the crew used oxygen tanks, but the actors had to hold their breath. The ad is considered a work of art.

The sex-sells-anything phenomenon applies to print as well. A naked woman, seen from behind, looking over her shoulder at the camera, sits on an invisible chair; the ad is for a chair exhibition. A photo showing the torsos of a man and a big-breasted woman embracing, he in leather, she in a clingy black dress, advertises a laundry detergent for dark colors.

Soon after I arrived in Paris, there was a battle of the *strings* in magazines and on giant public billboards. A billboard campaign for Sloggi showed two long-haired women from behind, dressed in *strings* (as thongs are called in France) and red boxing gloves, their posteriors buffed and shined, playfully menacing a smiling man in tight boxers as he defends himself. "Be sexy. Be Sloggi," the caption read.

Not to be outdone, a Bolero lingerie ad campaign showed a young woman removing what appeared to be tight pants, revealing her *string*. Turning toward the camera, she announced: "I'm a virgin. Are you?" The manufacturer insisted that the ad was nothing but a clever play on words. *Vierge* is the French word for "virgin," and it also refers to the astrological sign Virgo. The ad was for a line of astrologically signed, hologrammed *strings*. The model was wearing a "Virgo."

Sometimes the ads that are considered the most artistic and clever strike me as a bit creepy. Chanel was particularly proud of its two-and-a-half-minute film, *Train de nuit*, starring the actress Audrey Tautou and directed by Jean-Pierre Jeunet, one of France's hottest film directors, to pitch Chanel No. 5.

Set to Billie Holiday's "I'm a Fool to Want You," it shows Tautou exchanging fraught looks with a drop-dead-handsome mystery man as they board the Orient Express and head to Istanbul. Apparently, he has smelled her perfume. As night falls, Mystery Man stands outside her compartment, and a strange look comes over Tautou's face as she lies in bed in a nightgown. Is it terror? Longing? E.S.P.? Maybe I've taken too many overnight trains to bizarre places, but I had the feeling he was stalking her. When I asked Jacques Polge, Chanel's chief perfumer, whether the ad seemed a bit frightening, he did not disagree. "Yes, yes, it's true . . . ," he said. "The film has its qualities—and its defects."

I asked Florence, my researcher, who had studied advertising for her master's degree in communications, for her reaction. She shared my uneasiness but at the same time found the Chanel ad mesmerizing. "He sees her and smells her, and you can feel there is danger here," Florence said. "Her scent stays behind even when he can no longer see her. She knows he's on the other side of the door and feels his presence, his desire. The perfume is the link between them. It evokes a dark instinct in this man. He is a predator, but he is also under her spell. You almost believe it could happen—and almost want to try it just to see if it will."

The goal of French advertising gives little importance to climax or resolution. "Rare is the woman who likes to be pressured," said Lévy. "Women prefer that things move progressively. Advertising is a little like that. If you use pressure, most won't like it. You have to lead, with the head, with the heart, with emotion so that you make yourself part of the life of your female consumers."

Creating a connection to potential consumers and taking advantage of a certain distance from them at the same time is just what the Bibliothèque Nationale did in 2007–08 when promoting a most unusual exhibition: its vast, secret archive of erotic art. As part of a campaign to attract a broad public to the exhibit, the library and the Paris mass transit system, one of the show's sponsors, constructed a teaser on the No. 10 Métro line. The platform of the Croix-Rouge station, near the Saint-Germain-des-Prés neighborhood of the Left Bank, had been closed since World War II. Now, it was dressed up to look like the foyer of an underground bordello.

As the trains passed, slowing down around a curve but not stopping, black strips of curtain fluttered open. Commuters got a six-to-nine-second glimpse of erotic engravings lit in shocking pink. It was a now-you-see-it, now-you-don't experience, a "furtive flash of hallucination," according to the artist who designed it, and the ultimate in X-rated subtlety. One of the loftiest, fustiest institutions in France connected with ordinary people over pleasure. The public responded. The erotica show was so popular that the wait to get in was more than an hour.

•PART THREE•

Written on the Body

8

The Allure of the Flesh

. . .

> Nothing is more beautiful than a naked body. The most beautiful clothes that can dress a woman are the arms of the man she loves. But for those who haven't had the fortune of finding this happiness, I am there.
>
> —Yves Saint Laurent

> She dressed badly.
>
> —Françoise Giroud, the writer, upon learning of the death of Simone de Beauvoir

On the day I met the queen of French lingerie, I didn't expect her to show me her bra. But there I was, with Chantal Thomass in her boutique on the fancy rue du Faubourg Saint-Honoré when show-and-tell seemed like the right thing for her to do.

We were in her private pink-and-black boudoir on the second floor, sitting on soft pink love seats and armchairs. Thomass was wearing a high black turtleneck, a long black ruffled jacket, and black bolero pants. Her black bangs fell into her eyes. Her only color was a slash of crimson across her lips.

Our subject was style, that renowned specialty of the French, as interpreted in the garments closest to the skin. When outsiders focus on French fashion—a multibillion-dollar contributor to France's economy as well as a pillar of its mystique—underwear is rarely the first subject they consider. But lingerie is important in France, as foreigners realize when they walk French streets and see how many shop windows are filled with elaborately constructed and decorated panties and bras. Lingerie is central, too, in the psychology of French seduction. It exists at the nexus of the two great themes of the personal presentation of the body: enhancement and revelation. Or, put another way, artifice and nudity.

As a young fashion designer in the mid-1970s, Thomass started playing with lingerie as a sideline, slipping tiny, bold-colored confections of lace, satin, silk, and wiring into her runway shows. Her "boudoir" revolution clashed with the wave of feminism that was sweeping France and bringing liberties to women, most notably the legalization of abortion in 1975. Her early creations were ignored by the mainstream women's media but picked up by magazines for men like *Lui* and *Playboy*. The approach worked, and now hers is the go-to shop for wealthy and stylish Frenchwomen in search of underwear. Her motto is "Hide to show better," an expression of the French idea that partial concealment enhances the erotic.

As my interview with Thomass progressed, it occurred to me to ask about her own preferences. What did she wear?

"For lingerie?" she asked.

"Yes. Today, for example."

She smiled. "One that I like a lot."

She gripped the top of her stretchy black turtleneck and pulled it down almost to her navel to reveal a masterpiece of engineering: a body-hugging structure of black lace with a high collar and a circle scooped out of the front that showed off her cleavage.

"There you go!" she said. And then she asked me what I was wearing.

I gave her a brief peek. I'll say only that it was sporty, a neutral color, and without lace.

"Okay," she said flatly. "Well, it's very American."

The Ipsos polling agency found in one survey that 91 percent of French women and 83 percent of French men believe that lingerie is important in life. Another survey indicated that French women aged fifteen and older spend nearly 20 percent of their clothing budget on lingerie, more than in any other European country.

Thomass had recently coauthored a book on the history of lingerie that came wrapped in black tissue paper and set in a pink box. So she led me through the evolution of the undergarment in France: how several centuries ago when the French were afraid to wash for fear of catching disease, they wore loose white *linge* (underwear) to allow their bodies to breathe; why women dared to show more flesh in the eighteenth century but that modesty returned in full force in the nineteenth; how until well into the twentieth century, black lingerie was worn only by prostitutes and widows. In World War I, women were thrust into the workforce and needed to move freely, so petticoats and corsets went out of fashion. Decades later, after World War II, came the return of the bra. Couturiers like Coco Chanel and Pierre Cardin hired and trained their own staff *corsetiers* (corset makers). Lace for their creations was specially made in Calais, silk in Lyon.

Thomass knows a lot about the bodies of the rich and famous: that Arielle Dombasle (a client) could not have had work done on her breasts, that Carla Bruni (who once modeled for Thomass) was a size 32B.

I visited Thomass with a pretty, fresh-faced American woman of twenty-three who wore simple clothes and little jewelry and had grown up in Wisconsin. She had been quiet throughout most of the interview. But she had a French boyfriend and a burning question.

"For someone, for example, an American, who knows nothing about lingerie, where do you start?" she asked. "With all the different colors, different styles . . ."

Thomass began to show her various bras. One was white and very lacy, another was black, very lacy, and very racy.

"Umm, it's maybe a little too sophisticated for her," I said about the black one, trying to be helpful. "A little too showy."

They both ignored me.

"In white or in black?" Thomass asked.

"Well, I don't know," the young woman said. "The white is a little more innocent, but the black is more . . ."

"Yes it's more . . . ," Thomass replied.

"If I'm going to take the risk, I'm going to go all the way," she said.

"Straight to the black," Thomass commanded.

Then Thomass shared with her the secret of a successful lingerie seduction. "The game of seduction is to let them think that there are pretty things underneath," she said. "It is above all not to show everything. It's either wear a miniskirt or reveal a décolleté. Never both. A miniskirt plus a décolleté, it's a little frightening."

The young woman seemed surprised. "We don't have this same idea of 'hiding,'" she said. "It's really all about showing; it's sort of the opposite."

She bought the racy black bra. What did I know?

The human body is the basic tool of seduction. And as seductiveness is a cultivated art, personal appearance can't be left to nature unassisted. In France, the enhancement and adornment of the body is a matter of careful attention and enduring interest. What you cover yourself with—and how much you choose to cover—is crucial to your success.

The vastness of the lingerie universe helped me rethink a phenomenon I had noticed in the late 1970s the first time I reported on the Paris fashion shows. The refined appearance so often identified with the Parisian style, for both men and women, projects a kind of cool seductiveness. Fine materials, exquisite detailing, a put-together, intentional look—all contribute to the message: *I am on a high plane, in control of my destiny and my beauty. I am not easy to attain. Do you think you are up to my standard? If no, stay away. If yes, come and try to get me.* Ideally, the body must be adorned, scented, nourished, but in a certain way.

On the flip side is the hot, universal seductiveness of bare skin. And here, the French exhibit another kind of intense interest and expertise. They like to play with the skin, frank and yet teasing. The bikini (invented by a French man), the elaborate lingerie, the unembarrassed fascination with fetching body parts, the partially concealed nude bodies shown routinely in advertising—all are part of a national game of peekaboo.

Of course, not everyone is equally adept at physical allure—or equally fit for it. Like people everywhere, the French are heterogeneous in style and body shape. Contrary to the stereotype, most French women wear sizes larger than 2 or 4, and many are badly dressed. Indeed, on the escalators of train stations at rush hour, in the classrooms of working-class public schools, and in bars, bistros, and boutiques throughout France, I have seen women who wear mismatched clothes and who by any standard would be considered fat, often paired with men who stray equally far from the ideal.

That said, I agree with all those authors of books on French elegance that there is a certain type of woman, plentiful on the streets of Paris and sometimes seen in other pockets of France, who projects the much celebrated French sense of style. The look appears effortless, but it is strategic and deliberate, achieved by following tacit rules. These women are looked at and appreciated by both men and women—and of course, they know it.

For Vanessa Seward, the artistic director of the fashion house Azzaro, whose natural beauty is matched only by her generous spirit, one basic rule might be called the "old Chanel factor."

"People always ask me what makes a Parisian woman different, and I say they have a very good way of balancing," she said. "It's very snobby to do maybe, but I never wear a new Chanel bag. I love wearing a battered one, because it doesn't look so glitzy. It is probably much more chic. Then I can wear something new. And I won't wear any makeup." The result, she said, is "a kind of balance and it all looks completely normal, without any effort."

The former supermodel Inès de la Fressange had a slightly different take: "A Parisienne won't wear a handbag, pants, and a sweater all from the same designer," she said. "Never. And she won't wear only new clothes. The French think that style is what you create yourself. Maybe that's the difference from an American, who says to herself, 'I have to have the coat of the season.' And when a German walks down the street, you can tell right away."

The younger French women I know have refined that thought. They say they sometimes wear all-new clothes; they just make sure they don't all look new. New clothes can't look flashy. They have other rules. Less is more. Dangly earrings and a big necklace aren't worn at the same time, even if they match. Zara, Mango, and Maje all make fun, well-fitting, and affordable dresses but not for a wedding or a big party because at least one other young French woman is likely to be wearing the same dress.

A French friend told the story of an American who visited her country house outside of Paris. "In two seconds, we knew she wouldn't fit in," she said. "She was overdone. She didn't have the right shoes. She was wearing too much makeup for the country. Plus, she was boring. We never invited her again."

The flip side of this kind of trial by fashion, of course, is the fear of being judged as inadequate. Parisian women inspire particular fear. "They have the ability to size you up, check your shoes, your jewelry," said Celestine Bohlen, an American journalist who was born in Paris as the daughter of a senior diplomat and has lived there for many years. "You get the once-over, as if they are saying, 'Which category should I put you into?'"

A cardinal rule of style for both men and women is that the elaborate effort behind a sophisticated look must not be apparent. It has to seem as if it simply happened.

"I know an American lawyer who has lived here for thirty years," a friend told me. "He speaks perfect French. He is always dressed perfectly, with cuff links, and a monogrammed shirt, perfect suit, perfectly tanned. He can talk as easily about opera as about football. I was looking for the flaw but I couldn't find it. I don't trust him for a minute. I keep thinking, 'Where's the flaw?' He seems to be too perfect to be honest."

French men—especially those with wealth, social position, elegance, or ambition—wear their look with such seeming effortlessness that foreigners often assume they have some sort of natural knack. But their stylish air is, in fact, no more natural or unstudied than the carefully cultivated appearance of chic French women. A recent full-page article in the newspaper *Le Parisien* informed men of what errors they should avoid for the summer season. There were seven guidelines: do not fully button up your polo; do not wear shorts too short; do not perch sunglasses on your head; do not drape a sweater over your shoulders; do not tuck a T-shirt into your jeans; do not wear a "wife-beater" undershirt; do not wear oversized, short-sleeved, button-down shirts. Allowed were a properly tied small cotton scarf, a Panama hat, and flip-flops.

In pursuit of a better understanding of what gives some French men their polished look, I asked for advice from some of my male colleagues. Bertrand de Saint-Vincent, the style columnist for *Le Figaro*, walked me around the crowd at a champagne-filled awards ceremony for the "best novel of emotion" of the year. We happened on the former television anchor Patrick Poivre d'Arvor, whom Bertrand calls "Mr. Seduction." Poivre d'Arvor is so famous that he once played himself in a French movie; a puppet with his face and voice is the television anchor on *Les Guignols*, the satirical political television comedy.

Poivre d'Arvor was wearing a well-cut black velvet jacket, pressed jeans, a white dress shirt, and black patent leather shoes. But his look was more than that. His shirt had been impeccably ironed, difficult and expensive to have done in Paris. Bertrand tugged at the bottom left corner of Poivre d'Arvor's shirt to show me that it had been discreetly monogrammed with his initials. In doing so, Bertrand exposed the elastic waistband of Poivre d'Arvor's checkered boxers. I presumed they had been ironed, too.

I got another, more personal lesson in how men cultivate style from Alain Frachon, a *Le Monde* columnist whom I have known for many years. Frachon is tall, slim, not at all classically handsome but with enough interest and darkness that he could play the Seductive French Journalist in an American movie, or at least look good in a beret. His French accent and liquid-chocolate voice fit well into his fluid and colloquial English.

In the early 1970s, Alain said, he donned what he called a "uniform": a velvet jacket, tight jeans, and Clark's desert boots. He chain-smoked Gauloises Bleues. He burnished his intellectual side and perfected a serious, thoughtful look. Then, as a young intern for ABC News in Washington and New York, he discovered that successful American journalists took notes in slim reporter's notebooks and wore blue, button-down, Oxford-cloth shirts from Brooks Brothers. So he bought slim reporter's notebooks and blue, button-down, Oxford-cloth shirts from Brooks Brothers. "I told myself, 'I am going to be a killer in Paris,'" he said. "I came back, fully dressed to impress all the women, like an American reporter."

Over the years, Alain said, his strategy was moderately successful.

He played hard to get until he was in his fifties, when he married and became a father. He still retains some of the aura of the seducer-journalist. But the secret of his success lies in his French charm rather than his Americanized dress. "I have to tell the truth now," he said. "If I have to give a priority to one of the weapons which helped me the most in my very modest career in seduction, it's that the girls realized that the others might be much more clever, but that, okay, I am nice."

That kind of allure doesn't come with a wardrobe.

French men are aware not only of their own look but also of the care and ingenuity that goes into a woman's demeanor and sense of style. There is a brief exchange in François Truffaut's 1977 film *L'homme qui aimait les femmes* (*The Man Who Loved Women*) that captures the centrality of women's clothing in the life of a certain kind of French man.

Bertrand, the film's protagonist, subscribes to a telephone wake-up service, and the same woman calls him every morning. He flirts with her; she resists. Then one morning, she lets him in on a secret.

BERTRAND: Tell me what you're wearing. No, don't laugh, it's very important.

WAKE-UP OPERATOR: I'm wearing pants today. Are you disappointed? You want to know if I'm naked beneath my sweater? Well, I'm not. I'm wearing a Lejaby bra—that's the brand.

BERTRAND: Ah yes, I know it. Lejaby, it fastens in the back, with adjustable straps and a plastic hook in the shape of a double S.

WAKE-UP OPERATOR: Bravo! You win a thousand francs.

No American man I know would know so much about the engineering of a particular brand of bra. In fact, no American man I know would know anything about a bra. What makes France different is that many men there are truly interested in the minutest details of what a woman wears.

Alice Ferney captured that sense in her novel about infidelity, *La conversation amoureuse*. The first time Gilles sees Pauline, long before they have an adulterous affair, he notes that her yellow dress is made of "fine poplin." Gilles, it seems, has a passion for knowing a lot about women. "He knew the names of fabrics because he was a man who loved women," Ferney wrote. "Whatever interested a woman interested him."

For an official visit to the White House in 2007, President Sarkozy arrived not with a wife (his marriage was breaking up) but with three women who worked for him: Finance Minister Christine Lagarde, Justice Minister Rachida Dati, and Rama Yade, a deputy minister of foreign affairs. Sarkozy was concerned with the way they would present themselves as officials, of course, but he also told them how to dress. As recounted in a memoir by Sarkozy's friend Jacques Séguéla, the advertising magnate, the president told Yade that she was "too beautiful for one of those 'frou-frou' dresses," instructed Dati that she "should not abandon her habit of Dior-ized elegance," and advised Lagarde to "leave her jewels in the safe."

Even Charles de Gaulle showed interest in the dress of women he found feminine and seductive. "Madam," he reportedly would ask, "what fabric is your dress made of?"

In France, knowledge about women's clothing is not only an indication of a man's appreciation of a woman's attire but also a tool of seduction. It shows that he is paying attention, and for a woman, this is important. In the sequel to the cult comedy *La boum*, a middle-aged couple is having dinner at a restaurant. As a playful test of their love, the wife asks her husband to describe what she's wearing. "How am I dressed?" she asks. He freezes. "There, below, under the table," she continues. "Am I wearing pants? Boots? A skirt with a slit? High heels? Black stockings?" He doesn't have a clue, demonstrating to her that he has been distracted by work and hadn't looked at her on their way to the restaurant. The relationship deteriorates, for other reasons. Later in the film, as they are saying good-bye at a train station, he says, "Ah, I forgot. Under your gabardine coat, you're wearing a straight navy blue skirt with a slit, the white blouse I bought you for Christmas, new navy blue sandals, and there, under your hair, little hoop earrings that no one can see, except me, when I . . ." He kisses her neck. The audience assumes he has won her back.

In France, as much attention is paid to specific body parts as to what covers them. In the United States, the focus tends to be on full breasts and flat bellies; in France the female body part that seems to get the most attention is not the breast, but the *fesses*—the curves perceived best from behind. The word *fesses*, which doesn't really translate well into English, is less formal than "buttocks," but more elegant than "ass" or even "butt." "Derriere" isn't bad, but then, that's a French word, too.

In 2003, the weekly news magazine *L'Express* devoted a fourteen-page supplement to the subject, with a caption on the cover that read: "*Fesses*: The rising curves." The supplement cited a poll by the BVA organization stating that only 38 percent of French men found the most fascination in a woman's breasts, while 50 percent preferred her *fesses* and legs. "The third millennium announces the return of the full posterior as the barometer of seduction," the magazine said.

A special report on *fesses* in *Elle* magazine in 2006 offered a guide to four different types: the hanging, the saddlebag, the flat, the fat. There was also a timeline of changes in *fesses* preferences over the years: "long and thin" popular in the 1990s—an androgynous silhouette where the *fesses* seemed to disappear—was replaced by rounder, "perfect curves" a decade later.

Naturally, a body part this important must be carefully presented, especially when it is clothed but even when it is not. For the one hundredth anniversary of her birth, Simone de Beauvoir was celebrated with half a dozen biographies, a DVD series, a three-day scholarly symposium, and the cover of the magazine *Le Nouvel Observateur*. The cover showed Art Shay's famous photo of her nude (except for her high-heeled mules) from behind, fixing her hair in her Chicago bathroom. The cellulite on Beauvoir's thighs and buttocks was airbrushed away, adding to the indignity and sparking a debate on sexism, feminism, and journalistic honesty.

The fact is, the *fesses* are accepted as a respectable topic of conversation in polite society. My French researcher, Sanae Lemoine, and I were talking about Brigitte Bardot, and she told me that for her grandfather, it was Bardot's backside that beckoned. "I remember my grandfather saying he would go see her movies for her *fesses*," she said. "If he wanted a 'beautiful' woman in a more classic and less vulgar or sexual way, he would go see a movie with Simone Signoret." Indeed, in the film *And God Created Woman*, a male admirer says of Bardot as he watches her walk, "She has an ass that sings."

The *fesses* are taken so seriously that a Frenchman wrote a book called *Brève histoire des fesses*, a scholarly history of them in art and society from classical antiquity to the present. The author, Jean-Luc Hennig, argued that the *fesses* are the voyeur's natural territory. They give pleasure not so much in physical interaction but rather as ideal objects for contemplation, in painting, prose, language, sculpture, and sexual attraction. At times forbidden objects of desire, at others flamboyantly accentuated and celebrated, the *fesses* give rise to a seductive practice and discourse all to themselves, he wrote.

French painters and songwriters have portrayed *fesses* in disarming and vulnerable situations. François Clouet's painting *Le Bain de Diane* (1565) demonstrated a bottom perfectly at ease and revealingly coquettish, while Gustave Courbet brought to life the white-skinned, working-class *fesses* in his *Les Baigneuses* (1853). In the song "Vénus callipyge," Georges Brassens proclaimed his attachment to them (though using *cul*, a more indelicate term than *fesses*) with lines like, "*Au temps où les faux culs sont la majorité / Gloire à celui qui dit toute la vérité!*" A loose translation would be: "At a time when hypocrite-asses are the majority, glory to the one who tells nothing but the truth!"

In late 2009, a book and a television documentary, *The Hidden Side of the Fesses*, broadcast by Arte, the European cultural television channel, charted how this body part helped shape civilization. The companion book was such a popular Christmas present that it sold out in most bookstores. The film was the most watched documentary in 2009, drawing even more viewers than a documentary purporting to tell the truth about Michael Jackson. Allan Rothschild, the codirector of the film, declared that France has a special relationship with the *fesses*. They are bared on advertising billboards, in fashion magazines, and in pharmacy windows, examples of what appears at first glance to be an exceptionally relaxed French attitude about nudity.

That first impression can be misleading. Nudity may seem to exist at the opposite pole of bodily allure from the elaborate dressing of couture, but in France the two have something important in common: both are the subject of careful presentation. To the French, showing the nude body to its best effect is not a simple matter of undressing. Even nakedness can be—and should be—a matter of style.

I discovered this truth most vividly on an autumn night in 2009, when I stood with dozens of other spectators waiting patiently behind metal barricades at Printemps, the elegant Paris department store, for a glimpse of an unusual window display. The night rain, steady and cold, could not keep us away. Shortly after 9:00 p.m., a screen covering a corner picture window lifted to reveal five female dancers in uniform. From afar, they seemed to be dressed as the Queen of England's guards at Buckingham Palace. Despite the dim lighting, on closer inspection, it was clear that they were wearing little except black fur hats strapped to their chins, high-heeled boots, black collars, red epaulets, white gloves, brass buttons, garters, and bits of ribbon. Shiny white tassels hung from their waists in front and in back to strategically cover their privates. Their breasts and *fesses* were stark naked.

The boulevard filled with martial music and the harsh voice of a male commander barking orders. The dancers saluted, strutted, marched, turned, and cocked their heads. They did not undulate or swivel their hips. Their breasts were firm and perky, their *fesses* taut and muscular. No body part bobbed or jiggled. The show—presented in cooperation with the Crazy Horse cabaret theater to "celebrate charm and seduction"—lasted for just five minutes.

I felt cheated. The dancers were so regimented that their performance seemed utterly unerotic. I didn't understand how precision and control could translate into charm and seduction.

The audience loved it.

The young French woman standing next to me marveled, "What dis-

President Jacques Chirac welcomes First Lady Laura Bush to Paris with a *baisemain*, a kiss of the hand. Chirac is an ardent hand kisser, who breaks protocol by touching his partner's hand with his lips, instead of letting his kiss hover in the air. His power kiss was one of my first lessons in understanding the importance of seduction in France. *(Philippe Wojazer/Reuters)*

Arielle Dombasle, singer, dancer, and actress on the dark side of fifty. "Seduction is not a frivolous thing," she says. "No. It's war." Women, she adds, should never be nude in front of their husbands: "You shouldn't. Otherwise, he won't buy you lunch." *(Erin Baiano/*The New York Times*)*

Alain Baraton, the chief gardener at Versailles, in front of the Grand Trianon. The author of several books, including one on love at the château, he calls seduction "the essence of life . . . the motor driving French society." France for him is "a country that built itself on love stories." *(Ed Alcock, www. edalcock.com)*

Seventeen-year-old Charlotte Marie, chosen as Joan of Arc 2010 for her spiritual devotion and her good works, during the annual celebration in Orléans of Joan's victory over the English. She wears twenty-five pounds of armor and a brass sword strapped to her belt as she rides around the center of town on a horse. For Marie, Joan of Arc was more than a virgin-warrior; she was also a coquette. *(Jean Puyo)*

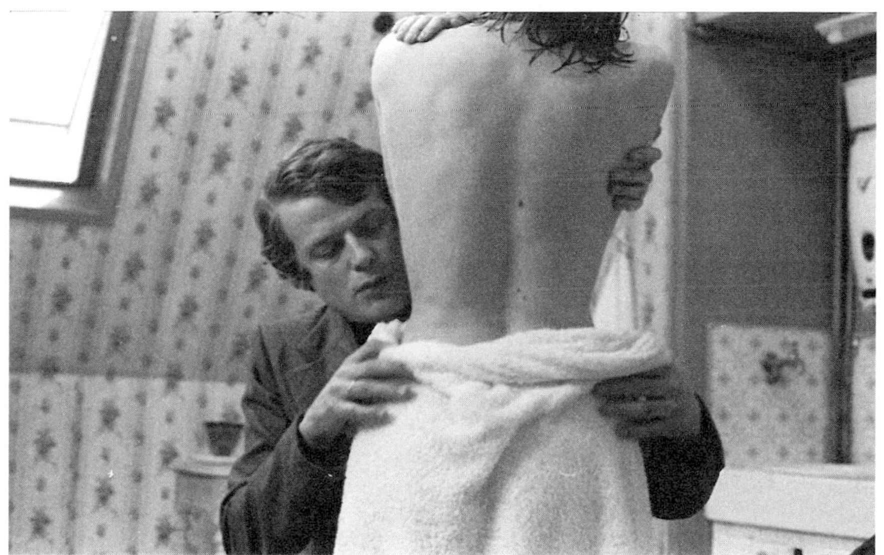

A scene from the 1972 film *L'amour l'après-midi* by Eric Rohmer. Frédéric, the narrator, a thirty-year-old married man with a stable job, a structured life, a pregnant wife whom he appears to love, and a young daughter, begins to spend time with Chloé, the ex-girlfriend of a close friend. They flirt; they kiss. But the movie ends without their ever having sex. In France, excitement often comes less from gratification than from desire. *(© Les Films du Losange—* L'amour l'après-midi *by Eric Rohmer—1972)*

An advertising poster dating from around 1925 for the Salle Marivaux theater in Paris. Frédéric Chappey, the director of the Musée des Années 30, explains the importance of *le regard*—the look—in the poster and how the men use it to signal to other women in the hall that they might be available on another occasion. *(André Marty, "Poster for the Salle Marivaux"/ © 2011 Artists Rights Society [ARS], New York/ADAGP, Paris. Photo: "Le Musée des années 30"/Pascal Cadiou)*

The Eiffel Tower is not only the world's most identifiable monument but also the symbol of France as a seductive nation. The philosopher Roland Barthes saw her as a woman, "a human silhouette; with no head, except for a fine needle, and with no arms . . . and yet it is a long torso placed on top of two legs spread apart." *(Ed Alcock/*The New York Times*)*

François Jousse, the lighting engineer who was responsible for illuminating more than three hundred monuments, buildings, bridges, and boulevards in Paris for more than twenty-five years. Paris succumbed to his charms. Unremarkable buildings glowed, much like ordinary-looking women who turn beautiful in candlelight. *(Ed Alcock/*The New York Times*)*

The windows of the Lancel handbag boutique on the Place de l'Opéra in Paris showing half-century-old photos of the sex icon Brigitte Bardot and the purse that bears her name. Bardot's power as seductress rests in an image that continues to grip the imagination: a carefree child-woman and a symbol of sexual liberation. *(Gabriela Sciolino Plump)*

MÉDITERRANÉE : LE BON COUP DE SARKOZY

Le Point

VOLTAIRE
ROUSSEAU
La guerre
sans fin

- Culture contre Nature
- Raison contre Passion
- Civilisation contre Pureté

par Roger-Pol Droit

The cover of the weekly newsmagazine *Le Point* showing the eighteenth-century *philosophes* Voltaire and Rousseau and the headline "The war without end." Intellectual foreplay—the clash of ideas—is part of the French national identity, from the corridors of power in Paris to the central squares of remote villages. *(Cover "Voltaire-Rousseau, la guerre sans fin,"* Le Point *no. 1870)*

A cartoon entitled "It Doesn't Take Much." The young woman smiles and thrusts back her shoulders when the young man tells her, "You are ravishing." *(Pénélope Bagieu/*Ma vie est tout à fait fascinante, *Éditions Jean-Claude Gawsewitch)*

An illustration by Sempé, the artist made famous in the United States with his work in *The New Yorker*. The workmen are whistling at the elegant woman as she passes, a sign of approval and playfulness on the street that is not at all considered rude or sexist in France, as it might be in the United States. (*Jean-Jacques Sempé*/Un peu de Paris, © *Éditions Gallimard*)

The butcher Roger Yvon wearing a necklace of his homemade sausages. More than a cutter of meat, he is a playful spirit, the soul of the staid rue de Varenne in the seventh arrondissement of Paris. Yvon is an available and faithful suitor, who entertains his clients by telling stories, sharing recipes, and introducing them to one another as if his business were a modern-day salon. The gratification is instant. *(Nigel Dickinson/*The New York Times*)*

Chantal Thomass, the queen of French lingerie and a firm believer that partial concealment enhances the erotic. Her motto, "Hide to show better," resonates with French women, who spend more of their clothing budget on lingerie than women in any other European country. *(Christian Moser)*

Dancers in the Crazy Horse cabaret show in Paris as soldiers in "uniform": black fur hats, high-heeled boots, black collars, red epaulets, white gloves, brass buttons, garters, bits of ribbon, and shiny white tassels that strategically cover their privates. On a cold, rainy night, they performed a five-minute mini-version of this show for passersby in a picture window of Printemps, the elegant department store. The event was billed as a celebration of "charm and seduction." *(Ed Alcock, www.edalcock.com)*

Jasmine flowers to be used in making Chanel No. 5 have just been picked on the flower farm near Grasse of Joseph Mul, who grows and processes flowers exclusively for Chanel. Most of the flowers used in perfume are now grown elsewhere—India, Bulgaria, Morocco, Egypt, Italy, Tunisia. But the French have made a global business of perfume to fit the image of who they think they are or would like to be: romantic, alluring, mysterious. *(Elaine Sciolino)*

The three-star chef Guy Savoy (*center*) with his father, Louis, and his mother, Marie, in the garden of his parents' home in Les Abrets, not far from Lyon. Savoy is holding the metal tin that held the first cookies his mother taught him to make as a child and that she still makes today. *(Elaine Sciolino)*

Le Bistrot de Pierrot in the northern French city of Lille, where the owner chats with diners. In France, conversation can be almost as important as the meal itself. *(Ed Alcock, www.edalcock.com)*

Dominique Strauss-Kahn, the director of the International Monetary Fund and a former French finance minister. Rumors that he is a womanizer have livened up Paris dinner parties for years, with some people expressing quiet admiration that such a high-profile political figure can find time for an active social life. *(AP Images)*

France is a republic, but it takes the history of its royals seriously. The cover of a special issue of *Le Figaro* magazine displays a portrait of King Henri IV, calling him "the adventurer, the seducer, the king." *(© Le Figaro Hors-Série "Vive Henri IV!"/2010)*

Former president Valéry Giscard d'Estaing and Britain's Princess Diana at Versailles, where they attended the theater and a dinner in 1994. Giscard, even in his eighties, remains determined to promote his image as a sexually potent male. In 2009, he published *La princesse et le président*, a novel that relates the "violent passion" between a French head of state and a British royal. It titillated readers with the suggestion that he might have had a love affair with Diana. *(John Schults/Reuters)*

The funeral of President François Mitterrand in 1996: Danielle Mitterrand, the widow; their son Jean-Christophe; Mazarine Pingeot, the daughter-out-of-marriage; her mother and Mitterrand's longtime mistress, Anne Pingeot; and the Mitterrands' son Gilbert. What upset the French public more than the existence of a second family was the revelation after Mitterrand's death that the French state had financially supported Pingeot and her daughter—even giving them full police protection. *(AP Images)*

NEWS EN COUVERTURE

SÉGOLÈNE ROYAL

Et dire qu'elle a 53 ans !

ENCORE UNE EXCLUSIVITÉ Closer

Sur une plage de la Côte d'Azur, Ségolène Royal vit les vacances de Madame Tout-le-Monde. Et affiche sa silhouette parfaite...

Retrouvez nos pages spéciales 50 stars à la plage

Ségolène Royal, the Socialist Party's candidate in the 2007 presidential election and a mother of four, in a bikini the previous summer. The caption in the celebrity magazine *Closer* reads, "And to say that she is 53 years old!" *(*Closer*, no. 60, August 7–13, 2006)*

President Barack Obama and Michelle Obama with Carla Bruni and President Nicolas Sarkozy in Strasbourg in 2009. Sarkozy is standing on the balls of his feet, a longtime habit that makes him appear taller. *(AP Images)*

President Sarkozy wooing the U.S. Congress in Washington in 2007 with a pro-American speech. As the members of Congress stood to applaud when he finished, he placed his hand on his heart for the third time, letting it rest there for a full five seconds. *(Susan P. Etheridge/*The New York Times*)*

The late American diplomat and emissary Richard Holbrooke with the author and the French foreign minister Bernard Kouchner on bended knee. Kouchner is telling the story of how in 1999 he wooed Madeleine K. Albright, the U.S. secretary of state, who had opposed his appointment as the United Nations chief administrator for Kosovo. He called on her during her vacation in Innsbruck, Austria, bringing with him a bouquet of edelweiss that he had picked for her. *(Ian Spencer Langsdon)*

In 2008, the French government unveiled a new logo designed to sell France as a tourist destination featuring Marianne, the symbol of the French republic. The "R" and the "A" in the word "France" form her bare breasts. To avoid offending the sensibility of some potential visitors, the word "France" was rewritten and the naughty nakedness eliminated. *(Above: first version of the logo created by Carré Noir for ATOUT FRANCE; below: logo de la marque France, ATOUT FRANCE)*

The food market in the Paris suburb of Saint-Denis is multiracial and multiethnic, an enclosed microcosm of layers of French history. Merchants and their clients—no matter their color, religion, age, ethnicity, or country of origin—seduce one another. They share a common purpose: buying and selling food products, of course, but also anticipation of the shared pleasure that comes with cooking and eating. *(Gabriela Sciolino Plump)*

Paris la nuit.
(Ed Alcock/The New York Times*)*

cipline! What elegance!" Another woman said she was "entranced by the absence of vulgarity. They are naked in such a way that they don't look naked anymore." A third was impressed by the perfection of the costumes and makeup that made the dancers "look like dolls." A male television reporter asked a number of spectators whether they considered the show to be a "sexy atomic bomb."

For them, French artistry was on display. The nude bits seemed beside the point. We were in front of an iconic department store on one of the busiest boulevards in the heart of Paris. We were a long way from Bloomingdale's. A long way from Las Vegas, too.

The director of the Crazy Horse, which is known for its nearly nude performers, is Andrée Deissenberg, a long-legged blonde who is half-French, half-American. I called on her at the theater one evening after the window display and before I watched the full show. I learned that most Crazy Horse dancers have studied classical ballet. They must measure between five feet six inches and five feet eight inches in height, with no more than ten and a half inches between their nipples and five inches between their navels and their pubis. They are weighed once a week. They are forbidden to have tattoos or undergo cosmetic surgery. Their identities are kept from the public: they are given stage names, and there will never be revelations about where they live, dine, or shop. They are never completely naked, even if their only clothes are strips of colored lights and high heels they never take off. "High heels enhance the leg line," said Deissenberg. "You walk differently; you act differently. When there is a little bit of artifice, there's the whole seduction thing going on. When you're naked, the audience is going to fall asleep."

She called the five-minute Printemps window show inspiring. "The dancers were in perfect control, perfectly lit," she said. "It was an act, on a stage. It was great, fantastic, and it inspires so many younger women."

Inspiring was not the word I would have used. "Inspired to what? To be sexy?" I asked.

"To be and to feel beautiful and desired," she said. "Women want to play with their sensuality, with their sexuality, with their femininity, to take control. And not just to be, you know, on the receiving end, but to be on the taking control end. On the dictating." In other words, she was saying, Crazy Horse dancers are feminist mistresses of their own destinies.

Deissenberg had worked in both Las Vegas and Paris, so I figured she was a good source on the differences between the two cities in matters of sexuality and seduction. Las Vegas is direct, not subtle or mysterious, she told me. "America is *Playboy* girls with big breasts showing everything. In Vegas, everything is lit up and bright. There is absolutely nothing left to the imagination. It's like Ya-ta-ta-ta, show me. It doesn't speak to your brain. It speaks to a few people's pants, maybe, but not to their brains. And the brain—that's where beauty is."

The Vegas dancers, she said, lack the power of their Crazy Horse sisters. "The typical girls in Vegas, they're almost victims," she said. "I'm sorry to say but there is a sort of 'I pump myself up with silicone. I put on little skirts to wiggle my ass.' There is no seduction. They don't bring out their own fantasies. They give in to the fantasies and demands of the guys. They lose something of themselves."

The Crazy Horse, by contrast, "is very intellectual," she said. "It's all about suggestion. It's in the imagination. It shows but you never really see." The choreography is disciplined and precise, the lighting mysterious—"more like watercolors dressing the body rather than lighting it up."

That night, the show was artistic and fancifully lit, not erotic. As I sipped champagne called Tsarine, I saw classic male sexual fantasies on display: a French maid with a duster; a female astronaut; a female executive who, when the stock market plummets, takes off her clothes, starting with her glasses and ending with her garter belt. There was a lot of *fesses* swiveling but no breast bouncing. The only act that brought the house down was a long comical tap-dancing sequence by two fully clothed, slightly balding, identical male twins.

It may be a bit of a stretch to cast the shows at Crazy Horse as an example of subtlety in the use of nudity, but it's clear that the French do enjoy playing a bit with nakedness rather than getting too quickly to the point. A recent poll by Ipsos revealed that only 3 percent of French women believe they are most seductive in the nude, and only 17 percent of French men feel that women are most seductive when naked.

The body, it seems, is more appealing when wrapped in mystery, however slight. Seeing a woman in clothes should awaken the desire of others to see her naked. It is a constant movement between what is apparent and what is not. The fashion designer Sonia Rykiel told me this many years ago, when she was promoting a line of clothing that opened and closed. There was no nudity but a lot of movement. "Naked," she said, "is not sexy."

Flirting and teasing as a means of enhancing nudity and prolonging pleasure is codified in the striptease. The French claim to have invented the modern striptease show. The first, *Le coucher d'Yvette*—Yvette's Bedtime Ritual—was performed in Paris in the 1890s. It featured a young woman slowly shedding layers of clothing as she searched in vain for a flea. In the succeeding decades, the Dutch dancer Mata Hari (later executed by the French as a spy during World War I) and Josephine Baker, the black American dancer and singer, brought their own styles to the genre.

The key lesson of the striptease is to master the balance between hiding and showing. To learn more, I sought out Violeta Carpentier, who ran a tiny striptease school out of a basement dance studio in the ninth arrondissement of Paris.

One Saturday morning, a dozen soberly dressed women, from the ages of twenty-two to forty-five, arrived for their class. They had been told in advance to come with easy-to-remove clothing: a blouse with buttons, a bra with no more than two hooks in the back, a skirt with a zipper in the back or on the side, a jacket that also could serve as a prop, shoes with no ties or straps, and, to maintain a modicum of modesty, a double set of underwear. By the end of the class, they'd be ready to perform a three-and-a-half-minute striptease act. One student was wearing a perky hat, another a black ostrich-feather boa. Sylvie, who was twenty-six, planned to give her husband a present—her performance. Thirty-two-year-old Laurence was there because her friends wanted her to shed her shyness and show off her body.

Charlotte, the teacher, dressed in a white pullover sweater and jeans, was tall and attractive but not red-hot sexy. She never took off her clothes as she took the class through the dos and don'ts. Pants are inelegant, jeans impossible. Removing a T-shirt or a sweater over the head isn't sexy. Clothes that are too tight can leave marks on the body. Underwire bras are recommended because they will stay in place when you slip the straps off your shoulders. Elastic-topped hose that stop somewhere above the knee accentuate thigh fat. Facial makeup that is too heavy will clash with the rest of one's skin color.

Long-haired ladies should pull their hair up in a chignon with a one-step, easy-to-remove pin, even a pencil, that will let it fly loose. The short-haired have to rely on hair ornaments like a flower or a scarf. The space for the performance should be free of furniture and lit with candles. The only other prop for each student was a chair that served as the centerpiece of the presentation.

And so the students got ready for action. They held on to the backs of their chairs, faced the mirrors, and swiveled their hips in figure eights as they lowered their bodies. They were told to imagine that the object of their affection was a handsome American. "We're going to call him Bob," said Charlotte. No one seemed very excited. "Unless you prefer we call him something else. Brad? We'll call him Brad!" (A lot of French women apparently like Brad Pitt.)

This was refined dancing, not the sweaty bump-and-grind you might find in an American striptease class. It required smooth movement, not furious flesh wiggling.

The women learned how to walk toward "Brad" while unbuttoning their jackets. "Don't walk like you think you're going to miss your Métro!" Charlotte warned. They stripped one side of their jackets off their shoulders and then covered up again. They stole a look at "Brad" and flung their jackets forward to avoid tripping as they walked away from him.

They were told how to show their profiles to advantage, how to move their knees, and how to unzip, drop, and step out of their skirts with deliberate slowness. Their sexiness would emerge through their elegance, mastery of illusion, and control. Martine, a short-haired redhead who had a blue-and-orange bird tattooed on her lower belly, asked, in a serious tone, "Why is the skirt taken off before the top?"

"To be able to show off the *fesses* for a longer time," Charlotte replied.

"But I don't like my *fesses*, so what if I don't want to show them?" Martine asked. I didn't see what the problem was with her *fesses*. They looked pretty good to me.

"Well, then maybe you should forget about striptease," Charlotte said, not bothering to disguise her irritation.

"Then I'm leaving!" Martine said and started to make her way for the exit.

Charlotte regained her composure and relented. "If you want to take off your top first, okay," she said. "I'm giving you the main course. Afterward, you can add whatever sauce you want."

Then the students mastered the arts of pole shimmying, hip swiveling, hair flinging, and breast thrusting, accompanied by a recording of "Mad About You" sung by Belinda Carlisle. They learned to unhook a bra in a swift, single movement, to pedal while sitting sideways and leaning back on an armless chair, and to slip off their panties without getting them stuck around their ankles.

Their success was unpredictable. One ethereally beautiful woman, with shiny waist-length blond hair and a perfectly proportioned body, couldn't master the moves or even the look. She stayed deadly cold and serious, as if this were a final exam for her baccalaureate. Then there was a twenty-eight-year-old engineer who was not especially attractive in her prim black suit but suddenly turned irresistible when she started to take off her clothes. Her flower-print pastel bloomers with dangling ribbons said naughty innocence. Without any prompting, she seemed to know which body part to stick out when. She was giggling so much that her breasts danced.

Whether dressing the body or flashing nudity, the French have strict ideas of what constitutes good taste and a horror of violating it. A striptease can be artful and therefore sophisticated and perfectly acceptable. On the other hand, a carefully chosen business outfit can be off-putting. Nowhere are French distinctions of taste on clearer display than in the attitude toward makeup.

Chic women don't wear makeup. At least they pretend not to.

While the dressed-up American woman will never leave home without applying a layer of foundation, then decorating with eye shadow and liner, mascara, blush, and lipstick, the chic French woman prefers to peel and polish rather than do a lot of painting. I asked Michèle Fitoussi to explain. Michèle is one of France's most important literary figures, a novelist and biographer, as well as a columnist at *Elle* magazine. She wears black-rimmed glasses and has perfect skin. She looks as if she wears no makeup.

And yet when I urged Michèle to show me what she was carrying in her purse, she dug out pressed powder, blush, mascara, a taupe-toned eye shadow, and a pale lipstick. So I asked her about the minimalist French attitude toward makeup. "Makeup dates you," she said. "It gives you lines. Like a tree." She had one word to sum up the painted-doll look that some American women swear by: *vulgaire*.

Vulgaire means more than "vulgar." It connotes a lack of style, taste, proper upbringing, and good manners. To avoid the *vulgaire* look, you could do only one dramatic thing at a time. "If I wear red lipstick, I wear all black," she said. "If I am wearing very high heels, they cannot be worn with a skirt that's too short. A big piece of jewelry, I wear it with a sober suit. You can be eccentric but not with more than one, maximum two signs. There's always a rapport with the erotic, but it's hidden. Beauty in France is very interiorized—like wearing a trench coat with a mink lining."

I asked the French women in my office about the subtle made-up look. Hélène Fouquet, a young reporter, explained the rule about balance. "It's either the eyes or the mouth," she said.

I told her I didn't understand; American women dress up all their facial features. "If you wear a lot of makeup on the eyes, you don't wear lipstick," she said. "If you wear lipstick, you don't do the eyes."

When makeup is not worn, in the bedroom for example, there are other ways to convey the idea of the beautiful. Marie-Louise de Clermont-Tonnerre, the head of external relations for Chanel, told me how she uses her bedroom to charm her grandchildren. "The seduction by a grandmother of her grandchildren depends on important details," she said. "She makes sure when they come into her bedroom that she is always dressed in a very beautiful nightgown. This form of seduction has nothing to do with fashion or makeup. It is seduction in a beautiful bedroom, with beautiful furnishings, and with her natural charm in her bed with its embroidered sheets. The grandmother must be magnificent when she is in her bed."

To find out more, I turned to Laura Mercier, the New York–based French creator of a line of cosmetics and skin-care products. Showy makeup, she explained, is reserved for women who either make their living on the streets or are trying too hard.

"It really astonishes me the way American women wear so much makeup," she said. "And when you are overly made-up, you send out the message that you are overly sexual." By contrast, Mercier said, "French women are not flashy. They must be subtle. The message must not be, 'I'm spending hours on my face to look beautiful.' "

Heavy makeup has its purpose, however. I asked a veteran showgirl at the Lido how it feels to dance practically naked night after night. She told me she has to sponge thick layers of makeup all over her exposed skin to give it a flat, uniform look under the lights. So she never really is naked, she said. But makeup is so much a part of her stage persona that she hardly ever wears it when she is not working.

Some things about French style, though, cannot be translated. Avoidance of the *vulgaire* takes special care when the art of dress and the game of revealing intersect.

Andrée Deissenberg of the Crazy Horse told me she always feels French in Las Vegas. "I don't dress like them. I don't walk like them," she said of American women. "There is French elegance, or better, Parisian elegance. It's restrained, nothing too fancy. Maybe a French woman will have her blouse a tiny bit opened, but she'll never have big boobs hanging out, or even small boobs. Much more sober also."

Details are crucial. "The heels will be the right height; the pants will be the right fit and the right material; the blouse will be the right transparency and the right cut. It will be sexy but you won't see anything, but you might be able to imagine. I will never wear something too tight. I will never put on a pair of opened-toed shoes if the painting of my nails isn't well done."

Okay, I got that. But then she threw me a curve. "The funny thing, in the United States, you'll go to a business meeting and you'll see the American woman next to you sitting there, and she's wearing the same black plants, the same nice blouse. Her nails are very well done. But actually, everything is wrong."

How so? I wanted to know.

"Frankly," she said, "I don't know how to explain that."

9

The Temptation of Scent

. . .

> According to the ancients, the panther is the only animal that emits a perfumed odor. It uses this scent to draw and capture its victims.
>
> —Jean Baudrillard, *Seduction*

> A woman without perfume is a woman without a future.
>
> —Coco Chanel

For the master perfumer Jean-Claude Ellena, who creates beautiful scents for Hermès, there is a passage in French literature that is deeply unsettling. It occurs in the 1930 novel *Regain* by Jean Giono. *Regain* is a pastoral tale celebrating the magic of tilling the soil. It is also the love story of Panturle, the last inhabitant of the ruins of a village in Haute-Provence, and Arsule, a woman who settles down with him to bring new life to the village and the fallow fields. Before that happens, however, Arsule falls into a life of wandering from place to place alongside an itinerant knife sharpener.

"There is an extraordinary passage," Ellena said. "The man is a grinder, someone who sharpens knives. He meets a woman who is a little lost. He decides to take her under his wing. We are not yet in a love affair, but we are getting there. She is pushing the wheelbarrow that carries his sharpening machine. She is in front, and she pushes the wheelbarrow along the country road, like this."

For emphasis, Ellena moved his body as if he were pushing something heavy, then continued. "Giono describes this scene very well. The man is behind the woman, and he smells her odor. He smells the odor of her sweat. And the passage is full of eroticism. Aaaah . . . Marvelous!"

Ellena paused suddenly as if he were afraid to continue. But he could not stop. "It is a smell that is truly that of an animal, a human but an animal at the same time," he said. "It has nothing to do with perfume. We are in the skin, in the flesh. I remember . . ."

His voice trailed off and stopped and started again. Ellena was aware of the significance of his words. "The story really disturbs me," he said. "I find this very . . . very . . . because I believe . . . as a creator of perfume, I believe the most beautiful smell is that of human skin. Much more than perfume. Perfume is nothing but clothing. That's all it is. It's makeup. A set of jewelry."

Ellena is said to be the most articulate perfumer in the world, capable of translating the scents he creates into poetry. It is this talent that sets him apart. A dabbler in watercolors and a collector of Chinese art, he professes to draw his inspiration from literary figures like Baudelaire, composers like Debussy, painters like Cézanne, and jazz singers like Stacey Kent. He spins his impressions into creations that trigger memories and fantasies.

He is usually a calm and controlled man whose movements are graceful, whose style is refined, and whose personality has the marks of an oversized ego. On the day we met, he was dressed in his "uniform": a perfectly pressed shirt, well-cut gray trousers made from an expensive fabric, and white shoes in soft leather. He knows he is handsome and playing at the top of his game, and he uses his dark brown eyes to destabilize his audience. That's what made his confession so daring.

Ellena may be an expert at combining scents from different flowers and extracts, but his story invites a conclusion that has little to do with those ingredients: that in the world of seduction, perfume is an extension of human sweat. Giovanni Giacomo Casanova, the great eighteenth-century seducer, knew that. "As for women, I have always found that the one I was in love with smelled good, and the more copious her sweat the sweeter I found it," he wrote in his memoirs. But if perspiration, unaided, produces the most seductive scent in the world, and man-made perfume is nothing more than a covering, like an article of clothing, or an adornment like jewelry or makeup, then there is no need for a multibillion-dollar perfume industry.

"In your profession, this must be a very dangerous thought," I said.

My words jolted Ellena out of his troubled state. He had slipped out of his corporate persona but now recovered his equilibrium. He embraced me with his easy charm, and he smiled.

"But this is not serious," he said, his voice turning to velvet. "I can exaggerate."

Of all the senses, smell is the most emotionally powerful and the most elusive. It sends its messages straight to the limbic system, a mysterious part of the brain that arouses emotions and feelings rather than ideas and thoughts. As Ellena's story illustrates, its connection to sexual seduction is natural and innate. But in France, the creation and use of scent has been refined far beyond the basics of sweat.

Perfume allows smell to be communicated in a pleasurable and compelling way. Even the names of its ingredients evoke the exotic and the romantic: Indian tuberose, Calabrian bergamot, Egyptian jasmine, Indonesian patchouli.

It is a medium that cannot be seen, tasted, felt, or touched. Its power is imagined, its allure a manipulation of time. The feeling it produces can linger long after the carrier of the scent has departed. That prolongation of the moment is the trick it plays on its target, by making its wearer impossible to forget. In that sense, it is the packaging of both possibility and remembrance.

Ellena used a simple demonstration to prove how scent plays with memory. He opened a tiny glass vial of an artificial version of vanilla and dipped a paper smell strip into it. He dipped a second strip into sweet orange. When he put the two strips together, they smelled like a madeleine. He dipped a third strip, this one into cinnamon, and made the smell of gingerbread. He dipped the fourth strip into lime, joined them all, and suddenly, I smelled Coca Cola!

"I play with your memory," he said. "I manipulate you." He was right. This was an old trick that I knew Ellena had performed before. But it proved his point.

Modern perfume, which relies on chemistry and technology, was invented in France in the nineteenth century. Yet the idea of perfuming was already alive on French soil thousands of years before, when Cro-Magnon man, living in the caves of what is now southern France, scrubbed himself with mint and lemon.

In the Middle Ages, French women wore *bijoux de senteur*, gold or jeweled containers for perfume preparations. In the seventeenth century, wigs were powdered with scent from flowers like jasmine, rose, hyacinth, daffodil, and orange blossom and sometimes spiked with musk, civet crushed with sugar, or hot amber oil. In the succeeding centuries, the French elevated perfume to a fine art, and their expertise at creating scent became part of the national mystique. Many perfume creators (known as "noses") consider the scents they make not products of chemistry but works of art, as important as paintings or poems.

Others are more down-to-earth, confessing that the romantic story lines may lure customers but bear no relationship to the hard work of perfume making. "Perfume companies and perfumers will tell you stories—of the queen of the night flowers that blossom once a year and by chance I was there and was inspired to make a perfume," said François Demachy, the chief perfumer at Dior. "What I do is far from that. Perfume is a science—the science of doubt. I'm an artisan."

But even Demachy allows himself to be swept away in the magic of what he does. He took me one morning to the Bagatelle gardens in Paris so we could see, feel, and smell the dozens of varieties of roses that are grown there for an annual competition. It is a ritual he follows every spring, to remind himself of the roses of his childhood in the perfume-making city of Grasse and to search for something new.

We dodged peacocks and British tourists carrying cameras and notebooks as we made our way along the paths. He showed me how to press my nose deep into each rose and take several sniffs. We smelled a large white rose tinged with fuchsia that didn't need much of a fragrance to attract insects because of its gaudy appearance. A yellow tea rose with glossy green leaves named O Sole Mio smelled like the color green, Demachy said. The small white Vierge Folle—Crazy Virgin—had no scent at all. There were roses with the smells of almond, lychee, peach, pepper, vanilla, cloves, and straw. I learned that roses get a slight honey smell when their petals begin to drop, that their scent evaporates as the day gets warmer, that older plants often produce fainter smells. "Every time I come here I discover another rose," he said. "Every rose has its own smell." He is a serious man, but here, in the rose garden, he was smiling.

Over the years, I have become conditioned to the smell of perfume as an integral component of the French ambience. It belongs to French culture, the same way lingerie and wine do, and I smell it a lot more often in Paris than in New York.

Proximity is one factor. Since everyone does a lot more cheek kissing than hand shaking in everyday life, there are opportunities to get close. The custom is to wear only enough perfume so that it can be detected when one is near enough to kiss. Getting close thus means being invited into another person's smell. A perfume becomes a form of intimacy, a gesture of sharing pleasure and a means to compel the other person to remember you.

A sophisticated and alluring perfume can play a central role in a seduction campaign. Drawn to the scent, one is drawn to the person. Lured by sensations that cannot be expressed in words, one is tempted to suspend rational thought and follow the lead of emotion. After an interview over lunch with Olivier Monteil, the communications head of Hermès perfumes, I stood to say good-bye, and he kissed me on both cheeks, close enough so that I could smell his scent. I asked what he was wearing, but he played coy. "An experiment," he said. "Rose, spicy, peppery. You cannot smell it from afar, only when I kiss you."

Each year the French spend more than forty dollars per man, woman, and child on fragrances, more than any other people in the world.

Americans spend only about seventeen dollars and the Japanese, four dollars. Spaniards and Brazilians consume more perfume than the French, but they spend less money on it.

And there is more. The sense of smell itself, not just perfume, is more important in France than many other places. As children, the French are taught to identify smells; there is a popular board game called Le Loto des Odeurs (The Lottery of Smells) that asks players to identify thirty smells, including eucalyptus, mushrooms, lily of the valley, hazelnut, grass, biscuits, fennel, strawberries, honeysuckle, and the sea.

Perfume is seen as an essential element in a woman's personal arsenal, and French men are invested and interested in it. They are more likely than American men to appreciate and recognize a woman's scent, to know what's on the men's market, and to wear a scent themselves.

While Americans are inclined to project the smell of cleanliness (deodorant soap comes to mind) or power (a scent that can be detected three feet away), the French prefer subtlety and mystery.

Ellena explained it this way: "The American vision of perfume is what I call performance. Americans talk about long duration, tenacity, power. Some perfumes—like Elixir Aromatique or Giorgio—immediately create distance, because their smell is so strong that I go like this." He extended his arm as if to push me away. "Perfume functions almost like a shield," he said.

The French vision of perfume, on the other hand, is based on aesthetics and discretion. "I prefer when a perfume brings people physically closer than when it creates a distance," Ellena continued. "You are present, through your smell, but you don't disturb me. I come to talk into your ear. We are in whispering mode."

Perfume may be an invisible whisper, but it carries the force of a weapon useful in a myriad of ways. Ellena revealed a battle strategy of long-haired women. "They put perfume just here," he said, placing his index finger behind one ear, then moving it slowly downward toward his neck, repeating the gesture behind his other ear. "When they walk, the wind enters into the hair, and it leaves a superb wake. And that I find very, very erotic. Devilishly erotic." He laughed out loud.

His response reminded me of one of Coco Chanel's most repeated sayings: "A woman should wear perfume wherever she expects to be kissed."

I experienced firsthand the sensitivity of French men to perfume one day after an accident landed me in a physical therapist's office. I was lying on my stomach as Alexandre was kneading my shoulder. He was explaining the difference between acute tendonitis and a torn muscle. We fell into silence. Then he raised a different subject.

"What perfume are you wearing?" he asked.

"I'm not," I replied. "But why in the world are you asking me about my perfume? No American man has ever asked me what perfume I wear." This is a fact. Not even my husband has ever asked me this question.

"I'm always interested when I like a perfume," Alexandre said.

He told me about a former client who wore the most exquisite scent. He forgot to ask her its name. The scent haunted him. It had a quality crucial for a great perfume: it persisted in memory.

He still had the client's phone number, but he didn't dare call her. The inquiry after the fact would be too direct and might be misinterpreted. He had missed his chance. He was so earnest that I felt compelled to help him identify the source of my scent. "It must be the hair conditioner," I said.

He smelled my hair. "That's it!" he declared. He smelled me again and said he detected mango.

The same question about my perfume choice came one day from Sophie-Caroline de Margerie, the writer and jurist.

"What perfume do you wear, if you do, and if I can be so bold?" she asked me in an e-mail.

I couldn't tell her that I suffer from allergies and rarely wear perfume. How unseductive would that seem?

"*Je suis infidèle*" (I am unfaithful), I replied "And what about you?"

"Very faithful to Guerlain, one for the summer (Après l'Ondée), one for the winter (Mitsouko)," she wrote back. "And a very secret one which I've handed over to my daughter: Iris Poudre by Frédéric Malle."

The next time I saw Sophie-Caroline, I asked her why she wanted to know about my perfume.

"I want to get to know you better," she said.

I told her I could not imagine how knowing her perfume would help me to get to know her better.

"A perfume gives an idea of the image you want to project," she replied. "So if you have a very strong, sexy scent, or if you have a lily of the valley scent, or if you have nothing at all, it tells me something about you. Maybe not who you are deep down but what you want to leave, to linger behind you. So that's why I asked. It's a very intimate question."

What did I want to leave behind? A perfume legacy as if I were handing down a country house or a wine collection? I was touched. She assumed I wore perfume. More than that, she assumed I had a perfume identity. And she wanted to know my perfume identity as a way to become closer.

I still didn't confess everything to Sophie-Caroline. "I don't have a very strong olfactory sense," I said.

I asked her what image she wants to convey with her perfume. "Ladylike and attractive, subtle and sexy," she replied. She likes her friends to comment on perfume as they would on a dress. And fidelity to a few perfumes allows the memory of her scents to live on.

"I want to wear the same perfume because I want my children to remember me one day by my scent," she said. "When I'm long gone and they're opening a wardrobe and remembering, 'Aaaah, Mommy.' "

Even men can go to great lengths to make sure their scents follow them. A young French friend told me about going to a party at the apartment of a man she found attractive. When the party was over, they went out dancing. They kissed. Before they parted, she realized she had left her expensive black cashmere scarf at his place. He promised to return it to her, as they were to meet again. Time passed, and he did not call her. She was forced to contact him, and when he met her, it was only to hand her the scarf in a sealed plastic bag. When she opened it up later with friends, she was hit with the velvety smell of iris. It was Dior Homme, the scent he wore.

"He wore my scarf!" she exclaimed, at once incredulous and amused. Her friends smelled the scarf and decided that no, the scent was much too strong; they said he must have sprayed Dior Homme all over it so she would remember him. She replied to the gesture with an unsigned text message citing a line from the best-selling novel, *Le parfum*, by Patrick Süskind: "The purpose of perfumes was to produce an intoxicating and alluring effect."

A week later, he sent her a Facebook message, asking her to join him for a drink. But she was already interested in someone else and never replied. For months afterward, however, she enjoyed his scent on her scarf. "It was absolutely delicious," she said. "And when it finally disappeared, it was sad."

The interplay of smell and memory is a familiar theme in literature and in memoirs. In "Another Memory," a short story by Marcel Proust, the narrator speaks of the power of a scent emanating from a room in a dilapidated, once-grand hotel. He is walking down a corridor to his room when he encounters a scent "so richly and so completely floral that someone must have denuded whole fields . . . merely to produce a few drops of that fragrance." The "sensual bliss" it produces is so intoxicating that the narrator feels compelled to linger outside the room. Later, when a pair of lovers leaves the room, he seizes one of the broken flacons they have left behind, capturing a few drops of the bottled remnants of their love affair. Recounting this memory, he says, "The scent of a weakened drop still impregnates my life."

The great perfumer Jean-Paul Guerlain once told an interviewer for *L'Express* that his earliest memory of smell dated back to when he was four years old. It was the smell of his mother's strawberry tart. For the adult Guerlain, the smell of strawberry tarts was synonymous with tenderness. "It moves me always," he said.

Sylvie Jourdet, a perfumer and the president of the French Society of Perfumers, told me that her epiphany came one day as she was working in a laboratory and sniffed an essence of the white privet flower. "We had rows of privet at our family house by the sea in Normandy," she recalled. "That smell brought me back to the great moments of happiness of my childhood. We all have our Proustian moments, and that was mine."

That makes exquisite sense. I recall the day my two daughters and I sorted through some of my mother's belongings after her death. We opened her velvet-lined jewelry box. "It smells like Grandma," my daughter Alessandra said. She was right. The scarves smelled of Johnson's Baby Powder. That was the scent Grandma had left behind.

A wonderful story about a perfume's power to create desire was told to me by Bernard Toulemonde, a trained botanist and food engineer who is a senior executive at International Flavors & Fragrances, or IFF. A giant American conglomerate with a headquarters in New York and a large operation in Grasse, it creates flavors and smells for, among other things, car waxes, laundry detergents, toothpastes, baked goods, and yogurts.

When Toulemonde was director of a global flavors research laboratory at Nestlé in the mid-1980s, he and his team of experts and scientists entertained themselves by playing games with smells during their morning coffee breaks.

"Even though we were working in food flavors, we were very much attracted by fragrance, fragrance being more, should I say, sexy?" he said. "More attractive, certainly than flavors, which are more technical. We had a really good time. One of our favorite games was to pick a theme and try to illustrate it with a perfume. We probably had something like fifty to a hundred perfumes to play with. One morning, the theme was, 'Illustrate the woman you would follow down the street.' And something unbelievable happened. There were twelve of us, and all twelve of us picked the same perfume, without talking to each other! It was the first time this had ever happened!"

"No!" I replied. "What was it?"

He told me it was First, by Van Cleef & Arpels.

Toulemonde said he couldn't remember exactly what it smelled like, just that "it produced a good mood in you, because you were following a woman and that put you in a good mood. Purely seducing, you don't know why. You're just seduced."

"But it's not based on any reality?" I asked.

"Not any rationale that I can explain," he said. "I'm totally unable. . . .

Perhaps a toxicologist would tell you, 'Yeah, that's normal because there is this molecule attracting you or doing something to your brain.'"

First is a classic soft scent created in 1976 by Ellena, who was then a young perfumer. And when I visited Ellena in his studio, I told him Toulemonde's story. He laughed out loud. He had created First, he said, to win his mother's approval. "I can admit today that in making First, unconsciously, I wanted to prove to my mother that I was able to make a very beautiful perfume," he said. Still, he added, he would not be tempted to follow a woman wearing it. When he smells First, his mother appears.

I went several times to the city of Grasse to search for the romantic past of French perfume. A tannery town set into a hill on the Côte d'Azur, Grasse first became known for perfume when Catherine de Médicis popularized perfumed gloves in the sixteenth century. As leather from Italy and Spain proved too competitive, Grasse left tanning behind and moved into growing plants and processing them into essences to make perfume.

Grasse is a small, closed place. It has retained its narrow, winding streets and centuries-old homes with hidden gardens. Doors do not open easily to outsiders, and families can still be referred to in the local patois as *estrangers*—foreigners—a generation after settling there. Most of the perfume industry has gone elsewhere. About a hundred companies remain, largely to furnish raw materials made from natural substances to perfumers and perfume companies around the world. In most cases, the substances themselves come from elsewhere—India, Bulgaria, Morocco, Egypt, Italy, Tunisia. Even so, the corporate heads of the big perfume houses remain fiercely proud of Grasse, bragging that the town bears witness to the rich history of French perfume and that the best French perfumers have learned the art of creating their scents there.

Despite globalization and competition from flower growers around the world, the French refuse to abandon the romance of the past. On a very small scale, they still produce their own flowers. One fall morning, I toured the farm of Joseph Mul, who grows and processes flowers exclusively for Chanel. Field trips there during harvest time—roses in the spring, jasmine in the fall—are a standard part of Chanel's polished publicity pitch to journalists. But Mul, who is now in his seventies, is the real deal, a fifth-generation farmer. His son and son-in-law are his partners and will carry on the business after he is gone.

Mul has the twanged accent of the south and the cracked skin of a man who has broiled too long in the sun. On the day of my visit, he wore jeans and a checked cap; the Lacoste polo shirt stretched over his rounded belly was a giveaway that he was no ordinary farmer.

About fifty pickers, most of them women, were sprinkled across the jasmine field. Most were from North Africa, Tunisia mainly, although there were a few Roma—gypsies—as well. Most stayed in dormitories on the farm. The pickers were exposed to the cruelty of the sun and the wind as they bent over the jasmine plants. They pinched and plucked the tender white blossoms one by one and placed them in wicker baskets. Many of the women wore colorful scarves and long skirts over pants. The scene was as picturesque as a painting by Millet, but it was not serene.

Mul is so attached to his flowers that he claims to have a permanent interaction with them. He knows when a rosebud is full and with a tiny movement of his index finger can coax it to open. He knows when his jasmine plants are "under stress" and not getting enough water. The stakes are high. About seven million jasmine flowers—six hundred kilos—are needed to make one kilo of absolute, the precious pure concentrate used in making fine perfumes. Produced here, it can be twenty to thirty times more expensive than the jasmine extract from India or Egypt.

The pickers arrived with their full baskets at a storage facility where workers wearing protective gloves and aprons poured the flowers into metal crates. The smell of fresh jasmine invaded the small room with such fury that all of the oxygen felt pushed out. My head ached; my heart raced. There was something overripe about the sweetness.

Later, over chilled wine with oranges, Fabrice Bianchi, Mul's son-in-law, turned the conversation to his childhood. "In the morning, we had to pick jasmine," he recalled. "Since then, this smell reminds me of having to wake up at dawn. Since we hadn't had anything to eat, by nine we'd have a *pan bagnat*, this sandwich with tomatoes, olives, hard-boiled egg, anchovy, olive oil. And for me, the smell of jasmine along with the *pan bagnat*, it brings back my entire carefree childhood."

The subject moved to a woman's smell, and Mul's eyes sparkled with play. "What I love in a woman is that even when I don't know she is in the room, I recognize her first by her perfume," he said. "This gives me pleasure. You know she's here because you already have loved her perfume," he continued. "It's exactly the same as when you go into a field of jasmine or of roses. Ah . . . you see. This is the poetry of scent."

"So it's anticipation that counts?" I asked.

"With all that can be foreseen," he replied.

The French have made a global business of perfume to fit the image of who they think they are or would like to be: romantic, alluring, mysterious. Chanel uses more sophisticated strategies than its flower growing to preserve and reinvent the romance of its scents. Above the Chanel flagship store in Paris, the third-floor apartment of Mademoiselle (as Coco Chanel was called) is preserved as a shrine. Chanel, who redefined the ideal woman as a free spirit, entertained here but slept at the Ritz. Her furnishings remain—seventeenth-century Chinese lacquered wooden screens, silver and gold boxes, Art Deco furniture, shelves of books bought more for their looks than for their content. I imagined I smelled her perfume there. Later I learned that the rooms are periodically spritzed with Chanel No. 5.

The goal today at Chanel, the company built by Mademoiselle and her famous fragrance, is much more than to keep her memory alive; it's to deepen, broaden, and control it. So Chanel markets the quality that comes with permanence. It needs to keep consumers convinced, for example, that Chanel No. 5 is made with the same ingredients as always, juices of centifolia roses and jasmine flowers grown on French soil near Grasse, not in far-off (read, inferior) fields of, say, Turkey or Bulgaria.

Yet Chanel is also caught between its commitment to tradition and its need to attract with something new. Chanel No. 5 is like a dependable but predictable wife, mother, or even grandmother. Where's the excitement if you look old and there's nothing to discover? The need to surprise was behind the marketing of Chanel No. 5's Eau Première. I was walking through the Bon Marché department store and was struck by an advertising banner for it: "As if it were the first time." The ad was schizophrenic—it evoked perfume "virginity" at the same time that it was trying to sell the history, reliability, familiarity, and experience of classic No. 5.

I recall a young French friend explaining why she would never wear a fashionable perfume. "You want a perfume with a story, and ideally your story," she said. "A perfume should be linked with your story forever."

She wears the same scent every day: Délices de Cartier Eau Fruitée. Its fragrance blends "fruits like iced cherry and zesty bergamot with the spice of pink pepper and feminine floral notes like violet, jasmine, and freesia, finished with warm amber, musk, and sandalwood," according to the Sephora website. Its style is "luminous, playful, delightful." My friend smells great.

I heard my favorite perfume story at the International Perfume Museum in Grasse. The director did not turn up for our appointment, so one of her young assistants offered to show me around. I'll call her Pauline.

First came the tour. In a show-and-smell room, we watched a short film on the sea as the salty scent of seawater was emitted from a small box attached to the wall. In a greenhouse, we studied plants like vanilla and patchouli. The permanent collection was a mishmash, including an Egyptian mummy of a dog (perfumes were used as a preservative), a silver toilette travel case that belonged to Marie Antoinette, a book dated 1168 on the art of preserving beauty, hundreds of perfume bottles, and oddities like tongue graters and bed warmers.

I asked Pauline about the relationship between perfume and seduction, unsure of the answer she would give me. To put it bluntly, she didn't seem to be trying very hard. Her full body was hidden under a loose black-and-white dress that nearly reached the floor. Large glasses sat crooked on her nose; her bangs fell into her eyes; no lipstick or rouge adorned her face. Her black shoes had square toes and clunky heels. She was a French version of Agnes Gooch, thc unglamorous stenographer in *Mame*.

But Pauline and I found a connection, and the conversation turned to her own life. "If you don't seduce in France, you're a nobody," she said. "I'm very shy, and if you're plain or if you're shy and if you don't put yourself out in front, you don't fit the mold. I tell myself that if I stay in a corner, it won't work, but if I'm smiling and really show I want something, then it comes. It's a kind of game."

"Do you wear perfume?" I asked.

"Of course," she replied. Her lips parted and she smiled. "My husband knew I always wanted Chanel No. 5, and a few years ago he gave it to me. When I opened it, I asked him, 'Must I do like Marilyn?' "

"Like Marilyn? Marilyn Monroe?" I asked.

"Yes, Marilyn said that all I wear when I'm in bed is Chanel No. 5," she explained. "My husband said he would like that. So I said to myself, 'Let me be quite crazy.' And I took off all my clothes."

Suddenly, right before my eyes, Pauline became a sex goddess. I think I was beginning to understand the power of perfume.

10

The Gastronomic Orgasm

. . .

> Truly, Chambertin and Roquefort make an excellent dish for restoring an old love and for bringing a budding romance to quick fruition.
>
> —Giovanni Giacomo Casanova, *Mémoires*

> This sumptuous velvet color, is it not the sensual gown of a voluptuous nudity plump with adorable and profane flesh? . . . On the other hand, do you not sense in it an immaterial purity, and the sort of generosity that suggests the human mingled with the divine?
>
> —Gaston Roupnel, writer and historian, describing a Clos de Vougeot Burgundy

I had never had a gastronomic orgasm before I met Guy Savoy. Sure, I appreciate good food. In our basement kitchen when I was child, my grandfather taught me how to pickle eggplant, simmer tripe in tomatoes, and grill lambs' heads with lemon and rosemary. He introduced me at the age of five to the wine he made in our backyard every summer and kept in two oak barrels in the cellar, next to his tools.

My father owned an Italian grocery store in Niagara Falls and sold provolone and parmesan, prosciutto and salami, homemade sausages and hand-cranked pasta-making machines, in the days when real Italians called it pasta, but everyone else still said macaroni. In the front of the store, he put wicker baskets of *petits-gris* escargots that came from France, until the government banned their importation. There was fresh-baked Italian bread on the family dinner table every evening.

Food was straightforward. As an adult, I sometimes thought the rapturous dining ecstasies described by brilliant food critics like Mimi Sheraton were over the top and a bit unreal. But there I was one morning in Paris with one of France's three-star chefs, allowing myself to get carried away.

I had declined Savoy's invitation for dinner—it could have cost five hundred dollars and would have violated my newspaper's ban on accepting a gift of value. But breakfast, I figured, should be safely within the rules.

Before then, I had seen Savoy only in his virginal whites: a starched, double-breasted chef's uniform that stretched tight over his belly and made him look older than his fifty-six years. That morning, he met me at the entrance to the modern restaurant that bears his name just off the Champs-Élysées wearing a black turtleneck and pressed gray slacks. The off-duty look threw me. It made his black eyebrows darker and contrasted nicely with his white hair and graying beard. He had lost his slightly rounded chef look. He led me into a private, dimly lit dining room with the window shade drawn and sat me in an armchair at a linen-covered round table. The room was small, and we were seated close together. A primitive African sculpture of a nude woman with breasts protruding like projectiles was just a few inches away. It felt naughty.

It was 9:00 a.m., but this was a moment for champagne, not orange juice and coffee. A salad of asparagus and Parma ham came first, an initial warming caress. Then fluffy soft eggs with specks of black truffle. Savoy likes to call himself a man of the soil, and the truffle portions must have seemed stingy. So he called for a truffle the size of a baseball and shoved it under my nose. "Breathe," he ordered. I inhaled. "Breathe again, deeper!" The aroma was musky and strong, penetrating my nasal passages and down into my throat. Wielding a small grater, he scattered slices of the fat, gnarled tuber over the eggs. Slowly at first, then faster and more frenzied. He couldn't stop. The slices flew past the plate and onto the tablecloth.

"Now I'll show you what real food is about!" he said. He cut two pieces of a crusty stick of bread, spread them with unsalted butter, and topped them with thick slices of black truffle. He handed one to me and took one for himself. We popped them into our mouths at the same moment. We chewed, slowly. We swallowed. We exchanged looks. Nothing was said. It was too intimate a moment. We both knew what we were feeling.

He had won me.

"I am seduced," he said, "by the magic of real taste. We are in the concrete here. You can see the truffle on the bread, anticipate it, feel it, smell it, taste it, savor it. This taste is exuberant but not violent. Alas, we live in a virtual world—of video games, blogs, financial bubbles. Gastronomy is not that."

Savoy railed about the pretension of so-called food artists who use chemistry to turn truffle oil into fake caviar and zucchini flowers into foam. "Cooking is about the art of creating, of transformation, of pleasing," he said. "The act of a woman preparing and serving a meal for her husband and children is nothing else than an act of seduction."

I asked him the source of his inspiration. He talked about his childhood and how his mother introduced him to the transformation of ingredients. He was about six years old, and they baked a simple cookie called *langue de chat*—cat's tongue. It was in her small restaurant attached to their home in rural France that he said he discovered the driving force behind cooking and eating: "Pleasure."

Here was the key to understanding real taste: it comes with *petits plaisirs*, small pleasures. Sure, we were enjoying ours on this day in a very fancy setting, and one pleasure was a truffle, one of the most expensive foodstuffs in the world. But Savoy was making a larger point: that satisfaction in life can come from a series of small, simple, everyday pleasures.

"Is your mother still cooking?" I asked.

Yes.

"Will you take me to meet her?"

Of course.

Savoy is a chef who is constantly surprised by food and who longs to turn it into something seductive for others. It sounds like a cliché, but Savoy makes food sexy. He supervised a documentary in which over the course of a year he visits ten people whose products he buys for his restaurants. In the film, he is constantly touching, tasting, licking, smelling, as if food were a woman and he a man obsessed with her. His odyssey of culinary sensuality is not just a show; it's genuine pleasure. He tastes snow. He dips a finger—twice—in walnut oil and then lets the oil dribble onto a slice of bread. He dips a finger at another point into melted milk chocolate and then into raw milk. He picks up a piece of hot white cheese with his fingers and eats it, saying it tastes like flowers. He licks his fingers as he pulls apart a lobster. For Savoy, the smell and taste of the golden wine from Château d'Yquem is emotionally "moving," the pale skin of a plump, raw chicken is "amazing," like "satin."

Long ago, France refined the preparation of food and the production of wine into seductive arts. But as much as Savoy reflects and upholds the country's gastronomic honor and traditions, he seems to be fighting the future. A downward trend line has been clear for decades: the food of France is in decline; French wine, while holding its reputation for quality, is facing stiff competition from every continent. Every year, with the French economy struggling and the global cachet of French food and cooking diminishing, the predictions get bleaker.

There is some truth to the frequent lament that France's rich culinary heritage—from the Michelin-starred restaurants to the neighborhood café, from the produce at neighborhood outdoor markets to the meat and fish at Rungis, the largest wholesale food market in the world—is suffering.

In his book *Au Revoir to All That*, the American journalist Michael Steinberger mourned the death of French food. Every depressing statistic was another dagger into the heart. A generation ago, the average meal in France lasted eighty-eight minutes; now it ends after thirty-three. Mega-supermarkets account for 75 percent of all retail food sales in France. Starbucks, which opened its first outlet in Paris near the Opéra Garnier in 2004, had more than fifty branches in and around the capital by 2011. In 1960, there were 200,000 cafés in France; now there are about 40,000. Wine consumption in France has dropped by 50 percent since the late 1960s. By 2009, McDonald's had more than

1,100 outlets in France; one had even opened at the Louvre! And, *quelle horreur*, France is McDonald's most profitable market after the United States. And on and on.

But the woe-is-me attitude somehow misses the point. There is a ritual at play in France—the search for the products, the preparation of the meal, the tasting and savoring, the memory of what is eaten recalled. The food on the plate is seductive, and the diner is eager to be seduced. This is not chemistry class but a love rooted in the soil, an appreciation of the classics and a feeling—shared by the simplest worker and the most lofty aristocrat—that food in France is about happiness.

"What I love about gastronomy in France is the idea of being led astray," said Basil Katz, a Franco-American journalist and a former chef. "A good dish will make you forget how much butter is used in the sauce, that you're eating what used to be a live animal, that the finished product is a clever mise-en-scène meant to deceive and prick your senses—from a sound like the crunch of crispy potatoes to the feel when you grab an asparagus and it is warm, slightly stiff with a little give but not too much."

The French take pride in sharing knowledge about what Americans may consider the most ordinary of tastes: water. Dominique Hériard Dubreuil, the president of Rémy Cointreau and a member of my French women's club, told me that water is the best medium for learning how to taste. Hériard Dubreuil's mother has trained the palates of her young grandchildren by serving them an assortment of mineral waters and teaching them to focus on the differences: which one is salty, which one is milky, which one is metallic.

Even as French patterns of cooking and eating change, an authenticity endures. The genius of French cuisine does not rest in theatrical presentations. Some cheeses disappear, but new ones—real farm cheeses—are being created. Old varieties of fruits and vegetables are being resurrected. Food produced in France remains among the most diverse in the world.

In 2010, the French meal was recognized as part of the world's Intangible Cultural Heritage by UNESCO, the cultural arm of the United Nations. The campaign had been launched by President Sarkozy in 2008, when he called French cuisine the best in the world and proclaimed his desire to make France the first country whose gastronomy would be so honored.

UNESCO did not declare French cuisine the world's finest or warn that its fruits, vegetables, poultry, or signature dishes were endangered. Rather, it honored the French mealtime tradition, with its rituals, table settings, multiplicity of courses, and the matching of wines with food. (At the same time, UNESCO also recognized Turkish oil wrestling, Azerbaijani carpets, and Croatian gingerbread.) It was only a symbolic gesture, and some food experts and critics called it a bit pathetic, but it fit in well with the French sense of national pride.

The guild-based industry of transformation still exists in France—the art and craft of turning raw food products into objects of desire through manual labor. Tightly hierarchical kitchens still contain armies of laborers who carve perfect florets out of carrots and cut vegetables into perfect eighth-of-an-inch cubes. There are no shortcuts.

Gilles Epié, the owner and chef at Citrus Etoile, who ran the Los Angeles restaurant L'Orangerie for three years, returned home a French chauvinist. "The turbot you find in New York—it's not what you find in Brittany," he told me. "The cèpe mushrooms in Washington State have no resemblance to ours. It's impossible to find fresh ducklings. When I asked a supplier in Colorado for a baby lamb, he looked at me as if I were a pedophile! He was ready to call the police.

"In L.A., they only want to eat salad. When you buy fish in a fish store, there aren't any heads, as if they aren't animals. You feel like you're in a pharmacy. I want my fish with heads! If a fish is served with bones, clients call their lawyer."

Food is consistently presented in France as a source of pleasure, and gustatory is so close to amatory delight that the lines may sometimes blur.

This is a country where I have switched on the morning news to find myself tuned into a scholarly discussion about the aphrodisiac properties of arugula or experiments on the use of escargot mucus to make a facial moisturizer. Artichokes are reputed to heal both body and soul; just about every French food writer praises truffles as helping to arouse lust. I have learned that tripe is a "sexual" food that can have "troubling" effects, along with certain mushrooms, shellfish, and strong cheeses whose smell is close to that of human sweat.

In 2010 Francis Martin, a plant biologist at the University of Nancy, and his team of researchers announced that the black truffle of Périgord has a sex life. In decoding the genome of the treasured fungus, they discovered that truffles are not asexual but are either male or female. Martin has advised truffle growers to encourage sexual intercourse by injecting oak tree roots (the truffles' habitat) with both male and female truffle spores.

French literature and cinema reflect this habit of association between love and food. In the dinner scene in Guy de Maupassant's novel *Bel-Ami*, the different courses are sexualized: "The Ostend oysters were brought in, tiny and plump, like little ears enclosed in shells, and melting between the tongue and the palate like salted bonbons. Then, after the soup, a trout was served, as rose-tinted as a young girl, and the guests began to talk."

Today, when Fauchon, the luxury-food emporium, advertises a new line of take-out box lunches, it starts with a classic place setting: two forks, two knives, two glasses. Instead of a plate, however, there is a woman's slightly opened mouth, her lips plumped up and painted in frosted rose that glints in the light.

In France, outsiders can be judged by their level of appreciation of food and knowledge of wine. James Bond, the fictional British secret agent, for example, spoke French, sported a French cigarette lighter and cuff links, drank Bollinger champagne, and ordered vodka martinis with a splash of Lillet. But his savoir faire—and therefore his seductiveness—apparently ended at the dinner table.

At a scholarly conference in Paris in 2007, the French researcher Claire Dixsaut cut down 007 in a way that his adversaries never could. Bond "never ordered a gastronomic menu," she sniffed. "He loved grilled chops, sole meunière, rare tournedos, and fresh vegetables. He was, at the table, as in his investigations, in search of the truth," nothing more. No raptures of culinary pleasure here. It got worse. "Bond," Dixsaut declared with the solemnity of a judge, "was a pitiful connoisseur of wine."

The French take their wine as seriously as their food. Wine is not just a product that is produced and consumed. It is an idea about France: a way of doing things, the celebration of a common past, the pleasure of sharing, the preservation of the magic and myth of the *terroir*—arable soil, but more like soul than soil, since the word embraces geology, history, family heritage, climate, and farming methods. Just about all the French people I have ever met, except for practicing Muslims, are interested in talking about, buying, storing, and drinking wine.

Roland Barthes captured France's proprietary, chauvinistic relationship to wine in "Wine and Milk," an article written more than half a century ago. "Wine is felt by the French nation to be a possession which is its very own, just like its three hundred and sixty types of cheese and its culture," he wrote. "It is a totem-drink, corresponding to the milk of the Dutch cow or the tea ceremonially taken by the British Royal Family." This helps explain why French wine continues to be so appreciated and exalted, despite the expansion, industrialization, and rationalization of winemaking in far-off places like America and Australia.

Barthes considered wine to be so strong a determiner of Frenchness that the leader of France was expected to identify with it. When René Coty, a president of the Fourth Republic, was photographed at home at the beginning of his term with a bottle of beer on the table, "the whole nation was in a flutter," Barthes wrote. "It was as tolerable as having a bachelor king. Wine is here a part of the reason of state." Decades later, Jacques Chirac was forgiven his thirst for Mexican beer because he drank oceans of French wine as well. I'm convinced that one of the reasons Nicolas Sarkozy is not more loved is that he doesn't drink alcohol—not even a flute of champagne when toasting another head of state or a glass of Bordeaux with a fine meal. The preservation of France's wine heritage is a duty: the wine cellar of the president of the French Senate, for example, is supposed to reflect the regional output of France as a whole.

Universally, according to Barthes, wine has a practical social function: it enables the worker to do his task with ease and the intellectual to become the equal of the worker. The French do that and much more: "Other countries drink to get drunk, and this is accepted by everyone; in France, drunkenness is a consequence, never an intention." A drink is felt as "the spinning out of a pleasure," a "leisurely act." Barthes called "knowing *how* to drink" a national trait that demonstrates the French man's performance, control, and sociability.

Growing up in France, my two daughters were allowed to drink legally as teenagers. Champagne was served at their senior prom. They developed a healthy respect for moderation. Perhaps the biggest cultural shock they faced in college in the United States was binge drinking.

The integration of wine into daily life starts early. Schoolchildren learn wine-drinking songs like "Fanchon," which is also sung by Boy and Girl Scouts, sports teams and military units, and people of all classes from all over France. Some of the lyrics:

Friends, we must take pause.
I spy the shadow of a cork.
Let us drink to adorable Fanchon,
Let us sing something for her.

Ah, how sweet is her company,
So rich with merit and glory!
She loves to laugh, she loves to drink,
She loves to sing, like us.

Many high school students spend the tail end of at least one summer doing *les vendanges*—harvesting—at a vineyard. They handpick grapes in a sleepaway camp setting that often comes with a small salary, food, lodging, and a vast amount of local wine to drink. While American newlyweds might freeze a piece of their wedding cake for a year, a French couple is more likely to keep a case or two of wine from the wedding party. When a baby is born, parents sometimes invest in a fine wine produced that year; the expectation is that both child and wine will get better with age.

The language used to describe French wines relies heavily on gender. In its color, texture, and form, wine is a woman. "Wine has a dress, legs, thighs, tears, curves," said Véronique Sanders, the manager of Château Haut-Bailly in Bordeaux. I told her that this sounded sexist. "The definitions were done by men," she replied. "That's why they seem a bit macho today."

When the subject is the wine itself, the language can go either way. Wines with high tannin levels are masculine: robust, beefy, sturdy. Wines with soft tannins are feminine. "Wine can be pouty, voluptuous, flirtatious, charming, soft," Sanders said. The gender issue gets even more complicated for the wines of Bordeaux and Burgundy. "Metaphorically speaking," wrote the French food and wine historian Jean-Robert Pitte, they are "hermaphrodites." He added, "Connoisseurs and poets characterize both as masculine and feminine."

Wines can also mate. That's what wine expert Enrico Bernardo told me. In 2004, after nine years of training to memorize the tastes of ten thousand wines, Bernardo underwent a grueling five-day competition that involved blind tastings and tested sensitivity to the minutiae of food, drink, and cigars. He won the title of "best sommelier of the world." Enrico is Italian-born, but he works as a promoter, educator, and seller of great wine in France, a country with the right sensibility to appreciate his peculiar perspective—that wine, not food, is the point of departure for a meal. Clients at his Paris restaurant, Il Vino, choose a selection of wines and leave the chef to prepare surprise dishes to match each of them.

For Bernardo, everyone is a wine. He is a Barolo: rich, complex, powerful, a bit exotic, and, of course, Italian. When he discovered that his Alsatian-French girlfriend was a Riesling, he knew she would become his partner for life.

"A Riesling has a very pale dress and is very clear, crystalline, with an incredible transparency like water," he said. "It has a nose that is very timid, reserved, fresh, floral, citrus, and has a very straight, very long spinal column in the mouth, very fair, honest, pure. The woman I fell in love with is timid upon first approach. She is very pure and honest. It took a long time before she revealed herself. I did not fall in love with a woman who is a fleshy, full-bodied Chardonnay or Marsanne, who is extroverted and more Latin. I fell in love with a Riesling." In time, he added, she may even be a Riesling *grand millésime*, the best one of all, because of her persistence and dependability.

Like perfume, wine plays with memory, but in a different way, because it conjures up the sense of taste as well as smell. The journalist Jean-Paul Kauffmann survived on a diet of memory as a hostage for three years in Lebanon in the 1980s. He kept his mind in shape by reciting daily the famous 1855 classification of the greatest wines of Bordeaux. He imagined their aromas and tastes from the dark and cramped dungeon where he was held chained and sometimes blindfolded. "I never forgot the taste of wine," he wrote after the ordeal was over. "Sometimes in the deep dark well of reality, a miracle happened: The taste of cedar and blackcurrant from the Cabernet Sauvignon, the plummy aroma of the Merlot, returned to me." Submerged in the past, Kauffmann was a free man, because, he said, "wine is synonymous with liberty."

I knew I'd never be one of those people who could tell the difference between the Côte de Beaune and the Côte de Nuits or detect the taste of wild strawberries and the odor of fresh dirt combined with the faint aroma of eucalyptus and the lingering aftertaste of leather. But I am aware of wine's seductive power, its capacity to draw a person in by revealing itself slowly, deliberately, over a long period of time. Walter Wells, the former executive editor of the *International Herald Tribune*, became a devoted student of French wine during his three decades living in France, and he told me that wine is not easily understood at first blush.

"If you know nothing about wines and go into a wine shop and ask questions, you're probably going to leave even more confused," he said. "It's not something that can be intellectualized. You have to taste it, experience it, year after year. You can learn how much wines can change from one town or village to the next. You can know a lot about Saint-Émilion and not know anything about a Saint-Julien. It just takes a lot of drinking."

Walter's path would not work for me. I am a very light drinker; I'll never be able to drink enough wine to know it even as a casual acquaintance. I did, however, come to appreciate that one can learn the basics even as an outsider. I once took a wine tour of Châteauneuf-du-Pape and Gigondas with an American friend and four Britons. Our guide, François, was wearing a baseball cap and vest with his company's insignia. "I hope this day will be unforgettable," he told us in English. Then he pressed a button on the dashboard of his van to play Nat King Cole singing "Unforgettable." The visit was well-organized and ritualized: we arrived at each château; the iron gates opened; we were greeted by a smiling host and a big dog that we were not supposed to fear.

Then François taught us how to drink. We held our glasses up to the light to examine the wine's "dress"—its intensity, clarity, and color. We swirled the wine to release its aroma and watch whether "legs" of liquid curved slowly enough down the side of the glass. We sniffed twice, first in sharp, short bursts to get acquainted, and then in deep, long breaths for a more profound understanding. Only then did we taste. We held the wine in our mouths for several seconds so that it could reveal its secrets and extend our pleasure. We rolled the liquid around with our tongues. Only then did we swallow, as slowly as possible. Still the act was not over. We chewed the residue lining our mouths for several seconds. We moved our empty glasses up and down and swirled them yet again, still hungry for a final sniff of contentment.

This was not at all like the instant gratification that comes with chugging shots. It was a ritual designed to prolong the moment. It became an intimate experience of pleasure sharing. "The best way to appreciate wine is to enjoy it in harmony," Sanders had said. Now I knew that she meant in harmony with oneself and with others.

On a hot, sunlit day in June, I met Guy Savoy's mother. Unadorned, unprogrammed, and unspoiled, Marie Savoy is proof that the seductive power of French cuisine is alive. She is in her eighties; her hair is gray and cut short. A life of hard work is traced in the deep lines of her face, and her body is sturdy. She wore a blue floral print dress covered by an apron.

When I asked her why she had decided to cook for a living, she did not say it was to help support the family or to have her own career. She used the same word her son had chosen to explain what drives him: "pleasure." It was the pleasure that came every day from sharing her creations with her clients and watching them enjoy.

My visit to the Savoys started when Guy Savoy met me at a train station not far from Lyon and led me to his white Saab convertible. He was wearing a gray linen shirt, faded blue slacks, and tennis shoes and was not recognized by anyone in the station.

As we drove along a winding road, he showed me the France that had shaped him. In the town of Ruy, he took me to a small, sad-looking restaurant set on a hillside amid two-hundred-year-old plane trees. We could see Formica tables and plastic chairs from outside, but the restaurant was closed. This place, he said, had once been his mother's *buvette*—a tiny refreshment bar and restaurant—attached to their modest home. Savoy's Swiss-born father, Louis, the town's gardener, had grown the fruits and vegetables for the restaurant. He had such a good eye that he could spot a morel mushroom poking through the soil hundreds of feet away.

"There was a huge terrace, and there were tables and flowers everywhere," Savoy said. "My parents grew everything they needed. The first morels, the first cherries, the first ripe tomatoes—these were big events every year. Here I cooked my first omelets, my first trout, my first escargots."

The subject changed to anticipation, the anticipation of the andouille sausage that we would eat at lunch at his parents' house. "You like it, andouille? With potatoes from the garden?" he asked.

Andouille? That fat sausage filled with smoked pig stomach and intestines that can smell like parts of the body where you don't want to go? I had been exposed to cuisine with odd animal body parts as a child. I was ready.

"*Bien sûr!*" I said. "I love it!"

As we drove through rolling hills of grapevines and corn, Savoy was eager to show and tell and smell: the scent of the newly cut grass, the building stones made round from the glaciers, the stillness of the lake, the backdrop of the mountains.

His parents, long retired, now live in a nondescript house with an adequate but by no means grand garden in the town of Les Abrets. Louis Savoy gave me a tour of his domain: beds of lettuce, carrots, peas, string beans, turnips, potatoes, onions, shallots, bordered by dahlias and marigolds.

The kitchen was small, old-fashioned, and dark, with a four-burner electric stove, a small oven, mismatched plates, and only a few knives and wooden spoons. There was neither a microwave nor a Cuisinart here. But the space clearly belonged to Marie Savoy. "I don't know how you can do it—you really have to have talent to cook on this stove," Guy Savoy lectured his mother, his voice tinged with exasperation as he struggled to sauté green peas in butter. A guest here, he had no right to treat her as he would his kitchen staff. But he was cooking, after all, and therefore unable to cede control.

"But it's not bad!" his mother said in protest.

Everything had to be cooked to the right doneness and served at the right heat, so Savoy, his mother, and his father engaged in a three-way conversation of hurriedness and joyful confusion. Savoy told his mother the potatoes were ready. "Cut them!" she told him. He said no—they wouldn't stay hot. He found a small wooden cutting board for the shallots but not a good knife. "A knife that cuts well!" he shouted to no one in particular, hoping, I guess, that one would magically appear. It did. He picked up a jar of his mother's homemade hazelnut oil, screwed off the lid, and ordered me to sniff hard, just the way he had with the truffle at breakfast. The pale yellow liquid smelled of concentrated nuts, sugar, and fat.

We moved to a round table under an umbrella in the garden. "Champagne!" Savoy commanded. "The glasses! Where are they?"

He served a simple salad with lettuce picked that morning, full, delicate leaves that folded easily under the fork. The lettuce generated excitement. "Oh, I adore this lettuce," he said. "The lettuce has real taste—the leaves, so tender!"

"At ten this morning," his mother chimed in, "the lettuce was still in the garden."

The andouille came out of the oven. "The real andouille," said Savoy. "The real, from here! It's the real thing here!"

It certainly was real andouille. He sliced and skinned it. It drooled juice onto the platter and gave off a rich, carnal smell. The thick rounds stayed firm, patterned like textured mosaics in brown, red, and beige.

The potatoes were small ovals, their brown skins taut over their flesh and glinting in the sunlight. "A potato!" Savoy said. "It's the meal of the countryside. It's pure simplicity. Mama, do you know where the corkscrew is?" he asked, holding a bottle of 1998 Bâtard-Montrachet.

We ate the andouille, whose taste was milder than its smell and tempered by the sweetness of the potatoes. Savoy wanted us to have more andouille and served himself a second and then a third helping. "You still want a little more? Another small piece, Elaine?" he asked. I knew there was a lot more food to come, but how could I say no to the real andouille?

The conversation shifted to his mother's *buvette* in Ruy. Savoy bragged that she had run it alone while he needed twenty-five people to run his restaurant. It was "nothing at all," she said, and then described it. She started her *buvette* with a dozen glasses and two big bottles—one that she filled with beer, another with lemonade. Gradually, she offered plates of cured sausages and ham, omelets, *fromage blanc*. Then she got the reputation for serving simple, honest, fresh meals. She raised trout in a concrete basin at the side of the house and made coq au vin, escargots, gratins. She worked from 4:00 a.m. until late at night on weekdays, and on Sundays she made fruit tarts, ice creams and sorbets, chocolate mousse, and *oeufs à la neige*. Her *buvette* had no name, but the regulars called it Chez Maman. Two of her regulars bought her a dressing gown as a gesture of appreciation.

Guy Savoy learned cooking by necessity, because his mother needed help in the kitchen. She kept working to the point of exhaustion, and her children forced her to quit when she was in her sixties. "Her passion engulfed her," he said.

A large *côte de boeuf* was now displayed and sliced. It was served with morels and shallots sautéed in butter that merged with the juices of the meat. Then came a bowl of green peas that looked like tiny shimmering balls of jade and a 1998 Château Léoville Poyferré Saint Julien. The peas were soft-skinned and slippery with hazelnut oil; they burst in the mouth with the sweetness of honeyed candy. The beef was so tender its flesh quivered under the knife.

"*Les petits pois, les petits pois*"—the peas, the peas—Savoy said softly, over and over, like a mantra. The morels, with their pungent odor and firm texture, excited him even more. "The morel for the mushroom gatherer is like the woodcock for the hunter," he said. "When I walk in the forest and see mushrooms that we can eat, it's an emotional experience. Even today, when I find a beautiful mushroom, my heart beats faster."

The joy was in the sharing, and when I asked if the green peas were from her garden, mother and son answered in unison. "Of course! The carrots, the spinach and—" said Marie Savoy.

"The shallots, the lettuce, the tomatoes," her son said, finishing her sentence.

For dessert, thick blocks of raspberry and vanilla ice cream were passed around, followed by *fromage blanc* made by a woman who lived on a small farm nearby. Savoy scooped piles of the creamy cheese into deep bowls. It was not enough. He drowned them in heavy cream and sprinkled white sugar on top. His mother brought out a rusty, dented tin that she has used to store cookies since the days when she taught her son how to make them. It is fifty years old. Out of it came meringues whose crusty shells melted on the tongue and crisp hazelnut cookies to dip into the strong black coffee.

When lunch was over, it was time to prolong the pleasure by recovering. Marie Savoy and I talked about marriage, children, and getting older. Her son took off his shoes, stretched out on the living room sofa, and fell into a loud-snoring sleep. Louis Savoy picked a chaise longue in a shady spot in the garden for his nap. When they awoke there was more discussion of the excellence of our meal and then long good-byes.

As Savoy and I made our way back to Paris by train, the meal was still in his mind. "*Les petits pois, les petits pois,*" he continued to say. He explained why he had been willing to take a stranger into his mother's home. "This was a family meal in the countryside," he said. "There is nothing better than when it is simple. Nothing. I do nothing more than try to cook as well as my mother. I wanted to show you that I invented nothing."

He told me he had never before taken an outsider to visit his mother. She had been terrified that she wouldn't make a good impression, and he had to calm her down.

"Why did you do it then?" I asked.

"I didn't do it for you," he said. "I didn't do it for me. I did it for France."

This was a bit over the top. But Guy Savoy is a showman.

It is not enough for great chefs to satisfy themselves. The artists of food crave aesthetic appreciation, and on a practical level, restaurateurs must seduce their customers. Guy Savoy talked about the day he served a sea bass with sweet tender flesh to the twelve-year-old daughter of a friend and all she could talk about was its bones. "People who don't want to be happy talk about the bones," he said. "They don't talk about the pleasure of the fish. They are permanently negative. What idiocy. To give you an example—take François Simon."

Simon is the anti-seducer of French cuisine, a dandy with sideburns, flyaway hair, bold tweeds, loud ties, and velvet vests. He regularly proclaims that France has lost its "culinary supremacy" and does his utmost to prove it by slashing and burning the reputations of restaurants. An ordinary-looking man with a fountain pen as razor-sharp as a butcher's knife, he may be the most feared and most read figure in France's culinary world. As the food critic for *Le Figaro* for more than two decades, he has skinned, sliced, grilled, and roasted his subjects, indifferent to the impact of his words on them.

I met Simon over lunch one day in an overpriced Paris restaurant attached to an overpriced hotel. When the sommelier started to refill his glass without asking, Simon stopped his hand in midair before a drop could fall. “I like to control the temperature of my wine,” he announced. “In a restaurant, I am horrified by having to obey,” he told me. “I want to be indulged.” He once wrote of sommeliers, “Perhaps we should drown them, to allow us to drink as we please.”

Simon has extended his reach with books, a weekly cable television show in which he hides his face, and a blog that includes his secret video recordings of some of the great and not-so-great tables of France. Not content to pass judgment on others, Simon claims to be an accomplished cook himself. On his blog, he boasts that he can cook a chicken two hundred ways. He once even closeted himself in the kitchen of the tiny Paris bistro Le Cochon à l’Oreille and cooked for the public for five nights in a row. Diners one night described the pumpkin soup as grainy, undercooked, and so dense it stood up in stiff peaks, the spiced chicken plentiful but stingily garnished, the zabaglione thin and runny. Simon had failed to seduce. But at least he tried, and that gave him some appeal.

If Simon is all about attitude, François Durand is all about love of the process. Tell me that French cooking is dead, that its power to charm the diner is exhausted, and I’ll introduce you to him. He is a cheesemaker, but he is also a warrior on the ground who does battle every day to preserve the best France has to offer. There is no improved, labor-saving route, in his eyes, to producing the perfect Camembert to suffuse the dinner table with allure.

Durand took over his family’s two-hundred-acre farm outside the town of Camembert when he was only nineteen and has run it for nearly three decades. With his sixty cows, he claims to be the last dairy farmer in Normandy to be making Camembert commercially from hand-ladled unpasteurized milk. He is delightful in spite of himself, so quiet and unassuming that it is hard to drag words out of him. But seeing him transform milk into Camembert is like watching a dancer. Standing erect, he fixes his left arm securely behind his back. Then he bends and sways as his right hand quickly ladles just the right amount of warm, curdled raw milk from a huge vat into hundreds of small white plastic cylindrical molds.

When visitors come, he welcomes them with perfectly aged Camembert on chunks of crusty bread. The cheese's white crust is slightly wrinkled and tinged with orange. Its pale yellow insides are neither too dry nor too gooey. The richness comes in its smells—of the farm, the grass, the cows, without the hint of ammonia in the industrially produced variety—and the feel in the mouth, washed down with homemade apple cider. Durand can't imagine a world without a real raw-milk Camembert. "What a loss that would be," he said. "We'd be missing a part of ourselves."

In politics and diplomacy, the preeminence of French food dates back to Versailles in the seventeenth century, when Louis XIV made cuisine an art form to compete with refined language, art, and architecture.

Cuisine became an important tool of French diplomacy, a weapon in the armament of persuasion. Charles Cogan, in his book *French Negotiating Behavior*, called this the "politics of gastronomy." "For the French," he wrote, "a meal is part of the negotiation itself in that it is an instrument or an accoutrement, and if France is hosting the talks, a meal gives the French an opportunity to display the sophisticated culinary skills they prize so highly."

But there is more to it than that. The meal is an instrument of seduction, of loosening the lips and softening the resolve of the adversary by giving pleasure. One of the best guides to understanding the French mastery of the weapons of diplomacy is still *The Art of Diplomacy* by François de Callières, a writer, a special envoy of Louis XIV, and a member of the Académie Française.

An ambassador's table, Callières wrote, "should be served neatly, plentifully, and with taste. He should give frequent entertainments and parties to the chief personages of the Court and even to the Prince himself. A good table is the best and easiest way of keeping himself well informed. The natural effect of good eating and drinking is the inauguration of friendships and the creation of familiarity, and when people are a trifle warmed by wine they often disclose secrets of importance."

A century after Callières's time, at the Congress of Vienna in 1815, France had to deal with its defeat on the battlefield and sought to compensate with the power of its culture. The French foreign minister, Charles Maurice de Talleyrand-Périgord, one of the most versatile diplomats in his country's history, wrote to King Louis XVIII, "Sire, I have more need of casseroles than written instructions." Food also colored Talleyrand's view of America, which he described as "a country with thirty-two religions and only one sauce."

It is bad form to decline the offer of a diplomatic meal. In 2003 I was one of several reporters accompanying Foreign Minister Dominique de Villepin on a grueling two-day trip to Afghanistan. We had flown to Kabul the night before. We started out in a Ministry of Defense jet with buttery leather seats, but only got as far as Tajikistan. There we donned flak jackets, helmets, and sound-muffling ear muffs and switched to a cold and uncomfortable military transport plane. A handful of my colleagues and I had been separated from the escorted French delegation and ended up wandering around Kabul, hot and dusty, for much of the time. On the way back to Paris, after another transfer in Tajikistan, we were bone-tired. I took a sleeping pill and went to sleep. Until the foreign minister's spokesman woke me up.

"I have good news for you," he said. "You have been chosen to dine with the minister."

Three of my colleagues and I were ushered into first class. I was so drugged that the cabin moved every time I blinked. I counted the forks on the white-linen-covered table. Four. Four courses. Four glasses, two for wine, one each for water and champagne. But there was nowhere to hide. I dug my fingernails into my palms to cause just enough discomfort to keep awake.

There were quail eggs topped with caviar and tiny pink shrimp, veal medallions with morels, then cheese, salad, and dessert courses. Villepin told stories to charm us, but his seductive powers were wasted on me. Afterward, my French colleagues told me the wines had been superb.

• • •

If France were to give an award for the most heroic champion of French cuisine in all its seductive glory, it would go to Jean-Claude Ribaut of *Le Monde*, the poet of French food critics. I imagine that Jean-Claude, who is about sixty, was quite a handsome youth. At the École des Beaux-Arts, he studied to be an architect. Eventually, he met a master chef who trained him to taste and to cook. Jean-Claude was initiated into the mysteries of Les Halles, then the largest wholesale fresh-food market in the world, where he met the food merchants and restaurateurs and learned their codes and rituals. He studied the history of French cuisine back to ancient Gaul and built one of the most impressive private libraries on gastronomy in France.

One evening, Jean-Claude and I dined at Jamin in the sixteenth arrondissement with a retired professor friend of his and a beautiful, twenty-three-year-old wine merchant named Fleur. It was close to midnight, and we had just finished dessert. Over coffee, I asked Jean-Claude what meal he would prepare if he wanted to seduce. The target did not necessarily have to be a woman, I said; it could be friends or family.

As Jean-Claude started to create a fantasy meal in his mind, his words fell over one another. He was so excited he jumped right to the main course. "I'd make a gigot of lamb, from a very young lamb," he said. "Well dressed, studded with anchovies. It gives an extremely subtle taste to the meat, a bit complex. It's cooked in the oven, so I'd serve it with its cooking juices—add a bit of clarified butter mixed with a mashed anchovy—as a sauce. Then an eggplant gratin on the side. It's a success; it works every time!"

Fleur was enchanted. "With just your words, I want to follow you and eat," she said.

The sumptuous meal we had just eaten was suddenly forgotten. We could taste the gigot and the eggplant.

We asked Jean-Claude to give us a course to start the meal.

"I'd start with a dish created around scallops," he said. "Scallops that have just been opened, cooked only a little, served with a sauce made from a reduction of white wine. There is a second sauce made from a wine a bit more elaborate, like Banyuls or Rivesaltes. When it's boiled down, it turns into a sort of syrup. Add a small spoonful of *crème fraîche*—not much. That melds the flavors and textures. But no flour, none. When the scallops are cooked, you sprinkle a little lime zest on them, so the contrast of the sweet Banyuls wine syrup with the creamed white wine plus the lime on the scallop—it's magical!"

He elaborated on the ingredients with the scallops—small fillets of sole and langoustines, soft leeks, a sauce with a strong, fine red wine and sugar and shallots.

"*C'est magnifique!*" Fleur exclaimed.

Earlier in the evening, Jean-Claude had been concerned that he didn't have a good subject for his column for Saint Valentine's Day. I told him he should write about his fantasy dinner, under the title "*Les liaisons onctueuses*"—the phrase he had used to describe the blending of flavors and textures.

"So, what's for dessert?" Fleur asked.

"I confess I don't know how to make pastries," he said. "But there is a magical dessert, magical, one I make almost all year round."

His dessert, fruits poached in wine, was foolproof. "Nectarines, peaches, apricots—fruits with pits—it's enough to poach them in a Sauternes or a Barsac or a syrupy wine for ten minutes," he said. "The wine has so much power! It's sublime! I add a little bit of sugar because the wine gets more acidic when it is boiled down, and you have to give them a little sweet emotion. I add some orange zest that I caramelize in a bit of melting sugar and that I put in this juice, in this syrup. There has to be balance. Then a night in the refrigerator! You make a few madeleines on the side. And if you are talented, then it's directly . . . directly to . . ."

Jean-Claude didn't finish his sentence. He didn't have to.

For the French, no food is too humble for seduction. One morning over another breakfast with Guy Savoy, the conversation turned to the sensual power of the most ordinary foods. I had overheard a famous food critic telling Savoy that his carrots were "sublime." I couldn't quite believe it and said so.

"Carrots are carrots," I said flatly.

Savoy called over one of his sous-chefs and ordered him to bring us some carrots. A few minutes later two plates arrived. Each contained two whole, peeled, cooked carrots, with one-inch stems. They had been sautéed in butter and laid on a lacy greenish-black bed of spinach and trumpet mushrooms.

Wine was served—a Puligny-Montrachet—and a lesson in carrot eating followed. Savoy said that the taste of the carrot was very subtle and sweet at the tip and got stronger and more forceful closer to the top.

"It's not true," I protested, trying not to laugh at him. But he was serious, so I corrected myself. "I had no idea," I said.

"You have to start at the tip," he explained. "You eat the carrot in little bits." We sliced a chunk of carrot, ate it, and sliced and ate again and again until we came to the top. "When you get to the top, you do like this. It is an incredible taste, you'll see."

My attitude toward carrots slowly began a transformation.

I told him that carrot leaves are inedible. He told me I was wrong. He popped a chunk of carrot and stem into his mouth. After he chewed and swallowed, the lesson resumed. "Taste up here. Okay, it is a bit tough."

I put the carrot top and the green in my mouth and began chewing the leaves and stems. I realized I was wrong. They were crunchy, like fried parsley, only sharper.

"Explosive!" he exclaimed. "Is it good? Me, I love it. Here it is, the concrete!"

I don't know whether it was the food on the plate or the excitement in Savoy's voice that made the carrot experience memorable. But it helps explain why the French don't eat alone. It is simply too delicious an experience to keep to oneself.

·PART FOUR·

Seduction and Public Life

11

Hide in Plain Sight

. . .

> The hiding must be seen: I want you to know that I am hiding something from you. . . . I want you to know that I don't want to show my feelings.
>
> —Roland Barthes, *A Lover's Discourse: Fragments*

> To live happy, live hidden.
>
> —Jean-Pierre Claris de Florian, eighteenth-century poet

Soon after I moved to Washington in the late 1980s as a diplomatic correspondent, I was invited to dinner at the residence of the Pakistani ambassador. I assumed more would be involved than fine dining and idle conversation. Still, the extent of my editor's expectations surprised me. "You should be able to get three stories out of it," he told me.

I was new to the Washington scene, and it would take a while for me to understand how much the city's dinner parties are an extension of the workday, offering opportunities for powerful people in government, diplomacy, business, and the media to pass on privileged information discreetly. Insider knowledge is doled out judiciously, and everyone understands that words exchanged over dinner and drinks are weighted. If the source is honorable, the facts are reliable and worthy of further investigation, since it is unwise to be caught in a lie. Revelations may serve as fodder for important decisions, to get information into the public sphere, to enhance or break reputations. I had to learn how to use these occasions to my advantage, and my newspaper's.

Little of this translates to France.

The French, too, have dinner parties where influential people get together. Plenty of words are exchanged. But the purpose is a lively contest in verbal jousting. And the first casualty of finely honed conversational rapiers is accuracy. When the aim is to be clever and engaging, the truth of what is being said is secondary. Transparency might make the speaker seem crude or boring or both. Embroidery and entertainment, for everyone's pleasure, trumps truth every time.

"*L'art de la conversation* is a national art," the writer and consultant Alain Minc told me one day. "It's not like in the United States, when after the fish is eaten, someone says, 'And now we will discuss seriously,' and everyone is supposed to discuss seriously. The rudest thing that can happen at a French dinner is for someone to say, 'We will now have a discussion.' "

Instead, said Minc, "If you want to speak lightly about serious subjects, you come up with false rumors and creative secrets. And that's a game. So when dinner is over, everyone has forgotten what he pretended to believe for a while."

"Wait, everyone forgets what he thought was the truth?" I asked. "But that's very different from America."

"Exactly," said Minc. "In America, everyone takes things seriously. Here, everyone takes things without any seriousness. Even when they are serious. It's the difference between an old country and a new country!"

"But what if the business is serious at a dinner party?" I asked.

"At a dinner party, nothing is serious. Never. Never."

The French relationship to the truth is not the simple "Thou shalt not lie" of a more puritanical nation. On a deeply moral level, the French would probably argue in earnest that a seriously damaging deception is no more common in France than anywhere else. It is not that truth has no value; rather, it has its place. And that place is determined to a large extent by the demands of seduction.

The French trade in secrets. They are titillated by rumors about powerful figures and politicians. The practice dates back to the era of the royal court, when information was power yet had to be handled carefully. Salacious stories, whether true or not, made for good entertainment.

Secrecy and concealment also present an unblemished facade. An exhibition at the Bibliothèque Historique de la Ville de Paris in 2008 crossed the line into too much truth by displaying more than two hundred color photos of life on the streets of Paris under German rule between 1940 and 1944. The photos had been taken by a collaborationist photographer, and they showed Parisians going about their business as usual—and even worse, having fun. One of the most jarring photos was the one used for the exhibition's poster and hung all over Paris: a group of pleasant-looking, well-heeled Parisians at a Métro entrance, a German soldier alongside them. The posters suggested that the French had adapted well to occupation. Some officials called for the exhibit to be closed; the mayor refused, although he authorized the removal of the posters.

The rules of what may be concealed or revealed are complex, shifting with circumstances, but the general principles are ingrained. Rumors create a fantasy and manipulate the way people see political or public figures. It is less important whether the rumor is true than whether it is interesting and appealing. Secrets, on the other hand, are more private and have more value. They play with the truth, depending on how much is given and how much withheld. Secrets lure you closer by revealing something to which no one else has access.

The very word "secret" appeals to the French public. The titles of the books I saw for sale one day at the main newspaper stand of the Gare de Lyon attest to the popularity of the concept: *The Secret Stories of Miss France. The Hidden Face of Banks. The Secret Story of Employers. Secrets of Happiness.* During slow news times, an investigative article or multipart television series about the Freemasons as the country's secret power center is certain to please.

But secrecy in French political and public life is more than a game. It is part of a national survival strategy. Choices about veiling or revealing information are tied to the desire to sustain a certain image of the country and its people. Ugly truths are easily covered up in the interest of maintaining a pleasant outer world in which anyone can operate. And where aesthetics conflicts with ethics, aesthetics often wins out.

That said, the secrets of the powerful usually stay secret, outside the mainstream media and the public pronouncements of politicians. As an

American journalist working in Paris, I had to learn to navigate in an environment where secrecy is valued and its inevitable counterpoint—telling the secret to the chosen few—is highly selective, with journalists expected to observe unstated rituals and rules that are never defined but don't fit an American newspaper. More often than not, the French media play along. It's a survival skill. As might be expected, the tradition of keeping secrets feeds lively rumormongering. The one who has access to the secrets has power, like the serpent tempting Eve with the promise of forbidden knowledge.

There are three reasons why rumors passed around in select, private circles are rarely put into public discussion.

First, because the French believe in the right to pleasure, they are highly tolerant of other people's private behavior, especially sexual behavior. They believe that private lives must not be invaded by outsiders.

Second, because they value a pleasurable existence, they do not enjoy ugly revelations that disturb the surface and threaten the social fabric. This is one reason that American-style investigative journalism is rare in France. (The French media's fear of retribution by the powerful is another.)

Third, libel laws are so protective of private lives that the smallest intrusion in print or broadcasting can lead to legal action and heavy fines.

Whenever there is a gap in the conversation at a French dinner party, all a guest has to do is mention the name of Dominique Strauss-Kahn, the head of the International Monetary Fund and a former finance minister, who is said to harbor presidential ambitions. Someone may innocently ask whether the rumors about his serial womanizing are true. It always livens things up.

Rumors can be exceptionally cruel and personal, even if not proven to be true: a certain former minister is a homosexual pedophile; a certain party leader may have a drinking problem; the father of another former minister's child is the former prime minister of a European country; the wife of yet another former minister caught him in flagrante delicto in a Morocco hotel suite; any number of intellectuals died by committing suicide. There is no hard evidence, that is, no attributable on-the-record testimony.

As an American who wants real proof, when I am treated to a particularly outlandish rumor, I ask my informant, "How do you know?"

Invariably, the answer is, "Everyone knows."

Because Paris is a small town, everyone in the political, literary, academic, journalistic, legal, and business world seems to know or be related to everyone else. France is so centralized in many domains that what happens in Paris is all that seems to matter. Almost everyone, as a result, is a self-appointed rumormonger. Politicians talk to their barbers. Policemen talk to their physical therapists. Chauffeurs talk to one another.

On a trip to the Doubs region in the east of France with agriculture minister Bruno Le Maire, I was ferried around by a governmental chauffeur. It turned out that he had worked for years at the Élysée Palace. We got into a discussion of French presidents. I learned which president had been reserved but flawlessly polite; which one had been arrogant; which one had liked to sit in the front seat, fiddle with the car accessories, change the radio stations, and jump out at stoplights to shake people's hands. "I had a ball," the chauffeur said. Still, he didn't dish. Not a word about anything specific that he had seen while accompanying French heads of state on unofficial trips or holidays. He just let me know that he knew.

During my time in France, the codes began to crack, the secrets to be revealed. The country became infected with a virus called *pipolization*—the hunger for personality-driven, tell-all tales. In addition, new technology made the rules ambiguous. The transformation of technology made it easy to record and film private meetings on a cell phone, contributing to a transparency that had never before existed.

I invited a well-connected friend over for lunch one day, and the conversation turned to the rumor that both President Sarkozy and his wife, Carla Bruni, were having affairs. Allegedly, the president was having an affair with a married junior minister in his cabinet, while the first lady was doing the same with a fellow pop singer.

The story had started with a vague posting on Twitter, which was picked up by a blog on the website of the weekly newspaper *Le Journal du Dimanche* but not printed in the paper itself. Then the story exploded in the British and Italian media. Denials and declarations by Élysée officials kept it alive and fueled new rumors.

Initially the mainstream French media ignored it all, although some news outlets ran stories saying they would not run stories of the current rumors about the private life of the president and his wife. They didn't say what the rumors were.

That was the moment of my lunch. The day after, my friend sent me this e-mail:

> Last night I had the confirmation that Carla is having an affair, which makes me sad, as I really thought that she had "*des principes*" [principles]. Officially she will stay with him! Poor Nicolas!

I wanted to ask her how she was so sure of her information. But I did not feel comfortable asking the question in an e-mail or a phone conversation. When I was a young foreign correspondent in Paris writing about secret negotiations to free American hostages seized at the U.S. embassy in Tehran in 1979–80, an official in the intelligence world told me that he could tell from the clicks and static on my phone that our conversations were being listened to. I also know that France still has an active intelligence surveillance system that has been accused of illegally phone tapping and physically following journalists and procuring their personal phone records in an effort to ferret out the source of their information.

Whether the rumors about Sarkozy and Carla were true didn't seem to matter much. One day, even before the story broke, a French editor told me that one of the paper's reporters had caught a glimpse of the president kissing a woman who was not his wife. I asked the editor why the story wasn't printed. "There was no proof," was the reply. "My colleagues know about the sex stories of the politicians they cover. Sometimes they witness things."

"Of course there was proof," I said. "There was an eyewitness. Your reporter saw it."

"Even if it could be proved, we wouldn't print it," the editor said. "Our readers are not interested in that sort of story. In fact, they would be upset."

In the United States there would be a rush to make the affair public. The American people would learn the truth about the deception; political wounds would be inflicted. Not so in France. This time, uncharacteristically, the rumors about the first couple became a matter of state, but it was one worthy of a Feydeau farce: finger-pointing at the glamorous former justice minister who was a friend of the president's ex-wife, formal investigations by the police and the domestic intelligence service, the freezing out of presidential advisers, suspicions of plotting by the Anglo-Saxon financial system to destroy the French economy, and declarations on state-supported radio by the first lady that the rumors were "insignificant." Like so many other rumors in France, this one failed to hold the public's interest, and it went away.

Official secrecy can also backfire in other ways. Journalists have the right—even the duty—to ask questions, not to titillate but to get at the truth. Their role is to get the record straight, usually to everyone's benefit. The absence of on-the-record transparency creates a breeding ground for rumors that get passed around so widely that eventually they are assumed to be true. I was confronted with this situation in September 2003 when France Inter's morning news show dropped a bombshell. In a swift review of that morning's press, the announcer cited reports of "a supposed illegitimate son of President Chirac in Japan." The Japanese love-child story had been rumored for years, but for the first time it was in print, in the pages of *Nos délits d'initiés* (Our Insider Trading), a book by Guy Birenbaum, a left-leaning political scientist, author, and journalist. Birenbaum devoted twenty pages to building an argument that Chirac, an expert on Japanese culture and regular visitor to Japan, had fathered a child there two decades before. The child, now an adult, was believed to be living in Switzerland.

There was no proof, just a lot of rich circumstantial evidence: forty official and private visits to Japan in the two decades before Chirac's 1995 presidential victory, the replacement of the head of France's foreign intelligence service in 2002 for his alleged investigation into Chirac's links to Japan, a legal investigation into Chirac's finances showing that he and his wife, Bernadette, had traveled to Japan in 1994 under the first part of Bernadette's maiden name, Chodron.

The mainstream French media did not go after the "love-child" story. The left-leaning daily *Libération* wrote a brief story about the report—only after it appeared in the British press.

When the story broke, I called on Claude Angeli, a managing editor and longtime investigative journalist for *Le Canard Enchaîné*. Much to my surprise, he said the love-child story was of no interest. "The only thing I would care about is whether Chirac misused public money to support the child," he said.

Then I asked Catherine Colonna, Chirac's press spokeswoman, about it. "No comment!" she replied. Then she said she had something to ask me: "How could you dare ask such a question?" Colonna had lived in Washington for many years, and I knew that she knew why I asked. The rules are different and the interest in a political leader's personal life is greater in the United States. There was no denial, however. To deny the rumor would have meant that she considered the exercise worthwhile.

For the philosopher and radio host Raphaël Enthoven, rumors are an inevitable part of French culture and cannot be disputed. Instead, rumors create a facade, an artificial image that can give protective covering. Enthoven is tall, dark, handsome, and mysterious enough to pose in any perfume ad. The first time I saw him, he was giving a reading and analysis of a text by Albert Camus, all about the wisdom of love and how it is harder to be happy than to flee happiness. He also happens to be the former partner of Carla Bruni and the father of their son. Several years ago, Bruni wrote and sang a song about a certain Raphaël: his low voice and "velvet glance." He "has the air of an angel, but he's a devil in love," she sang. I met Enthoven over coffee to discuss the role of seduction in French history. I also brought copies of some of the media stories about his life with Bruni. He took my pen and began to mark them up, saying, "So this is wrong! This is wrong!"

If these were all lies, I asked him, why not go public with the truth? "Because you can't change this, you can't," he said. "You can't correct an image. No denial can extinguish a rumor. People want to believe that the forbidden is the truth." Still, he said there was a perverse advantage in having a public persona that didn't conform to reality: he could hide behind it. "Sometimes, you can hide under what people think of you," he said. "It's a fantasy. It's an image. I mean, they are not talking about me; they are talking about someone who looks like me."

The same could not be said of Frédéric Mitterrand, France's minister of culture and communication and the nephew of the late president François Mitterrand. He chose to reveal his secrets, and that decision nearly did him in.

Mitterrand would never have made it as a cabinet secretary in the United States. In 2005 he published *La mauvaise vie* (*The Bad Life*), a memoir in which he revealed disturbing secrets through what the critics called beautiful prose. This combination made Mitterrand's confession an excellent exercise in seduction, a strategic (and perhaps also therapeutic) act of bringing the public closer to him. He triggered the reader's empathy; this made him even more appreciated in France.

In his memoir, Mitterrand told the story of his sexual coming of age. Then he revealed the secrets of his sexual practices, specifically, how he, as a middle-aged gay French man, craved good sex with "boys," especially when he paid for their services. Acknowledging that the "boys" had been forced into prostitution by poverty, he nevertheless reveled in the certainty that his dealings with them were business transactions and that he would get what he paid for.

"The profusion of very attractive and readily available boys puts me in a state of desire that I have no need to curb or conceal," he wrote. "Money and sex, I'm right at the heart of the system—a system that really works, since I know I won't be rejected." As the story progressed, the prose became more sexually graphic and, frankly, disturbing. A boy of an undefined age in Thailand particularly aroused Mitterrand. When he kissed the boy, he felt "his lips cool, tongue deep, the salty saliva of a young male with no trace of tobacco or alcohol. His skin is exquisitely soft, his supple body twists when I stroke and squeeze him, and I get the sense that he experiences pleasure wherever I touch him." In making love to the boy, he wrote, "I've never felt so blissful and so powerful." This sort of conduct was easier far away from France, Mitterrand wrote. "In

France, it can be a whole production to get most call boys hard, but we're definitely not in France now, and we use the washcloth, the soap, and the shower attachment to explore and measure ourselves against each other," he continued.

Morocco was another venue for pleasure seeking, and Mitterrand made the case that young male Arab prostitutes were the beneficiaries, not the victims, of their profession. They used people like him "as a substitute wife and, at the same time, as a savings account," he said, adding, "The beautiful '*gosses*' [boys] arrive as if for a sport, and to finance the appliances for their future marriages to the cousins chosen by their mothers." The secrets confessed were padded with elegance; the ambiguity of language infused them with mystery. The French literary elite considered it a courageous, moving, and well-written book, and refrained from passing moral judgment. Even after his appointment as culture minister, the center-right newspaper *Le Figaro* gushed, "He is a seducer, in the time of seduction itself. . . . [Mitterrand] has shown himself stripped naked in *La mauvaise vie*, his book of memoirs and confession in which he recounts his homosexuality."

I found the book troubling, creepy even. It was pornography, and not just that, self-indulgent exhibitionism. In a country where millions of people are of Arab descent, I couldn't understand how Mitterrand could exploit Arab boys and enjoy credibility with France's ethnic Arab population. I felt I understood one of the most famous lines in American Supreme Court history. Articulating his definition of pornography in a 1964 obscenity case, Justice Potter Stewart said, "I know it when I see it."

So I felt I knew it when I read it.

When I asked French scholars and friends about Mitterrand's book, few seemed distressed. Some told me I was being too American. "It's a very beautiful book, very dignified," said Frédéric Martel, a sociologist and former cultural attaché in Boston who has written books about homosexuality in France (he is gay himself) and about culture in America.

"Frédéric Mitterrand does not hide," Martel said. "He talks about homosexual prostitution without any mask. He is well known on television, and his popularity has protected him. The artist can say everything." But Martel predicted there could be trouble ahead: "Whether the popularity of a political man, who is now a minister, allows him to say everything is yet to be known."

The trouble came in 2009, when Mitterrand came to the defense—a bit too forcefully—of Roman Polanski, the Oscar-winning Polish-French filmmaker, after Polanski was arrested in Switzerland at the behest of a prosecutor in California. Polanski, who was living in Paris, had pleaded guilty in 1977 to having unlawful sex with a thirteen-year-old girl, and had fled the United States before the sentencing. A fugitive from justice for more than thirty years, he was now facing extradition.

Calling Polanski a "marvelous man," Mitterrand said, "If the cultural world doesn't support Roman Polanski, that would mean there is no culture in our country."

The issue played into the hands of the French far right. Marine Le Pen, the daughter of Jean-Marie Le Pen, the founder of the ultraright National Front movement—and who later would be named his successor—read excerpts from Mitterrand's book on prime-time television. She branded him a pedophile, and called for his resignation. Unconstrained by the code of silence that paralyzed much of the rest of the political establishment, she had pushed the matter into public view. Suddenly, Mitterrand's book and his personal behavior became an issue.

Mitterrand had tested the tolerance of the tribe. He had accepted an appointment as a high-profile minister and assumed he would not be judged for having immortalized his confessions in writing. He should have been more cautious. And when he went on the offensive in a prime-time television interview, the beautifully wrought confession was stripped of its magic, and the truth was laid bare.

He confessed that he had paid for sex abroad. "Yes, I've had relations with boys," he said, "but you can't confuse homosexuality with pedophilia." He called his behavior an "error," though not a "crime." When asked how he knew he had never paid for underage sex, Mitterrand replied that he could tell the difference between a youth and a "forty-year-old boxer." He vowed not to resign.

In the end, he triumphed over Laurence Ferrari, the interviewer, not because of the force of his arguments but because she hadn't done her homework. In the course of her questioning, Ferrari admitted that she had not read his book.

President Sarkozy backed his minister. To fire him or allow him to quit would have acknowledged that a mistake had been made in giving him the job. As time passed, the outrage subsided. Mitterrand threw himself into his work, traveling around France to open cultural exhibitions, sit on panels, deliver speeches, pin medals on artists and artisans. When he showed up at a festival of young filmmakers at Saint-Jean-de-Luz in the southwest corner of the country, he was greeted with a standing ovation.

The protection of privacy had trumped the calls for justice and punishment. A survey by the BVA polling firm determined that 67 percent of the French believed that Mitterrand should not resign.

Laurent Joffrin, the editor of *Libération*, defended the tradition that keeps lives private. He suggested in an editorial that it would be wrong to challenge Mitterrand's word and try to prove that he was not telling the truth. "This obstinacy would have consequences that all of us must think about," Joffrin wrote. Recalling that André Malraux, the country's first culture minister, had called man "a miserable little pile of secrets," Joffrin asked, "Do we want to reveal them? Do we want a society of total transparency, that is, a society of inquisition?"

The answer, obviously, was no. The French people wouldn't stand for it. The codes might crack, but the glue of the centuries-old construction of secrecy would hold.

12

La Pipe and *Le Cigare*

. . .

Kings should enjoy giving pleasure.

—Louis XIV

Yes, it's true. And so what? It's none of the public's business.

—President François Mitterrand when asked if it was true that he had an out-of-wedlock daughter

During his political life, Valéry Giscard d'Estaing was convinced that he had discovered the formula for winning elections. It was not a sophisticated polling operation or a massive grassroots organization. It was not an army of brilliant speechwriters or policy aides educated at France's top graduate schools.

Giscard had a much simpler solution: he went after the votes of women. And he did it not with promises of pay equity or better child care, but with *le regard*, the look, the electric charge between two people when their eyes lock and a bond is created.

Giscard served as France's president from 1974 to 1981. As befits a French politician, he transformed his presidency into a three-volume political memoir with the grandiose title *Le pouvoir et la vie*—"Power and Life." In it he boasted that he had worked hard on his *regard* and turned it into an effective campaign tool. "During my seven-year term, I was in love with 17 million French women . . . ," he wrote. "In all the demonstrations, parades, meetings, I would force myself to stare at each woman and each man who happened to be in front of me. Was there some method in this way of acting, some sort of trick to influence and seduce? Presumably."

His honesty was at once disarming and alarming. He even talked about how his system turned him on: "By doing this, I would receive the special radiation of energy that is transmitted from one being to another, and this sensation made me feel good and emboldened me. As a result of looking at the women of France, I saw them, and I fell in love with them."

He acknowledged that English-language readers would certainly find this way of thinking "very French!" He didn't seem to care. More important was that he wanted readers to know how adept he was at visually undressing women. "It is true that I directly felt the presence of the women of France in the crowd, that I guessed their silhouettes and that I would linger just a little longer to look at them, the duration of this extra half-second when, suddenly, the nudity of the human being appears in the eyes," he wrote. Though Giscard traveled widely and loved crowds all over the world, his special love for French women made him long to come home to them. Nothing compared to the erect, elegant posture of French women, which showed off their height. He praised their natural way of walking—"precise, without rigidity or a too-visible desire to attract attention." Most of all, he adored their "delicious smiles," because they conveyed both maternal and romantic love. It was, he recalled, a "pleasure and an anticipation that I cannot describe in a more precise way other than to compare them to the feelings you have when you are in love."

Giscard did not limit himself to generalities. His memoirs are peppered with descriptions of specific women who attracted him. During a political event in Corsica, he imagined a female member of his own team, Alice Saunier-Seïté, in bed. As she introduced him before one event, he noticed her "muscular" body, the "feline ease" of her movements, her tanned-looking legs. "A bizarre thought crosses my mind," he wrote. "When she makes love, she must put the same vehemence into it." Giscard appointed her as his secretary of state for universities.

Giscard's shamelessness and abundance of description touches on a fundamental rule of French politics: good politicians love and are loved.

Their brand of love must fit one of the unofficial pillars of the French Republic: seduction. Politicians in any democratic country must woo the public, but in France it is assumed that their powers should not only be personal and magnetic but also extend to the bedroom. Appealing political positions are not enough.

France has always been a feminine country, and I'm convinced that its male politicians have some strange connection to France as a woman. And not just any woman: not a maternal figure like Mother Russia, but the beautiful, bare-breasted Marianne.

An aura of virility and sexual potency is not merely a plus. It's a necessity. A political man who reveals his sexual prowess is proving his good health and vigor: he is showing his constituents that he is fully and physically capable of running the country. "To come to power, you have to seduce, and to stay there, you have to prove yourself *vigoureux*," wrote Jacques Georgel in his book, *Sexe et politique*.

Politicians are not hounded out of office for sexual indiscretions, and the public is often happy to let their secrets remain officially under wraps. But seduction flows as an undercurrent in public and private life, so it is natural that talking about politicians' personal lives is part of the national discourse. There is one exception to the sexual indiscretion allowance: gender. A female politician is expected to be faithful to one partner.

I called on Giscard one morning at his antique-filled home in the sixteenth arrondissement of Paris. Dressed in a sober dark blue suit and tie, he received me in his study at a table covered in green baize. He had agreed to talk to me about France's global stature and its potential for using "soft power" in the world today.

I gently moved the conversation to *le regard* that had created a special connection between him and the women of France. He nodded and pursed his lips in the subtlest of smiles. He did not hesitate in talking about the sexual tint of French politics. "Yes, that's absolutely true," he said. "It's exactly what I think. . . . And the touch of the body, body contact. It's a transfer of energy! When I see a smiling face, warm and pleasant, I want to touch it, and not just the face. The arm, the hand—to become energized."

As I listened to these words from a former president, I felt my Americanness all the more keenly. In the United States, sexual desire is considered a distraction from the hard work of governing. Politicians are supposed to be pure, or at least strive to be. Americans have proved time and again that they see a politician's cheating in marriage as tantamount to cheating on the voters and the country. Even the most innocently playful banter can have negative consequences. In France, the ability to seduce a lover and engage on the playing field of sexual pleasure, in or out of marriage, is regarded by both men and women as a basic male competency, and no male politician dares risk being seen as inadequate.

In October 1992 the popular magazine *Actuel* asked French politicians three questions: Have you completed your military service? Have you smoked marijuana? Have you cheated on your wife? These were the questions that had plagued Bill Clinton in his campaign for president that year, and in France, the exercise could have been considered an invasion of privacy.

Politicians on the left had no hesitation about the third question. Some of the answers were comical; all of them were ambiguous.

The former minister Claude Évin: "Cheated, no. Had diverse relations, yes."

Jean-Jacques Queyranne, a deputy from the Lyon suburbs: "What French political man, what man-child would be pure enough? There you go. I answered."

The former minister of commerce Jean-Marie Bockel: "The answer that I would have facing my wife, if she were here in front of me and if we were discussing this subject, is that I do not claim to be perfect."

Jacques Rocca Serra, a senator: "I will not lie to you. In Marseille, everything is known. I do not drink. I do not smoke. I never gamble. But I have one passion, and I repeat one passion: I love women. I have been a very, very, very great womanizer. This earned me a very bad reputation, even though I've always strictly kept it separate from my political or professional occupations. Yet, while I was married—which only lasted for four years—I refused to cheat on my wife."

Jean-François Hory, the president of the radical left: "I would respond the same way as Clinton: We have taken care of the problem, my wife and I. And it is no longer a problem today."

On the right, where greater lip service is paid to the teachings of the Catholic Church, the answers were just as creative.

Patrick Devedjian, a deputy from the Paris suburbs: "If my wife were here she would perhaps answer you. She knows the answer."

Alain Carignon, the mayor of Grenoble: "No. But I only recently got married. . . . I still have time. . . . Because life without seduction is death!"

During the Monica Lewinsky scandal in the United States, even French politicians associated with Catholic causes chose to congratulate Bill Clinton for his strength of libido rather than admonish him for his weakness of character. "He loves women, this man!" Marie-Christine Boutin, a deputy in Parliament and one of the major figures of the religious right in France, told a French interviewer. Boutin is an unusual politician in France because she brings her religious beliefs into the National Assembly. She is an anti-abortion activist, and she has held a Bible and shed tears in arguing against France's domestic partnership legislation, which she claims encourages homosexuality. But Clinton's sexual behavior was different. "It's a sign of good health!" she said.

The French never understood all the fuss about Clinton and Lewinsky, the young White House intern. "Americans are the puritan descendants of the Mayflower," Devedjian told the authors of *Sexus politicus*, a 2006 book on sex and politics in France, repeating an oft-sounded idea. "Our institutions originate in the decadence of ancient Rome. We are an old people. The mistresses of monarchs, from Louis XIV to Napoléon III . . . are part of our history. In truth, what is scandalous across the Atlantic is one of the favorite traditions in France."

The French media and political elite made much of the fact that the report by independent counsel Kenneth Starr on the Lewinsky affair noted the president's use of a cigar in a creative way. One of the funniest lines about the Lewinsky affair came from the parliamentary deputy André Santini, a center-right politician from a Paris suburb. "*Bill Clinton est l'homme qui a réconcilié la pipe et le cigare*," he said. "Bill Clinton is the man who reconciled the pipe and the cigar." *Pipe* has the same meaning in both French and English. But in French it also has a second meaning: it's a vulgar slang term for fellatio. Santini, a passionate cigar smoker, liked the phrase so much that he used it over and over. France's political leadership also felt Clinton's pain. At one point, President Chirac telephoned Clinton to assure him of his esteem and his friendship "in this personal ordeal."

The concept of sexual sin and forgiveness means little in French politics, and Bible-thumpers like Mark Sanford of South Carolina don't exist in France. As a congressman in 1998, Sanford called for Clinton's impeachment ("He lied under a different oath, and that's the oath to his wife," Sanford said); eleven years later, as governor of his state, he lied about his own extramarital affair. The French political elite was astonished when the sex antics of Sanford and María Belén Chapur, his "soul mate," as he called her, made news. A lead paragraph like this one that appeared in the *New York Times* would never be found in a French newspaper: "Gov. Mark Sanford said Tuesday that he had visited his Argentine mistress more times than he initially disclosed and that he had had inappropriate flirtations with several other women as well."

There is nothing unusual in France about a politician who is missing in action, as was Sanford when he secretly decamped to Buenos Aires to meet his lover. "Missing in action" is a tried-and-true component of French political life. Giscard, when he was president, was rumored to have crashed his car into a milk delivery truck returning to the Élysée early one morning after a *rendez-vous galant*, a romantic assignation. He neither confirmed nor denied the story. Chirac's chauffeur wrote in his memoirs that Bernadette Chirac would incessantly ask, "But in short, Mr. Laumond, where is my husband tonight?"

What really made the French giggle about Sanford was his need to babble on about his feelings. French commentators were bemused that he got teary about crossing the "sex line" with Chapur, admitted his sinfulness, apologized, and asked for forgiveness. It is impossible to imagine Chirac or Sarkozy or any French politician giving such a performance.

Compare the fallout after the Sanford revelations with the smooth-as-silk—and very French—handling of the Dominique Strauss-Kahn affair. Strauss-Kahn, the former finance minister and Socialist Party presidential hopeful, was rumored to have had a long and deep history of interest in women other than his wife. Even in senior governmental circles, there was surprise when he was named head of the International Monetary Fund. But Sarkozy pushed for the appointment. Strauss-Kahn had been an able finance minister, he was considered a gifted economist, and his new assignment would get a potential Socialist rival out of the country.

Hints about Strauss-Kahn's behavior had been the subject of rumors for years. In a kind of French parlor game, journalists and authors quoted one another as a way to avoid responsibility for the stories (and lawsuits). Press articles appeared with enough detail and innuendo that any reader could connect the dots and draw conclusions.

So many sources told so many stories that at least some of them had to be true, the French said. But the stories also made Strauss-Kahn a living legend, and some people expressed quiet admiration that such a high-profile political figure could find time for such an active social life. But then, as the media columnist Daniel Schneidermann told me, "There are no formal complaints; there are no judicial proceedings; there is no evidence with proof that you can print." Anne Sinclair, Strauss-Kahn's wife and one of France's most respected television journalists, was asked in 2006 if she suffered because of her husband's reputation as a seducer. She answered, "No, if anything I am quite proud! For a political man, it is important to seduce. As long as I seduce him and he seduces me, that's good enough."

A cover story in *Le Nouvel Observateur* in 2003 on group sex and "exchangism" clubs included a small sidebar headlined, "The Minister Is There." It recounted a visit to a "private libertine soiree" by an unnamed minister with presidential ambitions. "They are oddly calm, almost tense . . . ," said the article. "Women are in uniform: short dresses, sexy underwear, leather skirts." The minister looked taller than he appeared on television, "almost electoral," the article continued. The details of the group sex were a bit blurred, although readers were told that "the poor man, overwhelmed for a second, quickly masters the situation." One of the spectators remarked, "You really think he can become president?"

The minister was not identified, but the chattering classes speculated that the only person who could have fit the description was Strauss-Kahn. When I asked Jean Daniel, the magazine's director, about the article, all he would say is that, in his personal opinion, it should not have been published.

When Strauss-Kahn was appointed head of the IMF in 2007, the French media did not investigate the rumors. The lone journalist to train the spotlight on them was Jean Quatremer, the *Libération* correspondent in Brussels. He wrote on his blog that Strauss-Kahn's "only real problem" was his "rapport" with women. "Too insistent, he often comes close to harassment," Quatremer wrote. "A weakness known by the media, but which nobody mentions. (We are in France.) The IMF, however, is an international institution with Anglo-Saxon morals. A misplaced gesture, a too specific allusion, and it will be a media scramble."

Quatremer's posting opened the way for other journalists to write coyly about whether Strauss-Kahn's rumored private life was appropriate to write about. A year later, the issue exploded. In the fall of 2008, Strauss-Kahn was put under investigation by the IMF for allegedly abusing his position after engaging in a sexual relationship with Piroska Nagy, an IMF economist. The French elite, right and left alike, rallied behind Strauss-Kahn and said his personal behavior was private. He hired a public relations firm and issued a statement in which he admitted infidelity. He called the affair "an incident in one's private life," accepted responsibility, and expressed "regret." Then he went silent.

His wife took the position that this was minor-league straying. "These things happen in the life of any couple," she wrote on her personal blog. "This one-night stand is now behind us. . . . We love each other as much as on the day we met." He was cleared of any wrongdoing.

Can these old French codes stand in a world of greater transparency and political correctness? In the wake of the scandal, Stéphane Guillon, a comic on France Inter's radio breakfast show, went after Strauss-Kahn just before he was to give an interview at the station's studios in Paris. To get ready for the IMF director's arrival in the building, Guillon said, "exceptional measures have been taken in order not to awaken the beast." As a precaution, women were advised to wear "antisex" clothing. High heels, leather, and chic underwear had been banned. The head of publicity would greet Strauss-Kahn in an Afghan *burqa*. At the sound of a siren, "all female workers must be evacuated." Guillon even alluded to Strauss-Kahn's penis as the "best-known organ of the IMF." Strauss-Kahn was not amused. On the air, he said, "Humor is not funny when it is essentially nastiness."

More generally, though, there was relief in the French government when the scandal passed. Among the French intelligentsia, there was also a willingness to forgive even his apparent excess. When I asked the historian Mona Ozouf whether Strauss-Kahn fit the tradition of the libidinous politician, she laughed softly and said, "Surely. He has exceptional energy."

The absence of a sexual aura can also hurt the politician who lacks it. The inability of Lionel Jospin, the Socialist Party candidate in the 2002 presidential election, to appear sexy contributed to his lack of electoral appeal.

Weeks before election day, *Libération* asked leading female editors about the women's vote. Claire Dabrowski, then the director of Téva, a satellite television channel for women, said that Jospin's subtlety and drollery were not enough. "If women don't appreciate Jospin, it is without doubt because he is not very sexy," she said. "Plus he has those big eyes. You think that's he's going to scold you. In short, we cannot imagine crazy nights of lovemaking with him." Françoise Le Cornec, editor in chief of *Jeune & Jolie* (Young & Pretty), a magazine for teenage girls, echoed these sentiments. "Lionel Jospin is not seductive at all," she said. "He has no charisma. He has an awkward air. He is as antisexy as possible. Chirac on the contrary has more presence. Plus, he's got this reputation as a womanizer, which gives him an aura among women."

I didn't find it comforting to know that female journalists were as concerned about the sexiness of their political leaders as Giscard was about the shape of his female voters' silhouettes. Still, I understood what they were saying about Jospin. I met him only once, on the Île de Ré, an island off the coast of France, where we were playing tennis on adjoining courts. During a break, I introduced myself. "It's an honor to meet you," I said. Except Jospin heard my pronunciation of the word *honneur* as *horreur*—horror. He lashed out at me. "*Horreur*! It's a *horreur* to meet me!" he exclaimed. His big eyes glowered. I was mortified. I fell over myself with my apologies and joked that my flawed French was to blame.

Still, I knew that Chirac would have thrown back his head with a loud guffaw and cracked a joke.

Unlike Americans, who are forced to take up the mantle of purity just when assuming high office might give them an advantage in the sexual game, French politicians are allowed to enjoy their enhanced opportunities. This reality flows from centuries of precedent. The kings took sexual seduction to new heights. There was a hierarchy to the women in their lives: wives, significant others (known as "favorites"), and women passing through the court who provided fleeting adventures. To make sure that no one forgets France's royal history today, the kings' escapades are routinely retold in cover stories in mainstream weekly news magazines.

In 2010, to mark the four-hundredth anniversary of the death of Henri IV, he was celebrated in exhibitions, books, magazine articles, and guided tours exploring his life. Did he really ride a white horse? (No one knows; accounts varied until the nineteenth century, when the Romantics made it white.) Did he really promise all Frenchmen the means to have a "chicken in every pot" on Sundays? (Yes, but promoting this dish from his birthplace was a political gesture, not a gastronomic initiative.) Did he smell as bad as people said? (Yes. Catherine Henriette de Balzac d'Entragues, one of his mistresses, told him he was lucky to be a king because otherwise she wouldn't have put up with it.) *Le Figaro* ran big color ads for a special edition on Henri: "The adventurer, the seducer, the king. Long Live Henri IV!"

Henri was married twice and was an indefatigable lover, with four important favorites, innumerable one-night conquests, and more than a dozen children. His letters to the favorites capture the depth of his passion for them. "Certainly, for a woman, there is no equal to you. . . . I cherish, adore, and miraculously honor you," he wrote to Gabrielle d'Estrées, considered his *grande* mistress. With Balzac d'Entragues, he was more graphic: "*Bonsoir*, my love. I kiss your tits a million times."

Henri's son, Louis XIII, considered a cold fish, contented himself with small, inconsequential affairs. Louis XIV built Versailles in part to facilitate his sexual adventures. Louis XV, shy as a teenager, became so sexually voracious that he went through women of all ages and classes of society, including four women who were sisters, and kept several women at a time in a mansion in a remote corner of Versailles. Louis XVI, by contrast, let seven years elapse before he consummated his marriage to Marie Antoinette and suffered politically as a result. "All of Europe knew well that Marie Antoinette's brother was explaining to him a bit how things worked," said Ozouf. "He was the laughingstock of Europe."

The tradition of seduction carried forward into modern times. Edgar Faure, a politician who wrote crime novels under a pseudonym and was a member of the Académie Française, liked to say that he had all the time in the world to succeed in his operations of seduction. When Faure became the president of the Council (de facto prime minister) in the 1950s, he availed himself of all the perquisites of office. "When I was a minister, some women resisted me," he told a friend, according to *Sexus politicus*. "Once I became president, not even one."

Edgar Faure is not to be confused with Félix Faure (no relation), a president of France in the 1890s. Tall and blue-eyed, he was better known as "President Sun" and "Félix *le Bel*" (Félix the Beautiful) because of his taste for luxury and young women. One of his lovers, Marguerite Steinheil, would enter the Élysée Palace through a secret door that had been built in the mid-nineteenth century by Louis Napoléon to give his own mistress easy access.

One evening in February 1899, the president drank a cinchona aphrodisiac. He and Steinheil met as usual, in a blue and gold salon. A few moments later, the president's chief of staff heard the young woman scream. Faure, dressed only in a flannel cardigan, was dead. Steinheil left the Élysée so quickly that she forgot her corset. The first lady called a priest to deliver the last sacraments, even though her husband was already dead. Upon approaching the salon, the priest asked, "Does the president still have his *connaissance*?" *Connaissance* means "consciousness," but it can also mean "acquaintance." An orderly replied that the *connaissance* had already been ushered out the back door. (The exchange is still considered one of the cleverest examples of *second degré* humor in French political life.) The real story was little covered in the French press, but the libertarian newspaper *Journal du Peuple* wrote, "We can say that he was not poisoned, but that he died because he sacrificed too much to Venus."

Rather than being embarrassed by these stories, the French seem to revel in them. In prime time one Saturday evening in the fall of 2009, French television aired a ninety-minute docudrama on Félix Faure's love affair. It showed the president and his mistress falling in love with one *regard*, and included several long scenes in which they did nothing except gaze at each other. "Americans would have no patience with this," said Andy as we watched.

An explanatory program on power and seduction followed—featuring interviews with former politicians, talking heads, and celebrities. The Italian actress Claudia Cardinale dismissed as "absurd" rumors that she had had a love affair with Chirac. The program also presented the far-right political leader Jean-Marie Le Pen, who was in his eighties, as having a certain "allure" because he was such a terrific ballroom dancer.

Even the most sober politicians seek to promote their virility. In 2004 Bruno Le Maire, the longtime chief of staff to Foreign Minister Dominique de Villepin, wrote a book about his boss, most of which is a straightforward defense of the man he served for many years. In the middle of the narrative came a personal confession about sensuality. During a trip with his wife, Pauline, to Venice in 2003, Le Maire recalled the sweet beginning of their day together. He had been in the bath. "I let myself be overwhelmed by the heat of the bath, the light of the lagoon that floated on the mirror of the door, the green tea soap, and Pauline's hand that softly caressed my *sexe*," he wrote.

We assume theirs is a requited love. And yet, the frank passage, coming in an otherwise straightforward book on Villepin's diplomacy, stands out. Maybe it is jarring only to my American ear.

For Le Maire and Giscard, and presumably for their readers, there is nothing unnatural about linking the quest for political power with the projection of an image of sexuality. I was on the road visiting farmers one day with Le Maire, now the agriculture minister, and I asked him why he included the sex scene in a book about French diplomacy. "There is an American puritanism that doesn't exist in France!" he said, defensively. That may be so, but his face had turned bright red.

"Not even for the most serious of politicians?" I asked.

"That's certainly my case," he replied. And then he laughed. "What I like about life is to be fully engaged in what I do," he said. "And this is as true in my personal life as it is in my work."

In the modern era, the seductive politician has found a new, expansive stage for his performances: the presidency of France. For the first half of the twentieth century, the country's constitution was based on a parliamentary system. There was a prime minister, but his power was diluted by the strength of the national legislators. The constitution of the Fifth Republic, created in 1958, gave France its presidency, an exceptionally powerful one with some of the trappings of monarchy.

The Fifth Republic did not begin with a seducer in the royal tradition. Charles de Gaulle, the first president, governed not with bedroom eyes but with austerity and moral authority. His *rigueur*, as it was called, meant that he did not succumb to the long-standing royal tradition of self-indulgence over principle. But de Gaulle had unusual personal charisma, the natural seductive power of the strong leader. And he added to that a great seduction of the whole French nation that was arguably as powerful as sex. He created a story line that appealed to the masses and convinced the world: far from being a nation of Nazi collaborators during World War II, the French had remained pure, even as they had been victimized, outraged, broken, martyred, and betrayed by an evil minority in their midst.

De Gaulle rewrote the narrative of the war in a famously improvised speech on the day of Paris's liberation, August 25, 1944. He portrayed the city as ravaged but liberated with the help of "all of France, of the fighting France, of the only France, the real France, the eternal France!"

It was a tour de force. For the previous four years, France had indeed been collaborating with the Nazis, but de Gaulle created a nobler image. She was a virgin in his eyes, "the princess in the fairy stories or the Madonna in the frescoes."

If the French followed him, they hadn't been cowards; they hadn't betrayed their fellow citizens; they weren't emotionally and morally hollow. They could convince themselves of this "certain idea of France," as de Gaulle called it, a heroic image of military bravery, courage in the face of hardship, and moral rectitude at a time of crisis. They could re-create "the eternal France": an old country with long-standing institutions built around security and tradition, not innovation and iconoclasm.

De Gaulle demonstrated a primal element of political seduction: the ability to promulgate a myth about a people. He embraced and reassured the French at a time when they were in desperate need of self-confidence and self-respect. Amid the chaos that followed World War II, France woke up, looked in the mirror, and was ashamed at what she saw. De Gaulle whispered in her ear, telling her exactly what she wanted to hear.

As a war hero, de Gaulle was not a womanizer and didn't need to be; his virility was assumed. According to one account a woman, exiting a particularly engaging meeting, hurried toward him and with ecstatic eyes said, "Oh, my general, if you only knew how much I love you." De Gaulle was momentarily surprised, then answered with a smile, "Well, madame, I thank you, but keep this secret to yourself."

One woman who managed to seduce him—intellectually—was an American, Jacqueline Kennedy. De Gaulle had been "irritating, intransigent, insufferably vain, inconsistent and impossible to please" during President John F. Kennedy's official visit to Paris in 1961, according to the president's aide Theodore Sorensen. De Gaulle was suspicious of Kennedy's promise to come to Europe's defense and vowed to continue France's project to develop its own nuclear arsenal. But Jackie chatted with him in her excellent "low, slow French" during lunch in the Élysée Palace, and he was charmed. De Gaulle told Kennedy that his wife "knew more French history than most Frenchwomen." By the end of the visit, de Gaulle had warmed up to both Kennedys, and from then on, he treated the American president better.

When de Gaulle resigned in 1969 after a defeat in a referendum, it was as if he had been abandoned by the love of his life. A year later, when his successor, Georges Pompidou, announced de Gaulle's death on radio and television, he said, "General de Gaulle is dead. France is a widow."

Years after de Gaulle's death, Jean-Luc Hees, the president of Radio France, interviewed Alain Peyrefitte, the de Gaulle confidant and former minister who had written several books on him. After the show, Hees asked Peyrefitte a critical question.

"I asked, 'Did he have lovers?'" Hees recalled. "He said, 'De Gaulle? Are you joking?'" Then Peyrefitte relented. "Well, maybe in Warsaw, and maybe in Beirut, before the war, but not after. There were rumors." Hees asked Peyrefitte if he was serious.

"Not after June 18, 1940," Peyrefitte replied. "He belonged to history after that. So he couldn't have any affairs with women, you know."

But by this time, Peyrefitte had become fully engaged in the topic. Out came another revelation. "Well maybe, there was an exception," he said. "To celebrate the victory of Bir Hakeim." Bir Hakeim, in the Libyan desert, was the site of a key battle in 1942 in which the forces of the Free French halted the advance of German and Italian troops. Peyrefitte stressed again that this was only a rumor. But that didn't stop him from keeping it alive and passing it on.

It is the fate of kings to be loved more in death than in life. And so it was that in January 2006, ten years after François Mitterrand's death and eleven after the end of his presidency, the French plunged into a warm bath of nostalgia for him. It came with a flood of books, magazine and newspaper supplements, no fewer than six television films and documentaries, and dozens of hours of commentary and speeches about his life. Although a Socialist, Mitterrand was among the most regal of French presidents, reviled by some, tolerated by others, loved by a few. He could be petty, cruel, vindictive, sadistic, secretive, and dishonest. He rarely apologized or admitted he was wrong. But somehow he became the gold standard for French leadership in the modern era. His election in 1981 was a revolution, the end of twenty-three years of conservative governments under de Gaulle and his successors Pompidou and Giscard.

In an era when a presidential term was seven years—not five as it is today—Mitterrand served two full terms, which made him the longest-serving head of state since Napoléon III (1852–1870). An intellectual who championed the causes of the left, Mitterrand ended capital punishment, strengthened regional governments, and promised a new economic model that would protect the ordinary Frenchman. A master of the nuances and rhetorical richness of French, he used lofty language, elegiac tones, and a religious-sounding register to evoke the necessity of socialism. He predicted that France would never be the same after he left office. "I am the last of all the all-powerful presidents," Mitterrand boasted.

He had no head for economics; he considered money base, and the French liked that, even though his policies—leading to universal retirement at sixty, a reduced workweek, and a bloated civil service—set the country on a downhill economic course that plagues it to this day. He wooed his people by spinning the myth they wouldn't need to get their hands dirty with work, money, or sacrifice but could still lead comfortable lives.

It was Mitterrand's personal aura, his mystery, his success in flouting convention that bred admiration, in life and death. "I know only one thing: to live outside the ordinary and to take to its maximum the intensity of living," he wrote in a letter to a friend in 1942.

He put women under his spell because he genuinely loved them, and they knew it. A magazine called *Influences* devoted an entire issue to him in 1988, in which this was made clear. The actress Marthe Mercadier called him "*un grand amateur de femmes*"—a great connoisseur of women. Yvette Roudy, a former secretary of state for women's issues, said that "the word seduction . . . is too limiting" in describing his aura, adding, "He takes time for you." Catherine Lara, a rock musician, described Mitterrand as a magician. "Everything in him seduces me," she said. ". . . Also, I find that he is aging marvelously well, like a good wine, a good Bordeaux."

My favorite comment came from Françoise V., a prostitute. "When I am with a client and I lack inspiration, I think about the rare men who still make me fantasize, including François Mitterrand," she said. "I find him marvelously gentle, sensual, and very gracious." I can't imagine an American prostitute in the late 1980s having the same on-the-job fantasies about George H. W. Bush.

In the fall of 1994, as his presidency neared an end, a *Paris Match* long-lens photograph offered graphic proof of what had only been whispered: that Mitterrand had fathered an out-of-wedlock daughter with Anne Pingeot, a museum curator and a scholar of nineteenth-century sculpture who had had a relationship with him for more than two decades. When the daughter, Mazarine, was ten years old, Mitterrand legally acknowledged paternity, with the caveat that it be kept secret from the public until his death. In her memoirs, Mazarine wrote that when she was asked at school to identify her father's profession, she crossed out the line.

Mazarine and her mother lived at government expense in a state-owned apartment near the Eiffel Tower. French taxpayers did not know that their president spent a considerable amount of time with a second family, including occasional weekends at a state-owned château. Mitterrand spent his last Christmas, before his death, with his mistress and daughter, not with his wife and their two sons.

Years later, Lionel Jospin revealed in a memoir a private conversation he had had with Mitterrand after the *Paris Match* photos were published. "He told me, 'Basically, there are two ways of doing it,'" Jospin wrote. One was to change wives, as Jospin had done, Mitterrand said. Or, he continued, "You can keep at the same time two women whom you have loved, whom you love, whom you respect." Explaining her father's choice of a double life, Mazarine said, "My father had an uncompromising concept of fidelity. One never betrays one's friends; one never betrays an agreed-upon pact. He would always be flabbergasted that people got divorced."

But for Mitterrand, as for the kings of centuries before, a wife and a favorite did not suffice. There were apparently other arrangements, including a lengthy relationship with the Swedish journalist Christina

Forsne. As described in her memoir, *François*, it began as a sexual liaison and then turned into companionship. She was a regular lunch and dinner companion at the Élysée; she accompanied him on trips. Though there were many errors in her book, no one in Mitterrand's circle challenged the main story line.

Assumptions were made about other relationships, in part because Mitterrand enjoyed the company of beautiful women. During a state visit to South Korea, he chose the actress Sophie Marceau, then in her twenties, to accompany him as the personification of French beauty. After Mitterrand's death, his widow, Danielle, turned confessional in a television interview. "Yes, I had married a seducer," she said. "And I had to live with it." One of the most enduring images of Mitterrand's funeral is a photo of Anne Pingeot, her eyes closed, the polka-dotted black tulle veil of her hat covering her face, her daughter by her side. There are still lively debates in polite circles about whether it would have been better if the mistress had stayed away. But what upset the French public more than the existence of a second family was the revelation that the French state had financially supported Anne and Mazarine, even giving them full police protection.

I thought of Mitterrand and his women when the story of a *burqa*-wearing French convert to Islam and her allegedly polygamous Algerian-born husband erupted into a political firestorm in 2010. The woman had been fined by the police for wearing the face-covering veil while driving a car, on the grounds that it was dangerous. The husband was accused by the government of having four wives who were claiming single-parent benefits for his twelve children. He was threatened with losing his French citizenship.

But the husband fought back, hired a lawyer, and claimed he had only one wife. The others, he insisted, were lovers. "If you can be stripped of your French nationality for having mistresses, then many French could lose theirs," he told reporters.

Unlike the immigrant husband, however, Mitterrand was irresistible to the French people. "Half-vampire, half-seducer," was *Le Monde*'s description of his enigmatic smile. Serge July, a founding editor of *Libération*, once called him "a master goldsmith in human relations."

Mitterrand wrote about France as if she were a woman whom he knew well, confessing his "passion for her geography, her living body." Jean Daniel of *Le Nouvel Observateur* said that this intense love of every part of France gave him universal appeal. "I took trips with him, and he knew its remotest nooks," Daniel recalled. "He knew all the people in town. There was something demagogic about him, a kind of subversive seduction. He'd ask things like, 'The butcher—has his baby been born yet?' "

The paradox is that Mitterrand also kept his distance, playing hard to get. That ambiguity appealed as well.

As a young politician, Jacques Chirac was rather dashing, a tireless campaigner who loved to throw himself into the crowds. On the road, he'd produce a fistful of cash—to buy a round of beers for the local guys or a bouquet of flowers for a woman he considered pretty. On the street, he'd sometimes sell his autograph to a woman for a kiss. In the early 1990s Brigitte Bardot called him "the only politician who makes me melt."

Chirac's amorous escapades were documented in a tell-all book by his former chauffeur, Jean-Claude Laumond, published in 2001. In the 1980s, Laumond wrote, the procession of women into Chirac's office was so constant that women staffers would joke: "Chirac? Three minutes. Shower included."

Laumond corrected the record. It took a bit longer, he said. "To an almost sickening degree, Chirac has had party militants, secretaries, all those with whom he spent five busy minutes," he wrote.

Chirac saw no need to hide his habits, and while he was in office, neither the press nor the public held them against him. In a series of interviews with the journalist Pierre Péan, he confessed that he had loved many women in his lifetime "as discreetly as possible." To reinforce the point, he repeated the line in his runaway best-selling autobiography in 2009.

For those who wonder how the wives of womanizing politicians tolerate their husbands' seductive successes, Bernadette Chirac offered some illumination. She alluded to her husband's extramarital affairs in her book *Conversation*, a question-and-answer dialogue with a journalist, published in 2001. "I have been jealous at times, very!" she said. "How could it be otherwise? This was a very handsome guy, with the gift of words besides. . . . The girls would line up at the door."

For the sake of the children and other family reasons, she decided not to dissolve the marriage. "Convention dictated that one put up a facade and hung on," she said, calling herself "a prisoner of familial traditions." He was stuck as well. "I warned him many times: 'The day Napoléon abandoned Joséphine, he lost everything.' "

During his twelve-year presidency, Chirac was never as monarchical, mysterious, or intellectual as Mitterrand. His appeal was as a man of the soil. He liked to pet farm animals. His favorite beverage was a Corona beer; his favorite dishes were peasant fare: *tête de veau*, charcuterie, sausages.

Chirac was the first French leader to acknowledge the guilt of the French state in the Nazi extermination of Jews during World War II. He pushed through reforms of the health care and pension systems and abolished compulsory military service. He was a keen art collector, particularly of Asian and African art. He once told an interviewer for a weekly magazine that poetry was "a necessity of daily life." But his dissolution of Parliament in 1997 led to an unwieldy and unworkable division of power with the Socialist Party known as cohabitation. And even when he had a united government afterward, he failed in fulfilling his promise to invigorate France's flaccid economy.

Toward the end of his presidency Chirac suffered a slight stroke. Afterward, he appeared less virile, indeed, like an old man. He sported a permanent tan and, according to some accounts, blackened his gray hair. When he was out of sight on vacation in Canada one summer, the puppet satire television program *Les Guignols* ran a skit speculating that he was off having a face lift.

As Chirac left office, his legacy was tainted by a string of corruption charges and unkept promises, but it was not long before he was once again beloved. An overwhelming majority of the French approved of his handling of foreign affairs, particularly his role as the European leader who had led the opposition to the American-led war in Iraq. In the age of Sarkozy, the French were nostalgic for Chirac's lack of pretense, his appetite for country cooking, his unabashed promotion of France, his gentlemanly demeanor. It seemed that the results of a 2002 poll were still true: more French women wanted to have dinner with Chirac than with any other politician.

Valéry Giscard d'Estaing's personal *opération séduction* was not enough to get him reelected for a second seven-year term in 1981. He had been the youngest president of the Fifth Republic and also the youngest ex-president. In his early years in office, he had projected an image of youthfulness. A bourgeois technocrat, he started out as a reformer and modernizer. He removed much of the formality and ceremony from high office, made use of television to promote his agenda, walked through the streets of Paris to official appointments, and organized meetings with ordinary folk, usually over the dinner table of a country auberge. Tall and slim, he wore soft cashmere V-necked sweaters and corduroy velvet pants.

There were stories about an active sex life, and I know women who claim they had to fight him off. He was rumored to have had a liaison with Sylvia Kristel, the star of the *Emmanuelle* soft-porn films. But after his defeat in 1981, Giscard took it as his mission to convince the French that he was more than lovable—that he was downright sexy—and that they had made a mistake in voting him out of office. He sought to burnish his image by writing a sentimental, melodramatic sex novel. *Le passage*, published in 1994, tells a story of hunting and of love in which Charles, a solitary, passive middle-aged man, becomes obsessed with Natalie, a mysterious blond twenty year old hitchhiker.

The first time he sees her, he drives past her, even though it is love at first sight. The second time he sees her, she is sitting by the side of the road and he stops and takes her home. She stays with him for a few weeks. Then one day she leaves abruptly. The book ends.

It is a classic sexual fantasy: a man stops on the side of the road to pick up a beautiful young hitchhiker and then seduces her. It also indulges a second, more complex fantasy: the older man seduced, then abandoned by a younger woman. *Le Monde* said that the novel "possesses a singular quality: its total absence of originality." Years later, *Le Monde* took another jab at it, branding it "an unintentional comedy."

In his eighties, Giscard remained determined to promote his image as a sexually potent male. In 2009, he published a second novel, which titillated readers with the suggestion that he might have had a love affair with Britain's Princess Diana. *La princesse et le président* relates the "violent passion" between a French head of state and a British royal named Patricia.

In the book, President Jacques-Henri Lambertye, a sex-driven widower, meets the princess at a banquet at Buckingham Palace. Like Diana, the fictional princess is trapped in an unhappy marriage to the unfaithful heir to the throne; she throws herself into charitable work while carrying on her own love affairs on the side.

Passion begins with *le regard*. "I stood up and I pulled back [my chair] to allow the princess of Cardiff to be seated," the president says. "She thanked me for it with one of those oblique looks that put me under her spell." Then comes a *baisemain*. "I kissed her hand and she gave me a questioning look, her slate-grey eyes widening as she tilted her head gently forward," the president continues. The princess becomes confessional, telling him, "Ten days before my marriage, my future husband told me he had a mistress, and that he had decided to continue his relationship with her."

In real life, Giscard is known to have been charmed by the young princess, but they did not meet until years after the end of his presidency. After spending an evening with her at an event at Versailles in 1995, he told a French women's magazine that she "is much more beautiful in real life. . . . I discovered she was also a cat, a feline. She moves without noise."

On a train ride back to Paris from a commemoration of D-Day, the fictional President Lambertye begins to seduce his princess. They make love for the first time at the Château de Rambouillet, where, as president, Giscard liked to hunt.

As narrator, the president is too discreet to describe his lovemaking with the princess: "I would not know how to do that. I only remember a great softness of warm skin, and being submerged in this flood of tenderness that I had felt coming at the end of the day and that had turned into an ocean."

Later on in the novel is a one-night stand with a beautiful Corsican doctor who ministers to the president after he survives an assassination attempt. He is less reticent here: "Her lips were opened and I felt, in her saliva and in mine, the acid net of desire. . . . It is that evening that I experienced love with the Venus de Milo, her strong shoulders and her sumptuous legs."

The media mused about whether it was logistically possible for Giscard to have bedded Diana or whether it was an old man's imagination run wild. "Total fiction, writer's dream, true story? Only the author has the key to this enigma," wrote *Le Figaro.* "The book may sell but it won't win any prizes unless there is an award for bad taste," the *Times* of London said.

On Europe 1 Radio, the comic Nicolas Canteloup did an impersonation of Giscard's haughty, marble-filled voice. "I used to be called the 'big gun' . . . ," he said, "I confirm it: Lady Di, I had her."

"You were with Lady Di?" the mock interviewer asks.

"To be frank, she's not the only one I had. I won't list them all." Then, the royalty-obsessed "president" goes on to list them: "I had the Princess of Luxembourg, the Duchess of York, Maria of Russia. I don't have the complete list."

Giscard ignored the criticism and insisted that the book was fiction. "It's a novel!" he exclaimed the day my researcher, a French woman in her early twenties, and I met him in his study. "Just let your mind go! The French president is not I. It's not my character. The British princess—I don't tell the whole story of Princess Diana. I tell you what one felt when one met her. It's a novel!"

The book ends with the president and the princess living happily ever after in Tuscany. Giscard said that he considered ending the book with the president going off with the Corsican doctor. "I thought about it, but I didn't do it because of Diana," he said. "Because I said to myself that this would be an insult to her memory if the president went off with the doctor. And well, this book, it's completely an invention, naturally, but Diana said to me—I knew her a little, but not much, a little, like that, in conversation—and she said to me, 'But you should write what would happen if there were a love story between two great leaders of the world.' "

So there he was, this man in his eighties, with wrinkled hands and a balding head and a lined face, enjoying his fantasy about a love affair with a young and beautiful princess. There was something poignant about Giscard holding on to a dream of gallantry and ideal love.

When we were saying our good-byes, his hand seemed to rest for a second on the derriere of my young researcher. It was not aggressive. Perhaps it was accidental. Perhaps it never happened. Then it seemed to happen a second time.

13

Bon Courage, Chouchou

. . .

His physique, his charm, his intelligence seduced me. He has five or six remarkably nourished brains.

—Carla Bruni, describing Nicolas Sarkozy, in *Carla et Nicolas: La véritable histoire* by Valérie Benaïm and Yves Azéroual

I listen to very few people. . . . I don't need people to tell me to smile, to reassure. I wish you knew how much I don't need this. I hate—and that's a weak word—to be told that stuff.

—Nicolas Sarkozy, quoted in *Dawn Dusk or Night* by Yasmina Reza

Valéry Giscard d'Estaing was not the only French president to get entangled with a princess. Nicolas Sarkozy had his own story, a brief but painful encounter with the heroine of *La princesse de Clèves*, a seventeenth-century novel of unrequited love. Like Princess Diana, this princess was young, beautiful, trapped in an unhappy marriage, and suffocating in a protocol-driven royal court. While Giscard was smitten with his princess, Sarkozy was contemptuous of his.

La princesse de Clèves was written by Madame de Lafayette, a countess close to the court of Louis XIV. It is considered the first authentic French novel and is a favorite on required reading lists in French high schools.

The story was daring for its time. A sixteen-year-old girl, brought up in the strictest morality by her mother, makes her entrance at court. A prince falls in love with her and asks for her hand, and she dutifully marries him. Then the unexpected happens. At a court ball one night, she exchanges looks with the rakish Duc de Nemours, and they fall immediately and passionately in love.

The princess comes to understand that the duke is "too seductive," a classic "infidel" who will abandon her for future conquests if she begins a liaison with him. The rituals of the court require the princess and the duke to see each other every day; the tension between them builds as they are forced to hide their feelings. Tormented, the princess confesses to her husband her love for another man and asks to be freed from appearing at court. She hopes that this will help her remain faithful. The prince, convinced that his wife has betrayed him, eventually dies from jealousy and sorrow.

In the end, an extreme sense of duty wins out over love. Instead of running off and finding happiness with the duke, the princess renounces what she considers a debased love. She enters a convent.

Sarkozy found *La princesse de Clèves* excruciating. During the presidential campaign, he railed that an official who decided to include questions about the princess in an exam for people applying for public-sector jobs was "a sadist or an idiot—you decide." He huffed that it would be "a spectacle" to ask low-level ticket agents their opinion of this difficult work. After he was elected president, Sarkozy felt compelled to attack the princess again, this time using a peculiar phrasing. "I have suffered a lot on her," he said.

But taking on the princess was not a wise political move in a country that prizes the rituals of seduction, romance, and intellectual discussion. Sarkozy was branded a literary midget for attacking what is considered one of France's best-written and most psychologically sophisticated novels.

I had my own theory: that the literal-minded, impatient, and thrice-married Sarkozy could not accept the ending. Unlike so many of his countrymen, he did not believe in foreplay that seemed to go nowhere. Without gratification, and as instantly as possible, the effort was not worth it.

Richard Descoings, the director of the elite Institut d'études politiques de Paris, known as Sciences Po, agreed with that notion. "No action, no result," he told me in explaining the president's antipathy for *la princesse*. "This is not a crime novel where at the end you know who kills the victim."

For many people in the academic and literary establishment, reading the book became an act of revolt against Sarkozy, whose blunt rejection of artistic pursuits and liberal political ideas had already made him a magnet for scorn. Sales of the book soared. The Paris book fair one year sold out of blue-and-white badges saying, "I'm reading *La princesse de Clèves*."

By 2009, the book had become a symbol of rebellion among university faculty protesting Sarkozy's proposed package of economic reforms. At an informal seminar at the University of Chicago's Paris campus, Sophie Rabau, a Sorbonne professor who had taken up the cause of the princess, described Sarkozy's statement that he had suffered a lot "on" the princess as a "lecherous" and "concrete" sexual allusion. "He is the horseman and she is his horse," she said. "A man is sweating on top of a woman, which contradicts the ethereal literary universe of the princess."

The truth is that Nicolas Paul Stéphane Sarkozy de Nagy-Bocsa is unskilled as a seducer in the classic French mode. Sarkozy is frank rather than indirect, prone to naked flattery and insults rather than subtle wooing, perpetually in motion rather than taking time for *le plaisir*. He is contemptuous rather than enamored of the complicated codes of politesse. Unlike François Mitterrand, who used language to caress and mesmerize, Sarkozy contracts his words and salts his sentences with rough slang. In a country where food and wine are essential to the national identity, he prefers snack gobbling to meal savoring.

Sarkozy is more than just a departure from the historic pattern of seductive leaders in France. He is a case study in anti-seduction.

Sarkozy's refusal to fit the expectations of French refinement stems in part from a lifelong habit of underdog belligerence. The son of a minor Hungarian aristocrat who abandoned the family, the grandson of a Sephardic Jew who converted to Catholicism, the product of France's outdated state university system and not its *grandes écoles*, he wears the pain of the outsider as both a burden and a badge of honor.

Sarkozy is so sensitive about his short stature (the Élysée is secretive about his height, but I would say he is no taller than five feet seven) that he uses a variety of techniques to appear taller. He wears shoes with thick heels. He has been known to stand on a stool when delivering a speech. (That trick has prompted cartoonists to portray him perched on a chair, or even more cruelly, as a dwarf.) Then there is the tiptoe maneuver. Sarkozy sometimes walks on the balls of his feet, a habit that gives him a distinctive, slightly off-balance bounce. The British tabloid *Daily Mail* ran a photograph of Sarkozy on his tiptoes with the much-taller Barack Obama in Strasbourg in 2009. To make sure the readers got the message, the paper circled Sarkozy's feet.

Sarkozy has called himself a "little Frenchman of mixed blood," even though he shortened his name to make it sound less exotic. His father, after all, had told him that with his foreign-sounding name, he would never be president of France. "For that," he said, "you have to go to the United States."

But Sarkozy worked his entire professional life through the party structure of the center-right UMP, and the party delivered. He ran an unusually disciplined campaign—American style—for president in 2007, and he hid his temper from public view.

The presidential election took place when the go-go economies of the United States and Britain made the French worry about being left behind. With the specter of economic stagnation pushing away other concerns, it was the right moment for the anti-seducer of French political life to make his move. In running for president, he sold competence over style and promised to break the chains of the past. He won not by reciting poems about beauty but by making promises that resonated with voters of different ages, classes, and priorities. Older, conservative men and women believed he would bring more law and order; younger voters felt he would make it easier for them to compete in the world economy; workers thought he would put more money in their pockets.

A believer in globalization, hard work, raw ambition, and the man on the street, Sarkozy at times seemed more American than French. "Subtlety is a French trait, as much as energy is an American trait," said Bertrand de Saint Vincent, a style columnist for *Le Figaro*. "We are less fat, we are less strong, but we compensate with subtlety. The French trait is a lightness and grace that can seduce. That's why Sarkozy isn't into seduction; he's into strength, and that's more American. The American bombards; the Frenchman is driven by lightness."

When Sarkozy spoke about France's future, he looked across the ocean to the United States. "The dream of French families is to have their young people go to American universities to study," he told an audience at Columbia University in October 2004, when he was finance minister, an exceptionally startling admission for a French cabinet member and one that he repeated as president. "When we go to the movies, it is to see American films. When we turn on our radios, it is to listen to American music. We love the United States!"

During a trip to the United States two years later, when he was interior minister, Sarkozy worked so hard to fit in that he struggled to speak English. I overheard him trying to make conversation with Nicholas Scoppetta, the New York City fire commissioner, at a ceremony honoring New York firefighters. This is what Sarkozy said: "I run. This morning. In Central Park. With T-shirt firefighters."

"Wonderful! Excellent!" Scoppetta replied, as if Sarkozy were a preschooler who needed positive reinforcement. Then Scoppetta turned to me and said, in a voice low enough that Sarkozy could not hear: "His English? He'd be the first to say he's a little embarrassed by it."

Sarkozy's unvarnished enthusiasm about imitating the United States seemed at first to work. But it was unlikely to endear him in the long run to the French, whose sense of national character is deeply imbued with notions of their superiority. And it looked a bit foolish when the Americans and British were hit hard by the bursting economic bubble in 2008, setting off a global financial meltdown.

A bigger problem is that even though they voted for him, the French just didn't fall in love with Sarkozy. They may not even have liked him. Once he was in office, economic events, the fear of change, the paralysis in the French economic system, and Sarkozy's own imperial style of governing all worked against him. Without a seductive aura to protect him, he was vulnerable. The pragmatist with a determination to modernize France now appeared as a cynic with a shifting set of beliefs and an overactive alpha-male personality. He couldn't stop himself from launching reforms that were ill-planned and smelled of desperation. Most of them went nowhere.

As he had never had a classic love affair with the woman that is France, the French people turned on him. Within a year they ranked him the worst president in the history of the Fifth Republic. And as the 2012 presidential election drew near, his popularity remained at historically low levels. Even so, nothing motivates Sarkozy like challenges and confrontation. "The more they attack me," he once said, "the bigger I become."

I never found Sarkozy a seductive interview subject. Indeed, it would not be going too far to say that he could be a boor. I saw that firsthand on the eve of the summit of the G-8 industrialized countries in June 2007. It was his third week in office, and he invited one journalist from each of the seven member countries other than France to the Élysée Palace for his first encounter with the foreign media as president.

He worked hard to be informal. Too informal for those of us who were used to elegance and protocol in interviews with heads of state. Sarkozy arrived more than thirty minutes late—in shirtsleeves. Before the hour-long conversation started, he ordered us to turn off what he called "these things"—the recording devices we had laid out on the long, wide table. The Élysée was not recording the interview either. There would be no transcript, no record of his first interview as president with foreign journalists. That gave him total deniability.

We needn't have worried; in terms of its content, the interview was unenlightening. More revelatory was Sarkozy's personal behavior. We did not have a relaxed man in front of us. He shifted uncomfortably, as if his body could not be contained in the gilded, brocade-covered armchair in which he sat. He casually leaned back in his chair and propped up one of his legs on the other, an incongruous sight in such a formal setting. At one point he swallowed whole a white pill almost an inch in diameter—without the benefit of water.

Even more surprising were his manners. On the table before him were four small china plates of assorted French charcuterie and cheeses. He ate from two of them but did not pass them around or offer them to us. The table was exceptionally wide, and so it would have been awkward for us to dare to serve ourselves. So we sat there watching as he chewed and talked, talked and chewed, without appearing to take a breath.

My second interview with him was even more unsettling. It was three months later, on the eve of his first trip as president to the United Nations General Assembly in New York. When Alison Smale, executive editor of the *International Herald Tribune*, and I arrived, Sarkozy greeted us with stiff handshakes and curt *bonjours*. He limped so noticeably that I almost asked him what was wrong. There was no smile.

During the hour-long interview, Sarkozy rocked back and forth in his armchair as if he couldn't wait for us to leave. He gripped the backs of the chairs on either side of him. His jaw muscles twitched. He stumbled twice on the word "multilateralism," laughing like an embarrassed schoolboy the second time he did so. Jean-David Levitte, his national security adviser, had to finish the word for him.

Sarkozy interrupted and even insulted us. At one point, when I pressed him on France and NATO, he replied, "I want to pay homage to your stubbornness, to the concern you have for raising burning issues in a perfectly banal way." I scribbled in a note to Alison, "Something is really wrong." We learned afterward that his marriage to his wife, Cécilia, was shattering that week.

The cold demeanor and nonstop movement vanished during a brief photo session afterward in his private presidential office next door, only to be replaced by another version of tone-deaf behavior. He closed the distance between us, gripping his arms around our shoulders and pulling us close for a photograph. "Mmm. I have a good job," he murmured. Sarkozy needed to make clear that he was the man, and we were the women.

It was a tactic he had used on the presidential campaign. At a café in the tripe pavilion at the massive Rungis food market outside of Paris, he kissed a waitress on both cheeks. Then he put his arms around two women in his press entourage, proclaiming, "I have an enormous success with girls!"

On another campaign stop, at a cheesemaking factory in the French Alps, Sarkozy wrapped an arm around the shoulder of an apron-clad female employee and kissed her on both cheeks. "I'm kissing you, eh," he said. "Look how good-looking we are! My heart is pounding!"

In a book about her year on the campaign trail with him, the playwright Yasmina Reza described how hard Sarkozy worked to convince her of his seductive side. Seated next to her at a dinner in Nice, he smiled at her and recounted his conversation with the blond woman sitting on his other side. "She's telling me, 'I dream about you every night,'" Sarkozy told Reza. "Isn't that moving?"

Sarkozy put his hand on the woman's bare back and continued: "She's charming, this girl. Have you seen how this one's decked out? Nothing cheap there." In the next breath he asked Reza: "Have you tried the white chocolate mousse?"

Reza replied, "Nicolas, behave; don't forget you want to be president."

But restraint is not in Sarkozy's DNA. France has a ministerial system with a clear division of labor: the prime minister is responsible for day-to-day governance while the president is more remote and above the fray, leading the country and taking responsibility for foreign and defense affairs. Sarkozy felt he had to do both jobs. Policy was run out of the Élysée, not the ministries. In a sense, France lost its president, because the president was trying to run the country himself; it also lost its prime minister because the president had crushed him.

Sarkozy's meddling in the tiniest of policy decisions fuels his short temper. This is a man who is so impatient that he has whistled to get the attention of aides, called for the elimination of the Foreign Ministry because it is "useless," and branded his press spokesman an "*imbécile*" during an interview on American television, before walking off the set.

One of the most detailed critiques of Sarkozy's governing style came in a series of classified U.S. diplomatic cables disclosed by WikiLeaks in the fall of 2010. They portrayed him as a "hyperactive," "mercurial," "authoritarian," and "thin-skinned" leader who tyrannizes his ministers and staff. Charles Rivkin, the American ambassador to France, said in one cable that Sarkozy functions in "a zone of monarch-like impunity," surrounded by advisers often too afraid to give him honest advice, and too impatient to plan or consult with other countries before launching "impulsive proposals" that often go nowhere. Rivkin also reported that Sarkozy's aides were so fearful of angering him that they supposedly rerouted his plane over Paris in 2009 to avoid his seeing the Eiffel Tower lit up in the colors of the Turkish flag in honor of an official visit by Turkey's prime minister. (Sarkozy opposes Turkey's bid to join the European Union.) In another cable, a U.S. diplomat said that Sarkozy seemed "less than gracious" during a visit to Saudi Arabia, refusing to try traditional Arab food and looking bored during the televised arrival sword ceremony.

"I shouldn't say this because it's politically incorrect," a Foreign Ministry official once told me. "Sarkozy—he's very un-French. It's not like the good old days with the formal politesse of the educated French, like all those American movies where the French servant is saying, '*Oui, monsieur.*' Courtesies and rituals don't cross his mind."

Subtlety also eludes him. According to Tom Fletcher, the private secretary to the former British prime minister Gordon Brown, Sarkozy once told Brown, "You know, Gordon, I should not like you. You are Scottish, we have nothing in common, and you are an economist. But somehow, Gordon, I love you." Sarkozy felt he had to qualify his love, adding, "But not in a sexual way."

Before meeting King Abdullah of Saudi Arabia, Sarkozy had to be told—gingerly—by his aides not to touch the body of the Saudi monarch in any way. When he tried to hug German chancellor Angela Merkel, her aides made clear that she needed her space. She couldn't stand his touching her all the time. Eventually, Merkel tolerated Sarkozy's hugging and sometimes even hugged him back.

There were times, however, when Sarkozy successfully used his style of "soft power" like a weapon of war. In 2008, during France's term as the holder of the rotating European Union presidency, he defused a crisis between Russia and Georgia. He went into action mode, traveling to

Moscow and Tbilisi and persuading the Russians to agree to withdraw their troops from key positions in Georgia. He returned France to the military wing of NATO after more than forty years, was instrumental in creating the G20 group of industrial nations, and took decisive measures when the financial crisis hit France.

Sometimes the rush to act has translated into damaging impulsiveness—the antithesis of both realpolitik and traditional French diplomacy, with its carefully plotted *opérations séduction*. Impulse was what led him to bound up several flights of stairs and burst into a conference room in Moscow after a meeting with Vladimir Putin. Sarkozy found himself on stage before the world's media, their cameras and recording devices trained on him. He was so winded, so off-balance that he was unable to speak clearly. Commentaries accompanying video clips posted on the Internet suggested that he was drunk. (He doesn't drink and never has.)

Even when he tried to be gallant he could be clumsy, as he was the time he kissed the hand of Secretary of State Hillary Clinton. As she walked up the steps of the Élysée Palace, Sarkozy took her right hand, raised it up too quickly toward his lips, and did not bend over far enough. He followed with a handshake and a pat on the back. She was so destabilized by all the movement that she lost her right shoe.

One way to understand Sarkozy's approach to seduction and politics is through his relationships with three tall, thin, beautiful brunettes who have been, or are, important in his life. There is the one who opposed him for the presidency in 2007, Ségolène Royal; the one who left him for another man, Cécilia Sarkozy; and the one who simultaneously stepped into the roles of wife and first lady, Carla Bruni.

When the storm over *La princesse de Clèves* first broke during the presidential campaign, Pierre Assouline, a leading novelist, biographer, and journalist, suggested on his blog for *Le Monde* that one of the reasons Sarkozy so disliked the fictional heroine was that she reminded him of Ségolène Royal. Assouline called it likely that Sarkozy saw in the princess the "unbearable metaphor" of the opposition candidate, who was called, among other things, "the woman in white," "the singing nun," "Snow White," "the socialist Immaculate Conception," and "Joan of Arc."

Ségo drove Sarko crazy right from the start. With her elegant profile, elite education, and stratospheric approval ratings, she seemed to have all of the seductive gifts that eluded him. Her imagined France was one of pleasure seeking. The title of her campaign association and website, which she described as a dialogue with the French people, was Desires for the Future. In two early polls, she edged past Sarkozy in a hypothetical runoff for the presidency.

Royal, however, was running on a Socialist Party ticket in a time when unbridled market capitalism seemed globally triumphant. A political infighter with a sharp tongue, she was not universally loved even within her own party. And as the first female presidential candidate from a major party, she was challenging tradition. "Who will look after the children?" quipped Laurent Fabius, a former Socialist prime minister. Another prominent Socialist, Jack Lang, declared, "The presidential race is not a beauty contest."

Ségo played with her sexuality, sometimes flaunting it, sometimes hiding it, a constant manipulation that for a while boosted her mystery and appeal on the campaign trail. She had work done on her mouth. When she had an upper tooth straightened, the newspaper *Libération* labeled it an un-French act, writing, "The French people's favorite Socialist is now endowed with an American smile."

The summer before the election, a celebrity gossip magazine published photographs of Ségo emerging from the sea in a turquoise bikini. Her breasts were ample and firm, her thighs cellulite-free. Her tummy gave no hint that she had borne four children. Later, the stand-up comic and actor Jamel Debbouze said he hoped that if Royal were elected president, the bikini photo would become her official portrait in every French police station.

As the campaign began in earnest, however, Ségo buttoned herself up and shed the flouncy skirts and gamine-like spirit that had led swooning male commentators to compare her to Audrey Hepburn. For the presidential debate with Sarkozy shortly before the election, she donned a tailored suit and a severe manner, aware that this was her best chance to prove herself.

Royal was on the offensive from the start. She interrupted Sarkozy with the line, "Let me finish," and defended her moments of anger.

"Calm down," he told her at one point.

"No, I will not calm down!" she replied. "No, I will not calm down! I will not calm down!"

"To be president of the Republic, you have to be calm," Sarkozy said, his voice taking on a patronizing tone. The scene was reminiscent of a couple bickering at the breakfast table, with the husband barely restraining his sense of superiority and the wife attacking him for not listening to her. The impact, though, was to rob Royal of her sensuality. Sarkozy kept his notorious temper in check; he neutralized her appeal, and when the votes were counted, he defeated her soundly.

When Sarkozy won the presidency, the first lady he brought along was Cécilia. He had met her twenty-three years earlier while officiating, as mayor of Neuilly-sur-Seine, at her wedding—to someone else. She was in her midtwenties at the time and very pregnant; her groom was a French television personality and singer almost twice her age. She and her husband began socializing with Sarkozy and his first wife. The two couples became close—until Nicolas and Cécilia took up with each other, then moved in together.

In their first days at the Élysée, admirers called Nicolas and Cécilia the French Kennedys: the president outdoorsy and athletic, the first lady beautiful and designer-dressed, the passel of children smiling and photogenic. A four-page spread in *Elle* on Cécilia (who had once moonlighted as an in-house model at Schiaparelli and Chanel) posed the question, "Something of Jackie?" The article ran side-by-side photos of the two first ladies, pointing out that Cécilia, like Jackie Kennedy, was "adept at minimalism," had "a prima donna style," embraced sports "as a way of life," and had "always been casual."

Le Figaro splashed an Internet poll on its front page under the headline, "The Sarkozy style seduces the French." Their detractors suggested that the Sarkozys were less like the Kennedys than like Italy's Prime Minister Silvio Berlusconi and his clan: showy, vulgar, acquisitive, more *nouveau riche* than old money.

Sarkozy's first act on the night of his electoral victory was to dine with Cécilia, other family members, and friends at Fouquet's, the glitzy century-old Champs-Élysées restaurant that had been bought by a luxury hotel group. His postelection victory trip with Cécilia and their son Louis aboard the yacht of a billionaire friend was mercilessly criticized. "You cannot identify with General de Gaulle and behave like Silvio Berlusconi," the philosopher Alain Finkielkraut wrote in *Le Monde*.

Soon Cécilia was missing from the presidential picture. Rumors came, with uneasy persistence, that she had left home. She was a no-show for a picnic lunch with President George W. Bush and his wife, Laura, in New England.

Cécilia had left Sarkozy once before, for Richard Attias, an events manager, in the summer of 2005. But she had returned several months later, and the couple had again appeared devoted. "Even today, it's hard for me to talk about it," Sarkozy wrote of their months apart in his 2006 campaign book, *Testimony*. "I never could have imagined being so devastated." He also said they would never again part, adding, "We're incapable of being apart. It's not that we haven't tried, but it's impossible."

Now it was clear that she had left for good, to marry Attias and move to New York. "France elected a man, not a couple," she said in an interview with the regional newspaper *L'Est Républicain*. "What happened to me has happened to millions of people: one day you no longer have your place in the couple."

The French embraced the news of the divorce with sangfroid and a collective shrug. In a poll conducted after the news broke, 79 percent declared *le divorce* of "little or no importance" in the country's political life. But without a woman by his side, Sarkozy was humiliated. His solitary existence became the butt of jokes. On Europe 1 radio, the comedian Nicolas Canteloup, impersonating Sarkozy, asked the host for help with a lonely-hearts ad. "I am going to put down, 'young man, athletic man, practicing jogging, recently divorced, in a good situation, looking for a serious woman for a relationship,'" he said.

The comic was interrupted by a call from a woman who identified herself as Ségolène Royal, who by this time had broken off with her own longtime partner, François Hollande. "It's not Madame Royal, but Mademoiselle Royal," the woman (also portrayed by Canteloup) said. She added that for some time she had wanted the job of France's first lady but confessed that Sarkozy was not her "type of man."

In the real life drama of Nicolas Sarkozy, the stage was set for Carla Bruni.

The "*Bonjour*" came out soft and smooth, part whisper and part song. As the mouth uttered the second syllable, the lips moved forward to form an O, and the O lingered on her breath. She said the word over and over, to the two pilots, the three security officers, the communications technician, the photographer, and the two journalists traveling with her on the thirteen-seat French military jet. The movement of these lips mesmerized. I couldn't stop staring at her mouth, waiting for the next word to fall.

Carla Bruni was traveling to Burkina Faso, her first official solo trip as first lady and as the first ambassador for the Geneva-based Global Fund to Fight AIDS, Tuberculosis, and Malaria. She had invited me and Anne-Florence Schmitt, the editor of the magazine *Madame Figaro*, on the overnight trip—a personal experiment in burnishing her image and projecting the soft power of France.

During the flight, she did not spend her time memorizing her talking points and statistics on AIDS in Africa; she was savoring *Le Horla*, Guy de Maupassant's short novel about anguish and insanity, pinching the edge of each page as she turned it, in slow motion. When one of the pilots brought her a heated hand towel on a silver tray, she unfolded it and pressed it between her two hands as if in prayer, closing her eyes and rubbing her open palms up and down slowly along the piece of warm fabric.

This was an encounter with a modern-day woman with the manners of an eighteenth-century courtesan, skilled in the art of movement and the rituals of conversation. If Sarkozy is an exemplar of anti-seduction,

Carla has the gifts to be his counterpoint and balance—a woman whose own mastery at attracting and charming others can translate into a clear political asset.

From afar, Carla is beautiful: about five feet ten, with a lean, long-limbed model's body and a high-cheekboned face that kisses the camera. But close up, she is not a fairy-tale bonbon of perfection. On this trip, her hair hung straight and thin. The tiniest of jowls were forming on both sides of her jaw. Her eyelids were slightly hooded. She confessed that her face had been lasered. She had her nose redone twice, the first time decades ago after it was broken, according to one of her intimates. It was the blend of vulnerability and ease that pulled me in.

As we talked, I came to realize where her true power lies and why so many men—from Eric Clapton to Mick Jagger—have been entranced. It is her voice. She has a dangerous voice, the voice of the Siren, the most ancient seductress of all. Lyrical, low, liquid, foreign, it does not rush but flows and relaxes and caresses. Carla was born Italian but has lived in France most of her life. Her perfect French and near-perfect, lightly slanged English have a touch of Italian.

In the two days I spent with her, her voice never became high-pitched or aggressive, even when I asked pointed questions about her personal life. Her speech pattern stayed slow, as if she had just stepped out of bed and had all the time in the world. At one point, we plunged into a discussion about the nuisance of phone taps by intelligence agencies and whether they inhibited phone sex with a spouse. But she never offered a definition of phone sex, and I realized afterward that I might have misunderstood. Phone sex for an American is simulating the sex act on the phone; for Carla, it might just be talking for a while in her normal voice.

At first blush, Carla Bruni seemed to lack the right profile to be the first lady of France. An heiress to an Italian tire-manufacturing fortune, she moved with her family to France as a child, studied art in Paris, became a fashion model, then turned to singing. Her politics were to the left, Sarkozy's to the right. She was savaged by some in the media as a sex-crazed foreigner—nude photos of her taken years ago were circulated on the Internet, and she herself had fueled the stories of her racy past. She had described herself as a "tamer of men," had called monogamy "terribly boring," and had declared herself faithful—to herself. Bruni was apparently the inspiration for a despicable character in *Rien de Grave* (*Nothing Serious*), a roman à clef by Justine Lévy, the daughter of the philosopher-writer Bernard-Henri Lévy and the former wife of the philosopher and radio show host Raphaël Enthoven, who left her and took up with Bruni shortly afterward. He was twenty-four; Bruni was thirty-two.

In the novel, Justine Lévy describes a Bruni-like character who has had plastic surgery and is "a leech of a woman," with "a Terminator smile" and the "look of a killer." The Enthoven-like character is bewitched by this woman as soon as they meet. Enthoven and Bruni insist that they began seeing each other three months after he had left Lévy; what was more unsettling was that Enthoven's father, Jean-Paul, one of France's leading literary editors, had been courting Bruni at the time. Carla Bruni and Raphaël Enthoven never married, but they had a son. In the spring of 2007, after they had been together for nearly seven years, Raphaël Enthoven decided to end the relationship.

The lives of Nicolas Sarkozy and Carla Bruni changed the night they met. They were brought together in November 2007 at a small dinner party hosted by Jacques Séguéla, the French advertising mogul and a friend of both of them. Séguéla included luscious details of the love-at-first-sight encounter in a memoir published in 2009. In the book, Sarkozy tells Bruni how delighted he is to meet a beautiful woman who smokes and drinks. He dismisses her past, saying, "My reputation is no worse than yours." He predicts that they will announce their wedding engagement and will be a better fit than Marilyn Monroe and John F. Kennedy.

"Engagement, never!" she replies. "From now on I will only live with a man who gives me a child." He takes her home. When she invites him in for coffee, he demurs. "Never on a first date," he says.

When I read passages from this book to Bruni as we flew back to Paris from Ouagadougou, an amused look came over her face. I could see that she was struggling: Should she deny everything? Say it was an exaggeration?

"I haven't read much of it, what Jacques said, but he was there," Carla said.

Séguéla quotes Carla as telling Sarkozy that he is "an amateur" in dealing with the celebrity press. "My relationship with Mick Jagger lasted eight years in secrecy—I disguised myself," she says in Séguéla's telling.

When I asked her about these lines, she denied ever talking about Jagger. "I never talk about Mick! I kept my habit. I'm just always surprised hearing quotes from myself that I never said."

Months later, I broached the story of The Dinner That Changed French History over coffee with Séguéla. He said he had reconstructed the dinner conversation from memory a few days later with the help of his wife, then gave it to Sarkozy and Bruni for a final vetting. He said they did not request changes. "Carla and Nicolas told me, 'We want this to be written as it happened, and you wrote it, unadorned, just as it happened,'" he said.

As he talked about how the evening unfolded, Séguéla described a Carla the world already knew, but also a private side of Sarkozy that few have seen. "It was an unexpected game of seduction between two wild animals," he said. "The two are *grands séducteurs*." He explained that he launched the conversation in telling them both to amuse themselves by playing their "seduction number." So everyone started playacting, as if it were a salon game with the task: "You have three minutes to seduce me."

"Like speed dating?" I asked.

"It was less formal than that," he said. "And then all of a sudden, in fifteen, twenty minutes, fiction became reality. The game became real life. In France, we have an expression that says, '*Ils se sont pris au jeu*'—They've been caught up in the game."

"So everything in the book is true, even what Sarkozy said about Mick Jagger's 'ridiculous calves'?"

"Absolutely," said Séguéla. "And besides, Jagger phoned Carla, saying to her gently, 'But listen, you could at least have defended my calves!'"

At first, the "Carla effect" worked against the president. While the French faced the New Year in 2008 with higher prices and a decline in their buying power, Sarkozy was touring the pyramids of Egypt in a whirlwind, paparazzi-documented romance with Bruni. An editorial in *L'Est Républicain*, whose readers live far from sophisticated Paris, opined: "He forgot that he should have a romance with France and not with himself and his paramour."

The French criticized the *People*-magazine style of their marriage, just eleven and a half weeks after their first meeting, and three and a half months after Sarkozy's divorce from Cécilia. At a formal dinner for the Israeli president, Shimon Peres, at the Élysée, Simone Veil, a French former cabinet minister and survivor of Auschwitz, declined to shake Carla's hand.

But Carla learned how to play the role of first lady even while keeping her career as a singer. She transformed the position from long-suffering pillar of support to bread-winning symbol of independence. She opened the private quarters of the Élysée to photographers from magazines like *Paris Match* and *Vanity Fair*. She turned demure, donning a gray midcalf Dior coatdress and matching pillbox hat and doing a perfect curtsy for the Queen of England. She wore flat ballerina slippers and kitten heels so as not to be too much taller than her short spouse. As an experienced ex-model, she assumed a goody-goody persona, looking down modestly, not up haughtily, at the camera lenses of the photographers who followed her.

Her approval ratings soared to more than double her husband's.

A passionate believer in psychoanalysis (she has been in psychoanalysis for well over a decade and once told an interviewer her dream was to train to become a psychoanalyst), Carla also made it her mission to change Nicolas. She told me she put him on a diet; he lost weight. She helped cure his migraines by persuading him to stop eating refined sugar and to break his chocolate addiction. She helped relieve his backaches by getting him to use her personal trainer. She tried—with mixed results—to curb his fits of anger. Soon his aides began asking before a trip whether she would be coming along. For the first two years of his presidency, Sarkozy had been ostentatious in his rejection of the arts. Then he began to be photographed with Marcel Proust's *Remembrance of Things Past* under his arm. On his Facebook page he bragged that he was reading *Pierre et Jean* by Guy de Maupassant and *Le lièvre de Patagonie* by Claude Lanzmann.

"You're reading?" one of Sarkozy's friends asked him in disbelief.

Sarkozy replied, "You tried for twenty years. It took Carla twenty days."

At times, Bruni seemed to be in charge, with Sarkozy following her lead. She was as soft as a kitten but tough like a man. She had the handshake grip of a wrestler and the cunning of a predator. She flirted with both women and men. Her manner wasn't necessarily sexual, but it enchanted the object of her desire.

She didn't seem to care what others thought of her. She reportedly told Michelle Obama that she and Sarkozy had been late to meet a foreign head of state because they were having sex, a story recounted by journalist Jonathan Alter in his book *The Promise*. "Bruni wanted to know if, like the Sarkozys, Michelle and the president had ever kept anyone waiting that way," Alter wrote. "Michelle laughed nervously and said no."

Her respect for her role as first lady did not stop her from writing lines in her new songs about orgasms and, most notoriously, about smoking her lover like a joint. In recordings, she included lyrics like: "I am a child / despite my forty years / despite my thirty lovers, a child." (She said that she never actually counted her lovers and chose the number thirty for its lyrical value.)

On our trip to Africa, Carla embraced small talk, telling me that Sean Connery was the best James Bond and that women should stop wearing makeup when they reach the age of twenty-five. She also turned confessional: she longed to have a child with Sarkozy but might be too old for it to happen; she hated politics and dinner parties. An American first lady would have stayed on topic, no matter what.

I asked Bruni if she was a predator, as others have called her. She formed her hands into claws. "Grrrrrrrrrrrrrrrr," she growled, rolling her Rs, Italian-style. "No, I don't feel like a lion or a tiger," she said. "I was never as wild!" She laughed.

I asked what comments by the news media were most painful. "The only stories I found unbearable were that Nicolas and I got married because of ambition, ambition for me, to have such a grand position, ambition for him, to get a woman from another world," she said. "I don't see who these people think they are."

One day, while Bruni was doing an interview with the women's magazine *Femme Actuelle* in the private quarters of the Élysée Palace, Sarkozy dropped in unannounced.

"Voilà, as soon as there are women around, voilà, as soon as there are ladies . . . ," she said when he arrived.

They kissed. Sarkozy perched himself on the arm of a chair, next to Bruni. She lightly rubbed his thigh.

"Oh là là. She's in great shape, huh, the first lady?" Sarkozy said. He added that he had had a meeting earlier that day with the prime minister of Iraq.

"Cool!" Bruni responded.

Then Sarkozy announced that he had been exercising and had just got out of the shower. He put his hand on Bruni's shoulder and rubbed it. After a bit more chitchat, he stood up to leave.

"*Bon courage, Chouchou!*" Bruni called out as he departed. *Chouchou* more or less means "sweetheart."

The video clip of Sarkozy's "surprise" visit—whether it was staged or not was an open question—became a worldwide hit on the Internet. *Femme Actuelle* posted a video of interview excerpts on its website. Sarkozy apparently liked the video so much that it became one of the first links on his Facebook page.

Other elements of the page suggested, however, that some of Bruni's lessons about refined appearances and subtle self-presentation might not have taken. Sarkozy's Facebook photo showed him tanned and grinning broadly, the top three buttons of his white shirt undone.

Under occupation, he had written, "Head of State."

14

The Civilizing Mission

. . .

> The emotional side of me tends to imagine France, like the princess in the fairy stories or the Madonna in the frescoes, as dedicated to an exalted and exceptional destiny. . . . France cannot be France without greatness.
>
> —Charles de Gaulle, *War Memoirs*

> Without France, the world would be alone.
>
> —Victor Hugo

Bernard Kouchner may have been France's top diplomat, but I wouldn't describe him as diplomatic.

A cofounder of the Nobel Prize–winning relief organization Doctors Without Borders, he challenged authority, destroyed convention, insulted opponents, and made up rules along the way. In the early 1990s, when he was filmed wading ashore in Somalia carrying sacks of rice provided for the starving by French schoolchildren, he was criticized for staging a manipulative media stunt. The satirical television puppet show, *Les Guignols*, features the puppet Kouchner permanently carrying a sack of rice on his shoulder.

Elegant, dapper, with movie-star looks despite his age (he is in his seventies), Kouchner had been France's most popular politician on the left for years before he joined the cabinet of the center-right government of Nicolas Sarkozy as foreign minister in 2007. Kouchner even fantasized about running for president himself. I once asked him whether anyone could beat Sarkozy in a presidential election. "Me, I believe!" he exclaimed. "I am not so arrogant to say I'm serious, but I'm more popular than he is."

"Do you *want* to be president?" I asked.

"Of course!" he replied. "It would be fun. It's not so hard."

No one has ever accused Kouchner of self-doubt.

At a reception at the residence of the American ambassador in January 2010, I was deep in conversation with Richard Holbrooke, President Obama's special representative on Afghanistan and Pakistan, when Kouchner joined us. Holbrooke and I were seated on a couch too small for the three of us, so Kouchner went down on bended knee.

I had known both men for more than twenty-five years, and although they were old and close friends, their styles were different. Holbrooke was at times charming, at times brutal, always strategic and well briefed; Kouchner was always charming, infuriatingly disorganized, and often unconcerned about the details of his portfolios. He addressed women—and men—as "my dear."

With Kouchner, formality could slide into familiarity with speed that could be disconcerting. "I'm with you . . . not enough," Kouchner said to me in English.

Holbrooke interrupted. He urged Kouchner to get serious and tell his Kosovo seduction story. So together, the duo recalled the time in 1999 when Kouchner had just been appointed the United Nations chief administrator for Kosovo. The UN secretary-general, Kofi Annan, and Holbrooke were fierce supporters of Kouchner; Madeleine Albright, the U.S. secretary of state, had opposed his appointment. She had never met Kouchner, but she had heard he was difficult. On top of that, he was French, and it has long been a staple of Washington lore that France can be an unreliable ally. She had told Annan that the appointment was a "mistake."

Kouchner discovered that Albright was vacationing in Innsbruck, Austria. He flew there from Paris to call on her. Before their meeting, he ventured into a field and picked her a bouquet of edelweiss.

"Like *The Sound of Music*," Holbrooke said.

Kouchner evoked an idealized vision of Albright's roots in the mountains of central Europe (even though she was born in a big city, Prague).

"I told her that she came from the mountains and from the flowers and that I was giving her more of them," Kouchner said. "And it was done!"

Kouchner turned her around.

"This is a true story," said Holbrooke.

"Well, yes, of course this is true! Obviously, it's true," said Kouchner. "And since then, Madeleine and I are friends."

"Isn't that the perfect story!" Holbrooke exclaimed. "It's Bernard at his best, really using seduction to solve an international problem!"

Indeed, in her memoirs, Albright wrote that Kouchner had arrived at their first encounter with edelweiss. She confessed she had found him irresistible. "As soon as we sat down, he said, 'I hear you don't like me,'" she wrote. "I tried to resist, but within minutes he was telling me all about his hopes for Kosovo. I was impressed by his deep convictions, humanity, knowledge and dedication."

And maybe by his charm as well. For all of his flaws, Kouchner, as Albright discovered, was hard to resist. While he was on bent knee next to Holbrooke and me, he balanced himself by firmly putting his right hand on my left knee. It was not a sexual advance but an instinctive act. Kouchner probably didn't notice that he was gripping the knee of a female American journalist or think about what it would look like in a photograph.

At least I was wearing pants.

Months later, at a reception Kouchner hosted after the screening of a new French film, he was just as hands-on. He took a bottle of red wine from a waiter and poured for his guests. He passed around a platter of chocolate cakes. "Look at this service!" he said. "You see, the French touch!"

As I was leaving, Kouchner kissed me—loudly—on both cheeks. "Don't forget that I'm in love with you!" he said.

I didn't know whether to be flattered, amused, or insulted. I know he says this to all the girls. The guys, too, I think.

What is diplomacy if not one never-ending seduction? You assemble all your best arguments and wrap them in pretty packaging to create a relationship with the other side. If you're strategic and clever and come to the table with attractive incentives, you may prevail. If the other side is also strong and determined, you compromise. The seduction may take one phone call between heads of state or decades of mind-numbing negotiations among teams of experts. It may take the forgiveness of a debt, the delivery of high-tech weaponry, a creative argument, or a humble bouquet of edelweiss.

Certainly, France has weapons other than words. It is a nuclear power and one of only five permanent members, with a veto, on the United Nations Security Council. It has a well-equipped and well-trained military, with troops deployed in places like Afghanistan and the Ivory Coast. It has a knowledgeable foreign-policy elite. It has the capacity to export its technical achievements: its passenger jets, high-speed trains, and nuclear reactors. This means that France is taken seriously on the global stage and that it projects a sense of power greater than its physical size, population, and economy might warrant.

But France's capability to use force to subdue others disappeared long ago. It was the dominant power in the world for a relatively short time—about 150 years between the victories of Louis XIV in the seventeenth century and the defeats of Napoléon in the nineteenth. Since then, it has had to rely more on powers of persuasion. In the years since World War II, France has had to adapt to its stature as a relatively minor power, learning how and when to woo the wider world. France is too weak an economic and military power to counterbalance the United States but too strong and too strong-willed to take orders from it. In addition, it has to compete with two sets of powers: established ones like the United States, Russia, and China, and emerging ones like Brazil and India, whose strengths and potential on many fronts are greater than its own. Natural as it may seem for a country skilled in the arts of seduction to win this contest, the record is uneven. In a permanent wound to its pride, it has lost one of its most powerful weapons—the supremacy of the French language, which long ago ceased to be the language of international diplomacy.

France is both blessed and cursed by the remnant of its colonial philosophy: its *mission civilisatrice*, or civilizing mission. This was the governing principle of French colonial rule in the late nineteenth and early twentieth centuries. In practice, French colonialism was exploitative, coercive, and often brutal. But as part of its mission as a world power, France felt it had a duty and a unique role among the European countries to bring light to the dark corners of Africa and Asia by "civilizing" their populations. This conviction was based on the belief in the superiority of French culture and the perfectibility of mankind.

Other colonial powers—the British, the Dutch, the Germans—conquered to enhance their wealth and power. They treated their subjects as "the other" and so allowed them to keep their customs and traditions. Wealth and power motivated France as well. But it adorned this imperial mission with a costume of "civilization"—and tried to assimilate the people it conquered. The French told the colonized that by adopting its culture, values, and language, they too could become model French subjects and, in some places, even citizens.

This has made France a country experienced in the art of "soft power," getting others to do one's bidding through attraction rather than coercion. The French have long sought to fine-tune the skills to woo, cajole, and persuade, at the negotiating table and on the ground. "If you look at the countries using soft power and the culture of public diplomacy, the French have been the pioneers," said Joseph Nye, the Harvard University scholar who coined the phrase.

But the art of influencing others through attraction (translated into French as *séduction*) often fails. The assumption that the rest of the world wants to dress like the French, live like the French, speak like the French, and become French is beautiful in concept but flawed in reality. It failed in the French colonies, most spectacularly in Algeria.

Algeria's bloody and violent popular revolution toppled the Fourth Republic, leading to a complete French withdrawal in 1962. Algeria symbolized the rejection of France's civilizing mission. This defeat—along with humiliation, guilt, and resentment—still haunts the French consciousness.

French diplomats are schooled in a diplomatic tradition dating back to the glory days of the eighteenth century, when France's intellectual influence and military power were at their peak. The eighteenth-century Prussian emperor Frederick the Great preferred to speak French rather than his native German and built a French rococo palace, Sanssouci, near Berlin. Russia's Catherine the Great detested France but loved French culture and made French the language of her court; she corresponded with Voltaire and welcomed Diderot to Saint Petersburg. Until the 1970s, the Westernized elite in Iran spoke French, ate French food, watched French movies, hired French governesses; Shah Mohammad Reza Pahlavi wrote his memoirs in French. When I first visited Iran during the 1979 revolution, I was struck that French words permeated the Persian language, even *merci* for "thank you."

These days, however, in the practical realm of diplomacy and in an era of French decline, the talent for constructing elegant arguments can be beside the point. More important for successful negotiation are pragmatism and flexibility. That's because diplomacy requires mastery of both the art of conversation and the art of persuading the other to embrace your point of view. The brilliance that may work in the salon, and that may have worked better when France was acknowledged as the leader of the European world, doesn't travel well to the twenty-first-century negotiating table.

"You have to be supremely confident and work in the sense of playing the game and prolonging the process," Gérard Araud, a senior French diplomat, explained to me. "But seduction fails when you run up against someone who refuses to play the game. Then you need to have a plan B. But in the French system, if you have a plan B you're presupposing failure. That's part of our problem. We use the seduction of words. But we may not be pragmatic seducers."

Even when the French try to use flexibility to nudge the other side to compromise, cultural misunderstandings can make the process difficult. Araud told the story of torturous negotiations with an American counterpart in 1999 over new strategic rules for NATO. Araud took the position that the text had to specify that any military intervention should be in accordance with the United Nations Charter; the American diplomat rejected that condition.

"What happens if you want to intervene and the Russians block it with a veto?" the American asked.

"I intervene," Araud replied.

"I don't understand," the American said. "You want us to say 'according to the UN Charter' and you tell me that you're ready to violate the UN Charter?"

"Wait a minute," Araud said. "When you marry, you say that you'll be faithful to your wife. After that, then there is real life."

The American looked at him in horror.

"Obviously, we had a cultural misunderstanding," Araud later recalled. "I was trying to say that in life, you need principles. You do your best to stick to your principles, but it happens that you don't stick to your principles. But here, there was a cultural impasse. So I said to him, 'Okay, forget it! Forget it! Bad example!'"

The story had a happy ending. "The matter was resolved by the two presidents, Jacques Chirac and Bill Clinton," said Araud. "They both knew a lot about marital fidelity."

More often than not, however, the French approach is more rigid. Jean-David Levitte, who served as national security adviser for President Sarkozy, acknowledged the influence of France's intellectual heritage. "Our problem is Descartes," he said. "The British method is pragmatic, empirical. The British come to the table with the interests of the United Kingdom in mind. They try to understand French interests and find a way to move forward. We are educated to give brilliant presentations: A plus B, in two parts and two subparts. That means our diplomatic presentations conform 100 percent to the interests of France and the formal instructions we have received. And then we exasperate our counterparts by giving them an impeccable, unanswerable Cartesian argument that is 100 percent right. Logic and reason would require them to say, 'It's perfect! I surrender.'"

The only problem, Levitte added, is that in the real world it doesn't work. He called the practice the *maudite dissertation*—the cursed dissertation.

Levitte learned that lesson the hard way, when he was serving as

France's ambassador to the United States during the most serious diplomatic crisis between the two countries in nearly half a century. It was triggered by President Jacques Chirac's opposition to the decision by the Bush administration to wage war against Iraq in 2003. France's approval rating among Americans plunged from nearly 80 percent to about 30 percent, below those of Saudi Arabia and Libya. French products were boycotted. French wine was poured down kitchen sinks. Vacations to France were canceled. French fries became "freedom fries" in the House of Representatives' cafeteria. The image of the idealized Frenchman as a lady-killer who could undress you with a look and soothe you with a bedroom voice vanished from the mind of America. It was replaced by the stereotype of the arrogant, effete snob who talked through his nose. Chirac was portrayed as a worm and as Joan of Arc in drag.

I'm convinced that there would have been a crisis in relations with France over Iraq no matter how sweetly the French said no to war. But the French negotiating style made things worse. Chirac, his foreign minister, Dominique de Villepin, and much of the French elite looked at the prospect of war with Iraq through two prisms, history and Cartesian logic, not as an issue where their opposition should be framed in an *opération séduction.*

In an interview in the fall of 2003, Chirac told my editor Roger Cohen and me that his experience as a young lieutenant wounded in Algeria's war of independence had helped shape his thinking on Iraq. "In Algeria we began with a sizable army and huge resources, and the fighters for independence were only a handful of people," he said. "But they won. That's how it is." Algeria proved to him that a vast and powerful army could be defeated by a small group of determined adversaries convinced of their right to run their own country. "We know from experience that imposing a law on people from the outside hasn't worked for a long time," he said.

Chirac also constructed a logical argument: there was no hard evidence that Iraq was linked to the terrorist attacks of September 11, 2001, or was developing weapons of mass destruction. When Chirac delivered a similar message privately to President George W. Bush at the United Nations just days later, Bush replied, "Jacques, I couldn't disagree more."

There was another, unstated reason why France was opposed to war: its citizens, including its large Muslim and ethnic Arab population, were overwhelmingly against it.

The American side was responding emotionally: someone had to be punished for September 11. And any ally who did not join the effort was no longer considered a friend.

Many French officials and diplomats understand that saving face for the other side, especially an adversary, is crucial to the success of the seduction. "It's better to seduce than to fight when you want to conquer an enemy," said Claude de Kemoularia, a former French ambassador to the United Nations. "You don't show your strength immediately. You have to create an atmosphere in which you've won your point but your opponent doesn't think he's been defeated. That's the best seduction."

During his time at the UN in the 1980s, Kemoularia had launched his own *opération séduction* as a means of reinforcing French influence there. He managed to fly himself and the other fourteen ambassadors of the Security Council on an all-expenses-paid trip via the Concorde to celebrate the annual grape harvest at the Château du Clos de Vougeot, one of the greatest vineyards in Burgundy. He raised private money to pay for it; it did not cost the French state a cent.

However, seduction is sometimes outweighed by the French love for romantic audacity in diplomacy and war. As Charles Cogan wrote in his book *French Negotiating Behavior*, slogans like "*Toujours de l'audace*" (Always Be Bold) and "*Impossible n'est pas français*" (Impossible Is Not French) feed into a taste for action and daring beyond common sense. The French have a tendency to use panache and bravura in the face of certain defeat. Such was the case in February 2003, during the Iraq crisis, when foreign minister Dominique de Villepin delivered the speech of a lifetime to the United Nations Security Council. Villepin is tall, elegant, handsome, and brilliant. Many of my women friends find him drop-dead gorgeous. But in this speech he failed the basic test of seduction: instead of finding common ground, he erected barriers.

Using the forum to slam the United States, he told the audience—and the world—that military action in Iraq was not justified. Essentially, he was telling the United States that France was right and the United States was wrong. On one level, Villepin played to the worst stereotype of the French diplomat: arrogant, self-righteous, narcissistic, and effete. He sounded as if he were talking down to the United States when he said, "This message comes to you today from an old [translation: wise] country, France." He won the applause of the chamber, but he humiliated and insulted the world's only superpower. As Alain Minc, the writer and unofficial political counselor to Sarkozy, said, "It was a magnificent gesture; it was stupid."

Years later, in retrospect, it was widely acknowledged that Villepin's message had been right. One after another, respected members of the American foreign policy establishment who had lined up to support the war effort came forward to confess that they had been wrong. Villepin had been one of the only opponents of the war to speak so clearly and passionately before the invasion of Iraq. "Dominique's speech was one of the most moving and strongest moments of my career," Gérard Araud told me. "The United States had lost its moral compass. He was saying what was right and what was wrong at a moment when nobody else in the world dared to do so. Sure, he delivered the message with his own style, as a *beau geste*. But he was right. And that is what matters." Yet Villepin's style had clearly done nothing to help influence the course of events, and for several years France's relationship with the United States suffered. Whether it was worth this sacrifice to take a principled stand is the kind of moral question that cuts close to the heart of all diplomacy.

There is irony that the diplomatic break between France and the United States happened during the Chirac presidency. Unlike Charles de Gaulle and François Mitterrand, who distrusted America, Chirac actually liked the United States. He also knew how to seduce by finding common ground with his partner or adversary. He was a man of the people—any people—and derived energy from plunging into crowds and sampling every sort of local food and drink.

Years before the war in Iraq, I traveled with Chirac from Washington to Chicago in the middle of a raging snowstorm. He was so eager to get there that when snow threatened to close down Andrews Air Force Base and prevent his departure the next morning, he decided to leave at midnight the night before. Our French Air Force jet bobbed and weaved through the stormy sky, and we arrived at our Chicago hotel at dawn. Chirac used slang-tinged English to sell himself and his country to America. He was praised for having received a special honor in his youth: a certificate from Howard Johnson's "for artistry in making banana splits." (He had worked as a part-time counterman to help support himself while attending Harvard summer school in 1953.) Chirac boasted another talent. Howard Johnson's "also had a very good turkey sandwich, which I did very, very well," he said. The audience applauded. He was down-to-earth, the Midwest's kind of French president.

He told American audiences the same stories over and over: how he worked as a forklift operator in an Anheuser-Busch factory in St. Louis and wrote a front-page article for the New Orleans *Times-Picayune*; how he hitchhiked across the United States; how he fell in love and was briefly engaged to a Southern belle named Florence Herlihy, who drove a white Cadillac convertible and called him "Honey Child." He wrote in his memoirs that he never contacted her after he returned to Paris, preferring to preserve the "delicious memory" of their romance.

I had also seen Chirac reach out effectively to more historically hostile audiences. He received a jubilant reception when he traveled to Algeria in 2003, the first state visit by a French president since the former colony won its independence in 1962. Hundreds of thousands of well-wishers turned out to shower him with confetti and flowers, to cheer and applaud him like a hero. Chirac was supposed to wave from his limousine, but instead he plunged into the crowd, zigzagging back and forth along the main boulevard like a driven man. Hungry for contact, he grabbed the hands of Algerians who had been kept back by iron railings. The policemen in white spats and gloves couldn't stop him. It didn't matter that the crowd was shouting "*Visa! Visa! Visa!*" and not "*Vive Chirac!*" That day, the failure of France's civilizing mission in Algeria, the violence and betrayal that seared the relationship was set aside. The Algerians seemed to be saying, "I want a visa to come to France and a chance to be like you." For Chirac, that was enough.

The French-American conflict over Iraq came to be about national identity. For both the United States and France, it underscored what the other was not. In the United States, Villepin was branded as "oleaginous" by one columnist and "diplomacy lite" by another. Instead of giving him pause, the criticism gave him more energy. He told me during one of our many conversations, "You grow with criticism; you are diminished with praise."

As foreign minister and then prime minister, Villepin saw himself as a modern-day Napoléon, a politician-warrior with a strong ego, a belief in the grandeur of France, and a conviction that he alone owned the truth. Even some of his closest aides considered him a bit mad and nicknamed him "Zorro." Following a champagne-filled dinner after midnight on an air force plane heading home from Afghanistan several years ago, he woke his aides for a meeting. "I like to kill one of them a day!" he joked. Villepin convinced himself that words could replace strategy.

I discovered clues to Villepin's thinking and temperament in his black leather Gucci briefcase, which he opened during a conversation in 2003, at the height of the break with the United States. Out came a thick, ecru-colored dossier tied in a ribbon that contained the still-to-be-published manuscript of the second part of his four-volume biography of Napoléon; a plastic folder containing a collection of his own poems that he was editing; the manuscript of a friend's book for which he was writing an introduction; a blue folder on painting; and finally, his official papers. "You see, I like to do many things at the same time," he said. "That's the only way to stay awake. At three in the morning you need to do something different than at two in the morning, because if not, you fall asleep."

Just the day before, Villepin said, he had written a poem. Its title was "Fire." He read it to me in French. It called on the living and the dead to preserve memory by letting the dead blend with life, holding high the banner of poetry, forcing open the locks and not burning the inventory. I'm not much of a poetry expert, and the poem sailed swiftly over my head. I praised it anyway. (Villepin would later become the inspiration for a satirical comic book that described life in the Foreign Ministry in his era. The tall, silver-haired, aristocratic minister, "Alexandre Taillard de Vorms," is permanently in motion, while musing about Greek philosophy, French poetry, and Stabilo marker pens. "The art of diplomacy is not to stay in your armchair," he tells his young aide. "You mustn't be scared of the flame. I leap into the flame. I become the flame.")

Villepin toyed with the idea of seeking the presidency in 2007, but he didn't have much of a chance. He had never held an elective office, did not have the apparatus of the conservative UMP party behind him, and, frankly, did not seem to enjoy mingling with ordinary French people. But he refused to abandon the political arena. He created his own political party, became one of the most articulate critics of Nicolas Sarkozy on the right, and launched a grassroots campaign to visit the rural areas and the troubled suburbs. He listened to the woes of his countrymen and vowed to help them. He was beginning to learn how to seduce.

Even in the darkest days of the French-American split over the war with Iraq, Jean-David Levitte, as France's ambassador to the United States, struggled hard to restore a positive image of his country.

Levitte turned his embassy into a communications war room. He gave dozens of speeches across the United States explaining why France opposed the American decision to wage war against Saddam Hussein. He appeared on late-night television talk shows and local call-in radio programs. He tasked his embassy with answering the hundreds of thousands of protest letters and e-mails that poured in. Diplomatic politesse and Cartesian logic were his only weapons against the onslaught of insults and obscenities. He invited Secretary of Defense Donald Rumsfeld, a neighbor, to dinner. (Rumsfeld refused.)

Most of his work went nowhere. The most brutal attacks came from Fox News, which night after night drove home the point that America had saved France from tyranny in World War II and that the French were traitorous ingrates and supporters of terrorism. At one point former secretary of state Henry Kissinger tried to mend fences by arranging a dinner at his home for Levitte and Rupert Murdoch, the owner of Fox. "I asked Murdoch to stop the French bashing," Levitte claimed. "He looked at me coldly and said, 'As long as it sells, I will continue.' I spent the rest of the evening charming his lovely wife, Wendy."

Such a strategy was necessary but only defensive. Even when the invasion of Iraq turned into a messy occupation and questions were raised on the American side about the wisdom of the war, there was a refusal in the United States to admit that France might have been right.

So Levitte also launched an unusual *opération séduction*, which he called a "reconquering of the heart." Traveling across the United States, he said, "I had come to understand perfectly what Americans reproached us the most for: our ingratitude as a people," he continued. The message was always the same: we liberated you French, so how could you not support us when we were attacked?

If Levitte was going to woo America, he needed to find a message that answered that question. The goal was to figure out what would bring pleasure to the Americans, what would make them feel appreciated and honored for the sacrifices of the past. He chose two solid-gold symbols: the Legion of Honor and the sixtieth anniversary of D-Day in 2004.

Levitte came up with the idea of marking the anniversary by giving Legion of Honor medals to one hundred American veterans who had participated in the D-Day landings. Two veterans from each of the fifty states would be chosen. They would have to be in good enough physical condition to travel, and they would be allowed to bring their families.

It was a record number of medals to bestow at one time. But in a personal letter to President Chirac, Levitte argued that Americans were woefully underrepresented in the roster of Legion of Honor recipients. His embassy had done its homework and discovered that Morocco, with one-tenth of America's population, had just as many.

Chirac signed off on the idea, but when Levitte sent the budget—more than a million euros—to the Foreign Ministry for approval, the response was swift. "Forget it," the ministry told him. Chirac would decorate one American veteran in France; the other ninety-nine would have to get their medals back home. "I wrote back and said, 'You forget it,'" Levitte told me. "'A hundred veterans are coming and I will be in charge of everything. I'll finance it myself.'"

Levitte had lived in the United States for several years, first as ambassador at the United Nations, then in Washington. He had learned the can-do American spirit. So he brought together the heads of several major French corporations. "I said to them, 'The loss of part of your market is catastrophic. This is a publicity campaign that won't cost much but will do a lot for your image.'" They all agreed to cough up the money for his D-Day plan.

He persuaded Air France to kick in a jumbo jet to ferry the veterans and their families. He persuaded the SNCF rail system to donate a special train to Normandy and four-star hotels like Le Meurice and Le Bristol to provide free luxury accommodations, meals, and ground transportation in Paris.

There was a three-hundred-foot-long red carpet at the airport in Paris, so royal looking that the veterans had to be coaxed to walk on it, and a gala evening with American swing music. Levitte got so excited as he told me the story that his words came out backward. "Woogie boogies! It was cool!" he exclaimed.

The veterans were awarded the medals at the Invalides in Paris as a French military band played. During the anniversary celebrations on the beach at Arromanches in Normandy, World War II footage was shown on huge screens. One scene showed a banner strung after Liberation, which read, "Thank you for deliverance." At Omaha Beach, thousands of French people formed a human chain that spelled out the words, "France will never forget. Thank you, America."

Every American grave was adorned with roses. The American Sixth Fleet band played the signature jazz tune of the Duke Ellington orchestra, "Take the 'A' Train." Fifty military planes flew overhead. The French frigate *Cassard* sounded a twenty-one-gun salute. In his speech, Chirac called D-Day "the day hope was born." When the veterans, dignified in their slow gait, marched past the reviewing stand, the Queen of England stunned the audience with a dramatic break in protocol. She joined the other world leaders in standing to applaud them. All of us there on that day—even some of the toughest among the White House press corps—became a bit weepy. "This was a moment of history," said Levitte. "Voilà. This was my thing. The veterans' celebration. This was my thing."

In his four decades as a diplomat, Levitte has become so adept at masking his feelings that he has earned the nickname "the Sphinx." But his victory at D-Day was the high point of his diplomatic career. As he told the story, he sucked in his breath and snorted in an undiplomatic fashion. He was struggling to will back tears. "I'm still crying now," he said.

Levitte understood the key to seduction in diplomacy as well as other areas of life: to find common ground and shared values and to build on them. Avoid confrontation and finger-pointing even if you are convinced you are right. Never let the other side lose face. Instead, get the other side to believe it is the winner. What Levitte did during the crisis over Iraq was to dig into French history and celebrate the best of the human spirit: generosity, courage, and sacrifice for the sake of freedom. What was needed was not elegant logic but the intellectual and emotional seduction that comes with good listening.

"It's crucial to feel empathy, sympathy, and love toward the people you are going to live with," said Levitte. "Within a negotiation, you have to establish a climate that will bring your interlocutor—who can sometimes be your adversary—to want to talk to you. My entire campaign in the United States was to say, 'We love you. We understand you. We are with you.'"

The D-Day anniversary in 2004 did not quickly repair the relationship between France and the United States. But it was an important reminder that the two countries were and would continue to be friends and not, as some in America proclaimed, adversaries.

Despite his failings as a *séducteur* in the French mode, Nicolas Sarkozy was able to seduce America. He told Americans what they wanted to hear. While Chirac and Villepin seemed arrogant and made the United States lose face, Sarkozy came off as an ordinary guy and expressed his love. Levitte helped teach him how to do it.

A key to his I-love-America approach came in a radio interview in 2003. When Arnold Schwarzenegger, the Austrian-born actor, won the governorship of California, some politicians and commentators said his victory reflected a dangerous American populism. Sarkozy, then the interior minister, gushed. "That someone who is a foreigner in his country, who has an unpronounceable name" can become the governor of the biggest state in the United States, "this is no small thing!" he exclaimed.

Sarkozy shared the official French view that America's war against Iraq was a mistake and that France was right to stay out. Nevertheless, he suffered during the French presidential campaign for being too pro-American, proudly proclaiming admiration for the American celebration of the work ethic and upward mobility. He wore the nickname "Sarkozy *l'américain*" not as an insult but as a badge of honor.

By the time he came to Washington on his first official visit as president, in 2007, he was perceived as a staunch friend of the United States. One of the greatest moments of his presidency was his speech before a joint meeting of the U.S. Congress—a rare honor for a foreign head of state. As part of the press traveling with Sarkozy, I was monitoring the speech on the House side. My *New York Times* colleague, Carl Hulse, came over from the Senate side to help me out. We predicted that it would not be a big deal. Few lawmakers were expected to show up, and congressional staffers would be rounded up at the last minute to fill the empty seats. After all, that's what had happened when I covered Jacques Chirac's appearance before Congress in 1996. (France had conducted nuclear tests in the Pacific not long before that visit, and much of the Congress boycotted the speech in protest.)

But this time turned out to be different. A few minutes before Sarkozy's speech, senators and congressmen poured in. Carl came rushing back to tell me what an extraordinary moment this was.

Congress was in the mood to embrace Sarkozy. He received loud cheers and a three-minute standing ovation as he stepped to the podium. Congress saw in him the imaginary good Frenchman who liked America, not the bad one who came with finger-pointing arrogance. Bertrand Vannier, Washington correspondent for Radio France, asked what was going on. "Bertrand, it doesn't matter what he says. America wants to love him," I said.

What none of us knew at the time was that Sarkozy's speech had been rewritten at the last moment to appeal to the emotions of the Americans. Henri Guaino, Sarkozy's top speechwriter, had drafted a text that criticized and lectured: the Americans had been wrong on the war in Iraq, Guantánamo must be closed, that sort of thing.

But Guaino missed the plane to Washington, and Levitte gained control of the text. He furiously rewrote it, injecting passages about friendship with the United States. He slashed the second half, which was full of criticism.

"We weren't here to give lessons," Levitte recalled.

Sarkozy delivered the sweet version. He spoke of his love of the American dream and of the cultural icons of the twentieth century, from Elvis Presley to Ernest Hemingway. He expressed admiration for American values and for the Rev. Dr. Martin Luther King Jr. He thanked the United States for saving France in two world wars, rebuilding Europe with the Marshall Plan, and fighting Communism during the cold war.

Even better, Sarkozy had been coached to put his hand on his heart. He did it with enthusiasm, twice in the first ten minutes. While Congress stood to applaud at the end of his speech, he again placed his hand on his heart, letting it rest there for a full five seconds as he smiled with satisfaction.

The strategy worked. Without sending a single soldier to Iraq, Sarkozy became, as President Bush called him later that day, "the kind of fellow I like to deal with." Senator Mitch McConnell of Kentucky, the Republican leader, said of Sarkozy's performance: "You just heard a Ronald Reagan speech from a president of France. It was an almost out-of-body experience for all of us."

The three-star chef Guy Savoy, who had been invited as part of the French presidential party, told me afterward, "I was so proud I had to hold myself back from singing the 'Marseillaise'!"

·PART FIVE·

The End of the Affair?

15

Seduce or Die

. . .

Certain nations stand out as possessing a peculiar power or charm, some special gift of beauty or wisdom or strength, which puts them among the immortals, which makes them rank forever with the leaders of mankind. France is one of these nations. For her to sink would be a loss to all the world.

—Theodore Roosevelt,
speech at the Sorbonne, April 23, 1910

I really love France.
If you don't like the sea
If you don't like the mountains
If you don't like the city
Then screw you!

—Jean-Paul Belmondo in
Breathless, Jean-Luc Godard's 1960 film classic

On a morning that grew gray and cold with the wind from the sea, Calais showed a little leg. After sixteen years of planning and an investment of about 28 million euros, this city in the northern corner of France unveiled a museum that pays tribute to the artistic specialty of its past: lace. The minister of culture was there, as were the mayor, local officials and residents, the architects of the modernist building, and dozens of journalists who arrived on a specially organized train from Paris.

Lace is the most seductive of body coverings. It evokes the idea of delicacy and femininity, showing without unveiling. In the early nineteenth century, the lace industry made Calais famous, and the new

International City of Lace and Fashion of Calais includes exhibits of handmade and machine-made antique lace, lacemaking machines as big as trucks, and couture ball gowns with lace as light as butterfly wings. The permanent collection holds 10,000 pieces of lace and 3,200 costumes and related objects. To mark the opening, a red, white, and blue ribbon of lace was cut with a silver pair of scissors. Promoters explained that lace is part of France's *patrimoine*, or heritage, and that it must be protected, preserved, and promoted; they touted a visit to the museum as "a spiritual, sensual, and sensory experience." Chantal Thomass, France's lingerie queen and the "godmother" of the museum, signed copies of her book on lingerie, her hands encased in tulle-trimmed fingerless black gloves. Eleven fashion designers showed lacy confections in a runway show.

But the celebration masked a sad reality: for nearly a century, France's lace industry has been dying, slowly and painfully, a victim of cheap foreign labor, changing fashions, and outmoded business practices and technology. Most lacemaking has moved to Asia. In 1909, there were 35,000 lace workers in Calais; in 2009, about 2,000.

Tourists have come to the lace museum since that opening day in 2009, but they have not transformed Calais into a must-see destination. The city was largely destroyed in World War II, and it is a place not of picture postcards, but of high joblessness. It is also associated with a darker side: as a magnet for immigrants and asylum seekers from far-off places of desperation like Afghanistan and Iraq. They carry on their backs the dream of crossing the Channel into what they believe is an El Dorado called Britain. Since the closing in 2003 of a refugee center near Calais and the eviction in 2009 of several hundred squatters from a wooded camp called "the jungle," the immigrants wander the city's streets, waiting for a better future that may never come.

The museum is a modern manifestation of nostalgia, an exercise in preserving a grandeur that no longer exists. In a sense, the dedication of a space for the "memory" of the "legend" of lace is an acknowledgment of defeat.

• • •

France today is stuck between two options, both of which are flawed. One is to embrace the tenets of a globalized world that demands technological advancement, physical mobility, and psychological fluidity. But that would run counter to traditional culture. The other is to celebrate and promote the attractive, seductive tools that worked for France in the past. But they are rusting with age and running less smoothly, like the lacemaking behemoths that need oiling and repair.

For decades, an awareness of the decline of France has bored deep into the national consciousness. There is an admiration for history and a reveling in past glory, but these are coupled with a fear of the unknown and a determination to maintain the status quo. Side by side with what is called *déclinisme* are valiant and desperate attempts to retain the country's reputation as a place of beauty and pleasure. Seduction is the best that France has to offer. When it works, it's magic: it is hidden, mysterious, and oriented toward a glorious, crystallized, ideal image. But it can also entail inefficiency, fragility, ambiguity, and a process that at any time can end badly. When the game comes up against the cold, hard wall of reality, when it reveals itself, seduction fails.

It can degrade into the antithesis of seduction, what I call anti-seduction, a kind of antimatter of the emotional world, canceling out the intent to attract or influence by producing the opposite effect. Pornography is anti-seduction. Bling-bling ostentation is anti-seduction. Talking about money is anti-seduction. Ending lively banter by declaring the conversation over is anti-seduction. Saying no for no good reason is anti-seduction.

When seduction fails, France fails. "Seduction is irrational; it is deceptive," said Bruno Racine of the Bibliothèque Nationale. "The seducer can instantly become despicable. When the terrible side of the seducer appears, his power of enchantment disappears. That is because seduction is the weapon of conquest. It cannot be the weapon of duration, because to endure you need other qualities as well."

I am convinced that, deep down, many French people feel bitter resignation that France is no longer as important as it was, even a half-century ago. On many levels, they are terrified by change. They fear losing their identity. They fear inhabiting a midsize democracy with beautiful buildings, becoming Germany with better food or, just as bad, a bigger version of Belgium or Switzerland.

Marc Fumaroli, the historian and member of the Académie Française, lamented the fact that the French language is in permanent and irreversible decline. Conversation, so crucial to seduction, is becoming a lost art, he said.

So that means France is doomed? I asked.

Not at all, he replied.

"One must not exaggerate," he went on. "These phenomena are terrible, of course, but ultimately, there remains the fact that everyone would like to come and live in France. We have at least ten centuries of civilization behind us. We have demolished, we have destroyed, but there remain enough traces. That is a source of happiness! There are entire regions that are inhabited by the English and Dutch who have settled here. If France is a museum, all the better! She must be a museum! It is by being a museum that she has a chance of survival, to be adored."

But adoration from the outside is not enough. The French know that they must find a balance between modernization (to avoid economic decline) and preservation (to avoid cultural annihilation). Like other nations and people shaken by economic retrenchment and globalization, the French are often confused by the difficulty of determining where the real threats lie. Like Americans, they sometimes focus on the small picture, what they see as threats to their identity, fastening on immigration and fear of the outsider.

The identity issue is so crucial that the Sarkozy government launched a three-month nationwide debate in 2009 to determine what it means to be French. About 10 percent of France's inhabitants are of Arab and African origin or descent, many of them Muslims, who offer a rich mix of history and cultures. But in announcing the initiative, Sarkozy proclaimed "the profound unity of our culture, and dare I say it, of our civilization." The government asked the country's one hundred prefectures to conduct town-hall meetings about the values of the Republic and sent them two hundred questions as a guide. The questionnaire was never made public, but it circulated quietly.

One question asked, "What are the elements of national identity?" Some of the choices were predictable: history, language, culture, agriculture, industry. Others less so. Where did France's wines and its "culinary art" fit in? Was the "countryside" an element of national identity? "Churches and cathedrals" were listed as possibilities, but not synagogues and mosques.

The grand national debate was an abysmal failure. It quickly degenerated into an ugly controversy about immigration and the rights of Muslims, ethnic Arabs, and ethnic Africans living in France. The majority of the French were convinced that the debate had been a ploy by the governing conservative party to win votes from the far right in the 2010 regional elections.

Only modest measures came out of the campaign, such as requirements that schools fly the French flag, display the 1789 Declaration of the Rights of Man in classrooms, and give students the opportunity to sing the "Marseillaise" at least once a year. "Many French doubt their identity because they do not have as secure bearings as they once did," said the sociologist Michel Wieviorka in the newspaper *Libération*. "The place of the country is no longer assured as before; its international influence is in decline. As a result, identity becomes the receptacle for all fears." He faulted the debate as an exercise by those in power "to confuse all sorts of historical symbols and meanings."

Even a seemingly benign promotion of France can backfire when the tools of seduction fail. In 2008 the government unveiled a new logo using Marianne, the symbol of the French Republic. The initiative, called Rendez-vous en France, was designed to sell France as a tourist destination. Tourism and communications specialists identified three values that make France so appealing: liberty (independence, creativity), authenticity (history, culture), and sensuality (pleasure, hedonism, Epicureanism, romance, passion, femininity).

The logo was a simple red-and-blue line drawing of a young woman with a slight smile, her head turned and tilted upward as if looking toward the future, the word "France" curving across her chest. When Finance Minister Christine Lagarde unveiled the logo, she praised it for evoking romance. “Why not?” she asked, quoting the twentieth-century writer Paul Morand: “When it comes to love, if you are French you are already halfway there.”

A close look at the word “France” showed just how cleverly the logo had been drawn. The “F” formed Marianne’s right shoulder; the “N” her left arm. The problem was with the “R” and the “A,” which clearly outlined breasts. Market testing showed that the evocation of naked breasts might offend people in some countries. A French business website pointed out that the image of a naked woman might be “banal” in French advertising but unacceptable in North America, Asia, and the Middle East. In the end, the word “France” had to be rewritten and the naughty nakedness eliminated.

One place to look for evidence of the change and displacement that feed French fears is on the farm. Three out of four French farms have disappeared in the last half century; in 1960 about a third of the French earned their living by farming; today less than 5 percent do. The United States saw a similar move away from the farm, but it took place earlier and was met with less alarm. In France, the trend is unsettling, and it is deplored.

Much of the French countryside remains resplendent, with rich farmland and pretty villages. But there is a darker side. The writer Frédéric Martel, who grew up on a farm, offered to show it to me. And so one weekend we went to visit his parents in Châteaurenard, once an archetypical French farming town in Provence. The neat rows of apple trees and grapevines that once lined the road heading into town disappeared long ago. In their place was a landscape of prefabricated warehouses, auto parts dealers, a halal chicken-processing plant, and fields overrun with weeds and scrub. This was not the romantic Provence of the author Peter Mayle, where the villagers are quaint, the views picturesque, and the farmers happy.

Châteaurenard, like dozens of other farming towns that were the bedrock of rural France, has lost its soul. The farmers, like Clément Martel, Frédéric’s father, are selling off chunks of their land and abandoning their unprofitable fields. The Châteaurenard area has 150 working farms, down from more than 800 in the 1960s. Local officials and farmers predict that by 2020, only 50 farms will be left. "Our farms are becoming the monuments of the dead, our town is a bedroom community that services others," said Bernard Reynès, the town's mayor. "We are losing our confidence that life will somehow get better, losing our roots, our rural identity."

Though it is near Avignon, a city that is one of France's top tourist attractions, Châteaurenard has little star quality. Half of its working residents commute to jobs somewhere else. The medieval fortress is crumbling, the church unlit and often closed, the museum a one-room collection of old farm tools. At night, the streets of the town belong to young men, most of them of Moroccan origin, whose fathers came to France as farmhands decades ago. There is no new industry, and the young men are repelled by the idea of farm labor.

"My father came here with his children to find success," said Mohamed Sghiouri, a high school student who hoped to become an electrician. "He was a farmhand for thirty years, and now he's at home on disability with back problems. Since I was small, he told me to 'work, work hard in school,' so I could do better than he did and stay off the farm."

The communities tend to keep separate. The ethnic Arabs congregate in one café; the Gallic French men in another. The first group gathers in the shade of trees around the central town square on hot afternoons; the second group retreats indoors. When the mayor walks the streets, he reaches out to shake the hands of the old-timers but leaves the ethnic Arabs alone. Every Bastille Day, the town celebrates the arts and crafts of daily life a century ago. A retired pharmacist grinds potions with a mortar and pestle. A baker makes loaves as big as casseroles in a communal oven. Residents dress in period costume to sing old French country songs. Children ride ponies. The ethnic Arabs stay home.

The malaise that hovers over the town extends to the vast wholesale produce market on its outskirts. There, six mornings a week during the harvest season, hundreds of farmers and distributors gather at six o'clock to buy and sell in a frenzied, one-hour ritual. They lament that the wholesale price of their lettuce is the same as the retail price in the supermarket off the highway and that boats docked in Marseille are filled with cheap pears from Chile.

And tomatoes. Tomatoes are the real losers here. First, there was the invasion of the Spanish tomato, followed by the Moroccan variety. But the decisive blow to the homegrown Provençale tomato was dealt several years ago when the Chinese industrial tomato giant Xinjiang Chalkis bought the local canning factory and began shipping tons of tomato paste all the way from China to can locally and sell as "made in France." Local tomatoes became worthless.

The decline of French agriculture is mirrored in a very different venue where seduction might be expected to hold sway: the world of international culture. "Grandeur" originally was a French word. But Paris, as the physical embodiment of French greatness, is no longer the cultural capital of the world.

In *Mainstream*, a groundbreaking book about the globalization of culture, Frédéric Martel identified the United States, along with India, China, Brazil, and South Korea, as the world's cultural powerhouses. France, he told audiences in the lively debates that followed the book's publication in 2010, had been left behind. Martel said that much of the French elite rejects the notion that to survive in the world, the French must learn and speak English. He documented a trend that began decades ago and continues today, the resistance to using English words in French society: the Socialist Party leader who is criticized for using the word "care" for one of her initiatives; the deputy minister who hopes to ban the use of "buzz," "chat," and "newsletters"; the former prime minister who proposes limits on English expressions in certain international organizations; the language commission that wants to substitute the words *ordiphone* for "Smartphone" and *encre en poudre* for "toner." Martel criticized President Sarkozy for not speaking English and for branding as snobs French diplomats who are "happy to speak English" instead of French.

Neither the French language nor French culture has the appeal it once did in the United States. Some of the best private schools in America have substituted Chinese for advanced French courses. Far fewer French books are translated into English, even as French best-seller lists feature translations of American authors like Philip Roth and Paul Auster. Some 47 percent of the citizens of the European Union speak English; 25 percent of the EU's official documents are printed in French, compared to 50 percent three decades ago. American movies and television shows are much more prevalent than they were in the 1980s. Ask a Frenchman who among his compatriots has the same cachet in the United States as George Clooney or Brad Pitt do in France, and he will tell you that such a person does not exist.

What my former colleague John Vinocur wrote in the *New York Times* in 1983 about the cultural retreat of France could be reprinted today: "It was a weak year for French films. . . . There is no hot new French play, no hot young painter. . . . France has fallen . . . among book-exporting countries. . . . The art market has moved to the United States." French films, he added, are "unexportable—chatty, obscure, non-visual, untranslatable."

For Stanley Hoffmann, the political scientist at Harvard University, there is nothing new in the concern over the French unwillingness to adapt. He said that when he first came to the United States from France in 1955, "there were all kinds of books on decline claiming that France was working against itself and would never outgrow its artisan and peasant mentality. This is a small country, very incestuous and also remarkably noncomparative. The French really don't look at what is going on elsewhere. Everyone knows there are blockages in French society. Some of them have been removed and others not. I wrote about them forty years ago! . . . We are rediscovering the same clichés."

Another source of anti-seduction in French life today can be found in the *banlieues*, or suburbs, on the edges of France's cities. Pockets of poverty, unemployment, and crime, they seize the headlines every so often, when daily life turns violent. The first time I went to a *banlieue* of Paris, however, was not to cover orgies of car burnings and rock throwing by roving gangs of young and restless men. It was to watch my younger daughter, Gabriela, who was then twelve, play soccer.

Gabriela had opposed our move to Paris. In Washington, she had been on an elite traveling soccer team, so I tried to appease her by promising that she would play soccer in France. Really good soccer. France, I told her, had won the World Cup in 1998. A French woman had just been named the most valuable player in the American professional women's soccer league. Soccer is to France what football is to America.

What I discovered, however, is that real French girls—at least real French middle-class Parisian girls—don't play soccer. Strapping on shin guards and kicking a ball up and down a dirty field is a boy thing. It is played by what sociologists call "the lower classes." So Gabby joined one of Paris's only *football féminin* teams. Most of the other teams were in the tough suburbs, so every weekend Andy and I stood on the sidelines with the other parents, most of them fathers with blue-collar jobs who had once played the game themselves and happened to have daughters. There were few soccer moms. Gabby discovered that soccer-playing girls smoke and talk back to the coach; she also learned how to curse.

Over the years, through Gabby's soccer, I got to know parents who were carving out a life for themselves and their families in the suburbs. But many of the *banlieues* are vast concrete wastelands built in the 1950s and 1960s as cheap housing for immigrants, mostly from France's former colonies. In these housing projects, unemployment among young men under age twenty-five is as high as 50 percent.

Discrimination against the residents of the suburbs is so deep-rooted that even well-intentioned people don't seem to know when they are guilty of it. I witnessed it on the day that Andy was sworn in to the French bar. The representative of the bar of Paris felt compelled to make personal observations as he granted the certificates. He congratulated a young woman with an Arab-sounding name from one of the suburbs for her accomplishments and told her that the suburbs needed good lawyers like her. To my American ears, it smacked of go-back-where-you-came-from. Would it have occurred to him that she might want to work for an international law firm or a big corporation or even the French state?

Life in the suburbs may be grim, but the residents still pursue everyday pleasures in ways that seem particularly French. Indeed, the food market at Saint-Denis, a vast glass-and-metal-covered expanse that dates from the nineteenth century, is a gastronomical pleasure palace. This suburb, just north of Paris, is also the site of the most French of French symbols, the Saint-Denis Basilica, perhaps the most overlooked religious gem in the Paris area, given its size and importance. According to legend, after Saint Denis, the first bishop of Paris, was decapitated near Montmartre during a persecution of Christians in the third century, he picked up his head, washed it off, and carried it about five miles to the north before he collapsed. A shrine was built, replaced by the basilica, which became the burial place for France's kings, from Clovis and Dagobert I to Louis XVIII (with royals like Catherine de Médicis, Henri IV, Marie Antoinette, and Louis XVI along the way).

The site has also served as a marketplace since the Middle Ages, when merchants from all over Europe came to trade. At first glance, the market appears to be run by and for North African Arabs and sub-Saharan black Africans. That's because to get to the food emporium, you have to pass through a long stretch of outdoor stalls with the feel of a raucous souk, where vendors hawk the paraphernalia of daily life: cheap fabrics, piles of clothing, costume jewelry, cooking pots, running shoes, even mousetraps and zippers.

On closer inspection, the food market is multiracial and multiethnic, an enclosed microcosm of layers of French history. The third-generation crêpe maker from Brittany makes crêpes and galettes to order. Parisian-born French men with tattoos offer pigs' heads and feet. The ethnic Portuguese and Italians, whose families immigrated to France decades ago, sell cheeses, oils, charcuterie, olives, and wine from back home. The Franco-Arab merchants who hold French identity cards in their pockets and Arabness in their voices lure passersby with deep-discounted trays of chopped chicken gizzards and homemade halal sausages. The greengrocers beckon with African root vegetables as big as melons.

Here the merchants and their clientele—no matter what their color, religion, age, ethnicity, or country of origin—seduce each other. They share a common purpose: buying and selling food products, of course, but also anticipation of the shared pleasure that comes with cooking and eating *en famille*. The process of acquiring the necessary raw materials needs time, conversation, and salesmanship. "Come and buy my tomatoes, madame, they are ripe from the vine," or "Let me mix a special curry for chicken, madame, and, oh, don't forget preserved lemons," or "Wait till next Tuesday and by then I'll have those special olives you like." If the customer is a young woman, the pitch is likely to start with something like, "Hey, you are *magnifique*!"

To change the mentality of the ethnic Arab and African population in the suburbs would require a redefinition of what France is—not the country of "republicanism" that ignores religious, ethnic, racial, and gender differences but one that embraces them. Diversity and ambition would be rewarded. The thousands of words of *verlan*, the ever-changing slang of the suburbs, would be put into dictionaries and used in schools. The popular culture of the streets would be celebrated—with scholarships, exchange programs, and support for the films, books, music, and art that struggle to get funded and noticed.

But that approach would require flexibility, which is not a French tradition. The Americans' strength "is that they put everyone on the same footing," the humorist Yassine Belattar told *Le Monde*. "They are not in the mind-set of 'labels' as we French are, but in the mind-set of action: 'Who's moving?' 'Who's proposing?' 'Who's innovating?' and not, 'What is your degree?' 'Where did you do your studies?' 'Who is your father?' "

Fear, together with the national habit of romanticism, also serves to hold back change. In the fall of 2010, millions of French people took to the streets to protest a modest reform of the state pension system: raising the minimum retirement age from sixty to sixty-two. Students, some as young as thirteen, joined with teachers, town-hall staff, train drivers, postal and utility workers, and other public-sector employees to stage strikes and celebrate worker solidarity. Even *casseurs*, or "smashers," young troublemakers who episodically confront police and loot a little, came out.

Jérôme Sainte-Marie, the chief political analyst at the CSA polling organization, argued that President Sarkozy had made a crucial error of presentation: he had cut off discussion with the unions and other opponents of the measure. "Social dialogue was interrupted," he told the *New York Times*, disapprovingly. The moment was not prolonged but abruptly terminated. Others made the point that Sarkozy the anti-seducer had brought the protests on himself.

In the end, the strikes neither shut down the country nor stopped most of the French from getting to work. But large swaths of the country were deprived of gasoline and diesel fuel; air and rail traffic was disrupted. The social action cost France billions of dollars. Still, Sarkozy did not blink, and the reform was implemented.

Sometimes I feel that the everything-is-possible American approach may never find a home in France. After so many years of living there, I thought I had accepted the quirky cultural differences between France and the United States that had frustrated me when I first arrived. When the French act in a way that seems to make no sense and wastes time, money, and energy (three visits by various technicians to get a hot water heater repaired, for example), more often than not I can let it go. Process is a natural part of French life, I say to myself.

I tell myself that France is also a place where promises of pleasure are deliverable. A melon bought at an outdoor market might be sublime. Women might flirt on the street. Men might be gallant. It is even possible, with playfulness, deference, a clever use of language, and staying power, to strip the French of their arrogance and get them to loosen up. That gives me the courage to fight bureaucracies.

Then came the drama of the kitchen. I decided that unless France changes its attitude toward the kitchen, it will never again be a great power.

French apartments are sometimes rented with empty kitchens. Except for a water source and perhaps a sink, there are no appliances, cupboards, or counters. Every new tenant has to install a kitchen—and pay for it.

Andy and I got lucky when we moved into our first apartment in Paris. The tenants who preceded us had left after less than two years, and we were allowed to buy their kitchen—with its top-of-the-line custom-made cabinets and appliances—at a bargain price. We were not talking *Architectural Digest*, but this wasn't IKEA, either. When we were about to move to a new apartment years later, the landlord ordered us to leave the kitchen empty, except for the kitchen sink. I made a case for at least keeping the cabinets, which still looked perfectly new. I harbored no illusion that anyone would buy them. But I just didn't think it was right to destroy perfectly good cabinets so that a new tenant could spend a vast amount of time, money, and emotional energy installing another set that might not be as good as this one. And I didn't feel like paying a hefty fee to have the cabinets pulled apart and hauled away.

"It's the rule," the manager of our apartment building told me when I asked to leave the cabinets. "Every tenant has to leave behind an empty kitchen."

Undaunted, I appealed to the landlord's representative. I tried the formal, obsequious French approach. "Would you have the kindness to consider allowing us to leave the kitchen cabinets for the next tenant?"

No. "The kitchen must be empty," she said.

I tried cultural outreach. "May I invite you for tea one afternoon to inspect them yourself?"

No.

I tried moral grounds and ecological correctness. "Isn't it wrong and a waste of energy and money to destroy a kitchen just so that the next tenant can install a new one?"

No.

I tried American marketing. "The cabinets will be a selling point!" I exclaimed.

No.

I tried Cartesian logic. "We are supposed to leave the apartment in the same condition in which we found it. The kitchen had cabinets when we first arrived. So it seems that there should be cabinets when we depart," I said.

"Things are different now," she replied. "We have streamlined our operation."

Finally, I tried the legal approach. "Why not write a clause into the new lease saying that the landlord takes no responsibility for previously installed cabinets?"

"The management has no need to take responsibility for cabinets that a tenant might complain about later," she replied.

And there I had it, a perfectly good French explanation about making the minimum effort that was required to avoid any possible complication. Innovative thinking, saving money, common sense, flexibility, and basic humanity were not part of the equation. It is this rigidity that fixes France in a time warp, depriving the country of the fluidity and the excitement that comes with solving problems. Fixed positions remain, no matter how absurd they are, like those governing the dismantling, for no good reason, of a perfectly good kitchen.

I had run up against the limits of seduction. I asked Bruno Le Maire, the minister of agriculture, what is to become of France if anti-seduction wins out in the end. He responded that seduction has limited power and must be constantly refined. It has to be based on finding common ground with the other and bringing the other to yourself. It ultimately can be done well, he insisted, and the French do it best.

"We no longer have military power, we no longer have economic power," he said. "The only force France has is its intelligence. It's very precious. I don't find it anywhere else in the world. The force of our intelligence allows us to talk to everyone, to understand the complexity of the real world."

Le Maire said that France's intelligence compelled it to argue years ago that the creation of the euro without a parallel European economic infrastructure was stupid. He said it was France's intelligence that understood that war with Iraq would be a disaster for years to come. "You can keep telling me France is a medium-sized power," he added. "I remain convinced it is a great nation. A singular nation."

"And if France continues to lose its global influence, its farms, its countryside that gives definition to what is France, if it loses its culinary arts, its art of conversation, what does it become?" I asked.

"We cannot lose that," he said. "If we lose that, we lose everything."

Le Maire quoted one of his favorite lines from a poem of Alexis Leger, the diplomat who under the pen name Saint-John Perse was one of France's best-known poets of the twentieth century and the recipient of the Nobel Prize for Literature in 1960. "Select a wide hat with the brim seduced." I didn't understand, so he explained: "To seduce means 'to pull toward yourself.' And when you 'seduce' the brim of your hat, you turn the brim toward the center of the hat. That's exactly what seduction is for the French, to pull the other toward yourself, to lead back to yourself."

Therefore, he continued, seduction requires concealed power. "That's what's at play," he said. "It's not a question of imposing power. It's not a question of forcing. It's to pull toward yourself with an operation in which you succeed by explaining, convincing, and making the other laugh. It's the opposite of Italian charm, which is given completely freely."

He cited the late Italian actor Marcello Mastroianni as someone who had an irresistible charm but was not seductive. "He was not adept at the process of seduction that brings one back to you," he said. "Fundamentally, that's the real French character. It's to see, even on a geographical map, that France is the heart of the world."

Epilogue: The Dinner Party

. . .

Just speak very loudly and quickly, and state your position with utter conviction, as the French do, and you'll have a marvelous time!

—Julia Child, on how to survive a dinner party in Paris

Ask the travelled inhabitant of any nation, in what country on earth would you rather live? Certainly, in my own, where are all my friends, my relations, and the earliest and sweetest affections and recollections of my life. Which would be your second choice? France.

—Thomas Jefferson

"Would you like me to give a dinner for you?" the elegant hostess asked over lunch in her apartment one day. "To discuss seduction?"

"I'd be honored!" I replied, perhaps with too much American eagerness.

The elegant hostess speaks elegant English, with considerably more grace than I speak French. So most often we speak in English.

The dinner, however, would be conducted in French. "How good is your French?" she asked.

The question was ever so slightly annoying. I had lived in Paris for several years. I wasn't one of those Americans who had never learned to speak the language, was I? Then again, I rarely initiated conversations with the elegant hostess in French.

"It's good enough to interview the president of France," I replied, giving her a broad smile of gut-it-out bravado.

"Good," she said, smiling back with more reserve. Then she put me on notice. "We're going to do it the French way," she said.

By this, I knew she meant careful plotting and preparation. A series of discussions followed by phone, by e-mail, and over lunch. She asked about my husband: his name, education, work, interests. She wanted to know whether we had dietary restrictions and how I wanted to be introduced.

This was to be an unusual event: not a casual, social affair but a strategically planned working dinner with twelve interesting people.

"More about these people when you next come to lunch," the elegant hostess wrote in one e-mail. "*Je t'embrasse* (if I may)," she signed.

During our next encounter, the elegant hostess told me about the professional lives and personal interests of the guests. There would be the famous novelist and biographer who worked on several books at once and his British wife, an intellectual in her own right; the creative thinker (a retired banker) and his wife, who produced and sold excellent Armagnac from their estate in the south; the former corporate president and his lawyer wife; the British foreign correspondent and his French businesswoman partner; and the hostess's husband, a Renaissance man who collected art, ran a think tank, campaigned for political reforms, and earned a living as a banker.

She said they were "thrilled and amused" by the prospect of the dinner. Thrilled, okay. But amused? I could accept that they might find the subject of seduction intriguing, but somehow I didn't see myself as the source of dinner table amusement. I enjoyed reading Edith Wharton and Henry James, both of whom had been gifted conversationalists in French at tables in Paris in their day, but I didn't think I had the skill to live up to their example in real life.

I decided to launch a two-pronged *opération séduction*. First, I would have to be presentable and glib enough to lure the guests into the game. Then, I would lay out questions and ideas about the role of seduction in French life in such a way that they would find the topic engaging and discuss it with relish. They didn't have to buy my ideas; they just had to be seduced into a good talk.

A formal dinner party is a test of manners in any culture. But sophisticated Parisians are different. They love to be seduced, expect to be seduced, and have a code of politesse and appearance that demands that everyone meet a minimum standard of seductiveness.

If you don't meet the standard, you can't really operate as an equal, certainly not in intellectual circles. Some slack will be cut for a foreigner. But this was a dinner party with me as the star attraction. I didn't care if I wasn't praised, but I wanted to be accepted.

Even after years living in Paris, I found that many of the codes of dinner party protocol eluded me. It wasn't enough that I was a correspondent for the *New York Times*, successful by the standards of my profession and my country. The French so easily can make an outsider feel awkward and *mal élevé*—badly brought up. All those centuries of drawing rooms and salons and minuets have given many of them a highly refined ability to throw others off.

My own experience in giving formal, catered dinner parties was limited. In all my time living in Paris, I had hosted only one. It was in 2003, to mark the occasion of Gérard Araud's appointment as France's ambassador to Israel. I had met Gérard in Washington in the late 1980s, when he was responsible for political-military affairs at the French embassy.

When Gérard was about to leave France for Israel, I threw a dinner party in his honor. I sent handwritten invitations on engraved stationery and ordered good wines and a lot of champagne. I covered cheap kitchen chairs in white linen. I hired a chef to prepare the perfect dinner and a waiter to serve it.

I consulted with French friends and came up with three criteria that have to be met for a formal Paris dinner party to succeed:

- The hostess must offer a beautiful meal, with effortless serving by hired help and first-rate wines. (The excellence of the food is less important than how it looks on the plate.)
- The guests must be seductive in appearance and level of charm.

- The conversation must be intellectually engaging, with all the guests contributing.

I did more research. One French friend warned me not to try to compete with the French in the table setting. They will always find a flaw, she said. I had no good crystal. My silver flatware didn't match. My set of good china was in storage in Delaware. So I decorated the dining table with miniature vegetables and satin ribbon instead of flowers. One guest, a senior Foreign Ministry official, announced that the table was perfect. Either he thought I was pathetic or he was very good at *second degré*.

Some guests brought flowers. One brought a bookmark with hanging baubles. A four-star general brought a miniature porcelain pot and his security officers.

I have no recollection of what we ate, except that the food was good enough and everyone praised it and that gooseberries and slices of starfruit decorated the dessert plate. The conversation was so lively that I broke with protocol and kept everyone at the table instead of retiring to the living room for coffee.

I had already made a much more serious protocol blunder. On the dinner invitations, I had invited the guests to say good-bye to Gérard as he took up his post as ambassador in Jerusalem. Israel claims Jerusalem as its capital; in the absence of a resolution on the final status of the city, the rest of the world does not. Gérard's post was in Tel Aviv, the city where foreign governments have their embassies. With a stroke of the pen, I had moved France's embassy, rewritten history, and insulted the French state.

This time, I would be better prepared. I consulted notes I had taken for an article several years earlier about the importance of politesse in France. As part of my research, I had attended a private seminar on proper table settings and dining habits. There I was, with a group of French and American women in a hotel suite adorned in silk brocade and velvet. All of us had paid the equivalent of ninety dollars apiece to raise our dinner-party consciousness.

I was taught that in the perfect French world, rules govern even the most trivial acts: how to greet a guest at the door, how to address someone you have just met, what gift not to bring to a dinner party. (Giving a bottle of wine can be considered an arrogant act that gives the impression you think you know more about wine than your hosts do. I once brought a one-hundred-euro bottle of 2004 Sauternes that I had purchased from a private domaine south of Bordeaux only to be told by the hostess that she and her husband had six one-thousand-euro bottles of Château d'Yquem in their wine cellar.)

Among the other lessons: Always arrive fifteen minutes late at a dinner party. The woman—not the man—extends a hand for a handshake or a kiss of the hand. A woman should leave her hands on the table and not rest them in her lap during dinner to avoid giving the impression that hanky-panky is going on below. She should also fold one hand over the other at the table, the better to show off her jewels.

You should eat asparagus with your fingers and sorbet with your fork. Do not say *bon appétit* at the start of a meal. (It's too direct a reference to the body.) Take only as big a helping as you intend to eat. (It is impolite to leave food on your plate.) Do not take second helpings of cheese. (The host may think you're still hungry). Never leave the table in the middle of the meal to use the powder room. (If you really have to go, wait until dinner is over and ask, discreetly, "May I wash my hands?")

In her pencil skirt and fitted cashmere sweater, our instructor looked as if she never ate. She compared a dinner party—for both guest and host—to mastering a sport. "You have to train hard," she told us. "But once you train and know the rules, it all comes naturally."

Most terrifying was her pronouncement that all can be lost in the first minute of acquaintance. "In the first twenty seconds, others will judge your look; in the second twenty seconds, your behavior; and the third twenty seconds, your first words," she said. "There is a code. If you do not follow it properly, it will be very, very hard to make a comeback."

The elegant hostess's dinner would require a layer of complexity that we hadn't learned in class: verbal quickness and playfulness. I knew that some of the nuances and sparring would escape me.

"If there is a conversational one-upmanship with a lot of light play . . ." I told the elegant hostess one day, my voice trailing off.

"There will be," she interrupted. "There will be a lot of *second degré*."

Ah, the treacherous *second degré*, where what is said is not really meant and you have to catch the second meaning, and then try to reply with a soupçon of humor and wit. I knew I was much too *premier degré*, too direct, too much in search of clarity. Even if I understood all the French expressions, I sometimes didn't get the jokes. I realized that it had been a mistake to tell the elegant hostess that my French was good enough to interview the president of France. Interviewing presidents is easy: the goal is to push them to make news, but in doing so, they have to express themselves clearly. *Second degré*—droll ambiguity—does not translate into good newspaper copy.

I confessed to the elegant hostess that her dinner party idea might not work; I was not nimble enough for *second degré*.

"I may just sit and observe," I said. "If I start thinking someone will judge me because I'm not using the imperfect subjunctive, so be it. If I don't do Edith Wharton, you're going to have to bail me out."

"They're all nice people, and they're my friends," she assured me. She repeated that they were "thrilled and amused" by the prospect of the dinner.

Once I had the list of the guests, I went to work. I asked Florence to do an electronic data bank search on each of them. I learned who had gone to a *grande école* and who had aristocratic roots, who had an ancestor who had helped bring the Statue of Liberty to America and who had launched a travel magazine, who had worked in the United States and who belonged to the exclusive Racing Club, who was seriously and who was casually religious.

I had to figure out what to wear. Michèle Fitoussi from *Elle* told me I needed a black dress that was elegant and sexy, but comfortable, and designer shoes with high heels, no matter how uncomfortable. I had neither. My "good outfit" for dinner parties was a Sonia Rykiel tuxedo jacket and pants that I had bought years before.

I consulted Olga Boughanmi, who runs a consignment shop in my old neighborhood. She picked out an Italian black silk wrap dress and a pair of Christian Louboutin high-heeled mules. I paid her two hundred euros. The dress was comfortable; the mules were not. Perfect.

I read and annotated a novel by the famous novelist that was entirely devoted to a chic Parisian dinner party. Along the way I found several references to the word *séduction*. One of the guests at this fictional dinner was a female journalist who had asked her assistant to do research on the other guests. I realized I wasn't being clever, just predictable. The famous-writer character in the novel ridiculed women who always came to dinner parties dressed in black. They gave the dinners the feel of a funeral, he said.

Another book by the famous novelist portrayed the dinner party as an exercise in stealth worthy of a sensitive military intelligence operation. One character had a habit of dropping his napkin so that he could position a video camera on the floor under the table to film the guests playing footsie. The fictional hosts installed a microphone in the elevator to monitor the comments of their guests as they departed.

Arielle Dombasle had been right: seduction is war.

Then came the preparation of my opening remarks. The elegant hostess explained that I would give a five-minute summary of the thesis of my book. Then she would turn the floor over to the other guests.

The French are particularly good at oral presentations, having been required from a young age to deliver what are called *exposés*—without notes. The *exposé* always follows a *plan*, a rigid, formal structure in which logic is more important than accuracy. I wrote a speech in French. Andy edited it. Florence corrected the grammar. I read the speech aloud until I got it down to five minutes.

"May I take notes?" I had asked the elegant hostess.

"A few," she said. "Thank you for asking. But no recorder on the table."

I smiled and thought of the time in Tehran, years ago, when I had interviewed the wife of President Mohammad Khatami. She had examined the bouquet of flowers on the table between us and exclaimed, surprised, "There's a microphone in the flowers! Someone is listening to our conversation!" Apparently, our conversation was being recorded.

For me, planting a microphone in a floral bouquet would have been bold and brilliant if it worked, humiliating and unforgivable if it did not.

On the evening of the dinner, I arranged to meet Andy in front of a real estate agency a few doors down from the apartment of the elegant hostess. The agency entrance was brightly lit, and I had arrived early. I pulled out the text of my speech for some last-minute cramming. I tried to concentrate, but the heel of my left foot felt oddly naked.

Balancing myself against the building, I lifted my calf behind me to inspect the damage. A thin run in my hose was making its way with determination up the back of my leg. A bad omen. It was too late to do anything about it. Across the street, a man with gray hair, glasses, and a tailored black coat looked at me as he walked past. He said something I couldn't quite make out. But he looked respectable enough.

"*Excusez-moi, monsieur?*" I asked.

"*Vous êtes superbe, madame!*" he replied.

I smiled, just a little. The good omen canceled out the bad. How could I be insulted?

We had been told that dinner was called for 8:45. Andy and I waited together under the lighted entryway until 8:55 so as not to appear rude by arriving on time. To our surprise, two other couples were already there when we walked in. Had I gotten the time wrong?

The elegant hostess was wearing a soft and clingy cashmere dress and dangly aquamarine earrings that caught the light when she turned her head. All of the other women were attractive and well dressed, but the elegant hostess dazzled. Only the lawyer and I were dressed entirely in black; the wife of the famous novelist dared to wear crimson Hermès.

The dinner party followed classic protocol. We drank champagne in the salon for nearly an hour. Candles set in front of the windows lighted the dining room table, which was covered in hues of red. The silver was English, the celadon-colored bone china French. As the guest of honor, I was seated in the middle, the famous novelist to my left, the British journalist to my right. The elegant hostess sat opposite me and announced that this would be a "working dinner" and that she would serve as "president" of the table.

But this was not an ordinary working dinner. The topic was not concrete, with arguments easy to organize, as French political leadership or the future of Europe would have been. This was a discussion that would be highly subjective and even confusing. Still, all the guests played the game, albeit with varying degrees of enthusiasm and insight.

"It's a book on seduction in France," the elegant hostess said, as a waiter served the first course—risotto with scallops.

"I don't understand why we're here then!" one of the men said.

Everyone laughed.

"It's to seduce Elaine!" another said. Another laugh. Okay, so they were "amused," as the elegant hostess had promised they would be.

"Listen, you sort it out however you like, but seduction in France is . . . it's a way of approaching France," the elegant hostess said. Did the guests understand the subtlety of her statement, that an "approach" could be interpreted as an act of seduction? I was grateful. The elegant hostess had signaled that she was my partner, my protector.

"She has a notebook!" the famous novelist exclaimed, spying the slim black notebook I had brought along in case someone said something unforgettable. I had positioned it to the left of my forks, rather than within the fold of the large napkin covering my lap, so there would be no secrecy.

Some of the other guests let out a long "Aaaaah."

I had been told that the famous novelist could play the role of observer. But he was so relaxed that he continued the banter with what he called a "very American" question: "Are we to be paid?"

Everyone laughed again.

What could I reply? I thought about explaining how American journalists don't pay for interviews, and then I stopped short. Think glib, I said to myself.

"Talk to my lawyer!" I joked, motioning across and down the table to my husband.

And then I started my speech. I thanked the hostess and the guests. I said that for me, seduction is a key to understanding France. I explained that the word has a sexual and often pejorative connotation in English, while it is much broader and more ambiguous in French. I said that while the French use the expression *opération séduction*, Anglo-Saxons say "charm offensive."

The British journalist interrupted. "But 'charm offensive' is originally a French expression used in diplomacy," he said.

Great. I didn't know that. He went on to explain that most diplomatic terms in English have French origins. My carefully crafted speech was left unfinished as the table drifted into a discussion about the paucity of English diplomatic vocabulary and the precise meaning of the words *galanterie* and *courtoisie.*

The elegant hostess brought the table back to order and urged me to continue my presentation. I said I had three questions for the group: "Does seduction act as a driving force in France? Is there a dark side and does anti-seduction exist, that is, the perversion of seduction that makes the process more important than ever getting a result? Finally, without seduction, is France condemned to death?"

The brilliant novelist liked the game. "Everyone knows that the Frenchman who behaves like a seducer is insufferable," he said. "On the contrary, the Frenchman who doesn't play at it is the one who truly seduces. If you have to make an effort, it's a failure. If there is effortlessness, it's an art!"

Some guests insisted that to succeed, seduction has to be a deliberate, conscious act. They were talking so fast I couldn't catch who was saying what.

"A willful act—" one male guest said.

"—but not too much at once," a female guest added.

"You can't see the mechanics behind it," said another male guest. Aha. That's exactly what some of the women in my women's club had tried to explain to me: that a good seducer in France is one whose strategies are invisible.

The creative thinker announced that "seducer" always had a slightly pejorative ring to it, although not at all as much as in the United States or Britain.

There was agreement that Valéry Giscard d'Estaing had been a *grand séducteur* in his prime, more so than Jacques Chirac. Maybe even now, although Giscard is well into his eighties. The talk moved to Giscard's novel about an imaginary love affair with Princess Diana, and I mentioned that he had signed a copy of his book for me.

"Did he include his phone number?" one of the male guests joked.

The female lawyer declared, "A very seductive woman—it's not only sexual. There are women who seduce all the time, all the time, seducing women as well as men. To seduce, you have to want to seduce, to keep your smile, for example."

I asked her directly—what do you do to seduce?

Andy cut me off with a warning: "Don't go too far, Elaine."

The novelist, concentrating on sexual seduction, proclaimed that the goal of the exercise is not to make a woman feel "seduced"; it is to make her feel *troublée. Troublée*? Disturbed? Perturbed? I asked him to explain. "When a woman says to a man, 'I have been *troublée*,' two days later—in the pocket." He said "in the pocket" in English. In French, the expression is *c'est dans la poche*, meaning, "It's a done deal."

I understood. I thought back to what Alain Baraton, the gardener at Versailles, had once told me, that the goal of seduction is to find the weak spot of the other and avoid an outright rejection at all costs.

There was chatter about a much-criticized YouTube video that showed President Sarkozy giving the Legion of Honor to Dany Boon, the actor. Sarkozy had tried to be funny, playing on Boon's Arab origins. His remarks were considered insulting.

"He tried to do it with humor—and therefore, seduce the public," the famous novelist said. "But it was zero degrees of seduction."

As the second course (a veal roast with apricots and prunes) was served, we landed on a subject that was currently gripping the politicians and thinkers of France: What does it mean to be French? The government had launched town hall meetings throughout France to determine what unifying values define the nation.

I pulled out a copy of the questions the government had sent to the prefectures across France to "enrich" the debates they were conducting. The table agreed that the debate on national identity was sheer folly.

"Look, it says 'churches and cathedrals,'" I said. "Why not also say mosques and synagogues? Or why not just say 'places of worship'?"

"Because that would evoke religion," one man said. "Churches and cathedrals are things of beauty."

"They are museums," another guest chimed in.

There was talk about François Mitterrand's campaign poster for the 1974 presidential election, which included the slogan "The Tranquil Force" and the bell tower of a church.

"This is France, madame," one of the male guests told me with a blend of gentility and condescension.

I recalled Giscard's admonition that as an outsider, I'd never be able to understand his country. I decided that this was a battle I could never win.

Inevitably, the conversation about national identity moved to the importance of desire, of pleasure.

"An identity for France is not an identity of the French people!" the British journalist proclaimed. He lost me there. I sat back and hoped no one would call on me as I had no idea what he meant, but people around me seemed to think it was important and nodded solemnly.

Then I understood where he was going. "How do you give people the pleasure of wanting to be French?" he asked. "With lectures, with gestures of welcome, with education, et cetera, and not at all with symbols, concrete things?"

For him, being French was an attitude, a state of emotion, a feeling—of contentment, of well-being, of belonging.

The famous novelist countered: "Pardon me, but when you say 'with education,' there is also 'La Marseillaise.' So you cannot remove the symbols. In education, there are the symbols of civic instruction."

The former corporate president disagreed. "For me, education is not symbols," he said. "It is the capacity to read."

The two of them embarked on a lengthy digression, a dialogue of subtle gamesmanship that was never impolite or angry but was not always comprehensible, at least not to me. It was also a classic exercise in the art of conversation, in the intellectual foreplay I had come to recognize. They seemed to be enjoying it.

The British journalist raised the issue of Dominique Strauss-Kahn, asking whether he could be the Socialist Party's presidential candidate in 2012 if, say, compromising videos were discovered and posted on YouTube.

But a woman said that Strauss-Kahn's reputation as sexually vigorous would add to—not detract from—his appeal as a candidate.

A male guest suggested that it was a statistical issue. "The big news in France is not that politicians who have had plenty of women win elections," he said. "This is not a question of nature; it's a question of degree. Between one and five, no difference; between five and a thousand, there is a difference."

Okay, now I got it. It was okay for a president to have had five mistresses but not a thousand.

But France had evolved, he explained. "The big news is that Carla Bruni has been accepted, even if she might have had dozens of men," he continued.

Not everyone agreed. A woman disapproved of the fact that Bruni was said to have had so many lovers. The guests tried to name all of them: the well-documented ones like Mick Jagger, Eric Clapton, and Raphaël Enthoven; then the rumored and imagined, including the son of a famous Nazi hunter, a former prime minister, Enthoven's father.

"She knew how to seduce the public," one woman said.

"It's true. She seduced, she really seduced," one man said.

As dessert was served (a charlotte with red fruits and meringues), the famous novelist defined the topic as very important. "In France, there has always been a rule," he said. "When a man sleeps with plenty of women, he's a Don Juan. When a woman sleeps with plenty of men, she's a whore."

"Yes! And Carla Bruni was the first—" said a woman.

"—to have turned this concept on its head—" said her husband.

"—who knew how to reconstruct her image," his wife replied.

I caught only one faux pas. One of the male guests got the elegant hostess's first name wrong. When he did it a second time, the famous novelist corrected him. The male guest apologized. When he got her name wrong a third time, his mistake was ignored. I figured it would have been too brutal for him to lose face once again. Frankly, I was relieved. My gaffes were noticed, too, I assumed, but perhaps more easily forgiven.

Strong espresso, herbal tea, and the Armagnac of the Armagnac couple were served in the living room. The "working" session was over. But even after the dinner guests were split up into several smaller groups, the conversation continued to focus on the subjects that had been raised at the table. "You could say, in effect, that these sophisticated dinner guests had been sufficiently seduced by the notion of discussing the subject that they voluntarily continued doing so," Andy said later.

There was a greater physical casualness than one might expect at a dinner party with such a refined group. Two of the women, including the elegant hostess, sat on the floor. The loosening up was more than the effect of champagne and fine wines. The nature of the dinner conversation had lent an unusual ease to the final act of the evening.

The brilliant thinker took me aside over coffee to say he had been struck by what had been left unspoken. I asked him to explain, but another guest joined us. The revelation that seemed to hold so much promise was put on hold.

The guests lingered until after midnight, even though it was a weeknight. The dinner had been a success. But what new insights had I gleaned about seduction?

There had been no disciplined Cartesian debate that culminated in a climax of sublime revelation and transcendence. But there had been an enthusiastic embrace of the subject. There had been agreement that the French *art de vivre*—art of living—was much superior to the "American way of life" because it was not work but encompassed pleasure and the appreciation of beauty. There had been disagreement over whether the art of conversation could take place in a bistro in a working-class suburb or needed a rarefied atmosphere like ours.

There had been no secrets spilled. The conversation had been directed outward, not inward. We were far away from America. No one spoke about work, money, or real estate. If anyone had been betrayed or unfaithful, or had committed adultery in his or her heart, Jimmy Carter–style, it was not confessed.

But there had been recollections of sweet memories. I found it touching when the brilliant thinker said that in his boyhood, his mother had taught him to dress well and look good even when he ran the most routine errand. He recalled a Coco Chanel line about anticipation and promise that he had learned from his mother: a man should never go out on the street without saying to himself that he is going to meet the woman of his life.

As for me, I came away both disappointed and elated. I hadn't been able to stop behaving like an American. I had wanted to appear a bit like Fanny Frisbee, a character in Edith Wharton's 1907 novella *Madame de Treymes*. Fanny was a New Yorker who had married a cold and rigid French marquis and was contemplating divorce so that she could marry an American who was both her lover and a friend from childhood. In the process of living in France, she had shed much of her American skin and become more French. In the eyes of her lover, this was a good thing.

But I hadn't transformed myself into Fanny. The influences of living in France had not made me mysterious, lowered my voice, regulated my gestures, or toned me down into harmony with the warm, dim background of a long social past. I had asked my questions with the brutal directness of a journalist, not the languorous sweetness of a siren.

Andy and I were the last to leave. As the guests of honor, should we have been the first? Too late.

We stood at the door with the elegant hostess and her husband. It was a special moment. We started to review what had been said and what had not. But now it was late, and the discussion was quickly suspended. We said they should come to our home, just the four of us, another time. Dinner that evening had been a gift, and also an act of intimacy. We had been let in. It would not be enough to write a note or call with a message of thanks the next day.

Andy and I made our way down the narrow winding stairs into the courtyard and the cold air of Paris after midnight. Late-night Paris belongs to the *flâneur*, the idle walker with no purpose except to roam.

There is always beauty to be discovered. So we decided to walk. There was no traffic; the only sound was the click of my impossibly high heels.

Andy told me about his conversation over coffee with the partner of the British journalist. "She considered herself the guest at the table most outside of the classic 'intelligentsia,' yet she said things that so perfectly capture the importance of seduction in her life," he told me. He said that she had described working long and hard on her appearance every morning, a French woman wanting to look good both for herself (for her feeling of well-being) and for others. She had told him how much she enjoyed French television programs—those endless roundtable talk-a-thons with no resolution at the end—that Americans find impenetrable and boring.

We walked past the real estate agency and the Saint-Germain church and the café Les Deux Magots. It wasn't yet 1:00 a.m. so the city of Paris had not turned off the lights on its buildings and bridges.

I had the feeling of comfort that comes with belonging, not entirely of course, but enough. I thought of a gift I had once given Andy: a David Sipress cartoon that first appeared in *The New Yorker*. It shows a small, serious, balding, bespectacled, middle-aged man sunk deep in an oversized armchair. He is reading a book. An image of the Eiffel Tower illustrates the back of the jacket. The book's title is "How to Be One of Those People Who Goes Off to Live in Paris."

Andy and I had gone off to live in Paris. And it had seduced us.

"Every man has two countries, his own and France," says a character in a play by the nineteenth-century poet and playwright Henri de Bornier. In our years living there, we have tried to make the country our own, even though we know that will never entirely happen. We will never think like the French, never shed our Americanness. Nor do we want to.

And like an elusive lover who clings to mystery, France will never completely reveal herself to us. Even now, when I walk around a corner I anticipate that something pleasurable might happen, the next act in a process of perpetual seduction.

BIBLIOGRAPHY

Every American who sets out to write a book exploring France and the French is aware of many fine books in English that have already been written on the subject. I'd like to single out a few that were exceptionally useful in my research and may be of interest to readers who can't get enough of things French.

One of the best overviews of France is still *Fragile Glory: A Portrait of France and the French*, written by my former *New York Times* colleague Richard Bernstein. First published in 1990, the book combines reporting, memoir, and analysis to produce an authoritative, first-rate account of the country.

Paris to the Moon (2000) by the master storyteller Adam Gopnik is an eloquent love letter to his wife and son and the life they all made together in Paris. His edited literary anthology, *Americans in Paris* (2004), a collection of delicious writings by Americans on Paris over the decades, is best savored with a glass of fine French wine.

Diane Johnson's 1997 novel *Le Divorce* is a superb comedy of morals and manners about the American encounter with France in the tradition of Edith Wharton and Henry James. I dip into it over and over—and I always laugh out loud.

A helpful guide for American women on the mystique of their French counterparts is *What French Women Know: About Love, Sex, and Other Matters of the Heart and Mind* (2009) by Debra Ollivier. Ollivier, who is married to a Frenchman and lived in France for ten years, is an insider who treats her subject with the right blend of humor and gravitas.

Then there is *French Toast: An American in Paris Celebrates the Maddening Mysteries of the French* (1997) by my friend Harriet Welty Rochefort, who has lived in France with her French husband for more than thirty years. She offers lessons on the French in a sassy tone, and even shares her mother-in-law's culinary secrets.

Finally, Charles Cogan's *French Negotiating Behavior: Dealing with La*

Grande Nation (2003) is an indispensable primer for negotiating with the French, in both diplomacy and life.

BOOKS

Ackerman, Diane. *A Natural History of the Senses.* New York: Random House, 1990.

Adams, William Howard. *The Paris Years of Thomas Jefferson.* New Haven: Yale University Press, 1997.

Ah, ces Gaulois!: La France et les Français. Paris: Courrier International, 2009.

Ardagh, John. *France in the 1980s.* New York: Penguin Books, 1983.

Assouline, Pierre. *Les invités.* Paris: Éditions Gallimard, 2009.

Azéroual, Yves, and Valérie Bénaïm. *Carla et Nicolas, la véritable histoire.* Paris: Éditions du Moment, 2008.

Bacqué, Raphaëlle, and Ariane Chemin. *La femme fatale.* Paris: Éditions Albin Michel, 2007.

Bagieu, Pénélope. *Ma vie est tout à fait fascinante.* Paris: Jean-Claude Gawsewitch Éditeur, 2008.

Bajos, Nathalie, and Michel Bozon. *Enquête sur la sexualité en France: Pratiques, genre et santé.* Paris: Éditions La Découverte, 2008.

Balasko, Josiane. *Cliente.* Paris: Librairie Arthème Fayard, 2004.

Balladur, Édouard. *Jeanne d'Arc et la France: Le mythe du sauveur.* Paris: Éditions Fayard, 2003.

Baraton, Alain. *L'amour à Versailles.* Paris: Éditions Grasset & Fasquelle, 2009.

Bardot, Brigitte. *Initiales B.B.: Mémoires.* Paris: Éditions Grasset & Fasquelle, 1996.

Barry, Joseph. *French Lovers: From Heloise & Abelard to Beauvoir & Sartre.* New York: Arbor House, 1987.

Barthes, Roland. *The Eiffel Tower and Other Mythologies.* Translated by Richard Howard. Berkeley: University of California Press, 1997.

———. *A Lover's Discourse: Fragments.* Translated by Richard Howard. London: Vintage, 2002.

———. *Mythologies.* Translated by Annette Lavers. New York: Hill & Wang, 2001.

Baudrillard, Jean. *Seduction.* Translated by Brian Singer. New York: St. Martin's Press, 1990.

Baverez, Nicolas. *La France qui tombe.* Paris: Éditions Perrin, 2003.

Beaune, Colette. *Jeanne d'Arc, vérités et légendes.* Paris: Éditions Perrin, 2008.

Beauvoir, Simone de. *Brigitte Bardot and the Lolita Syndrome.* Translated by Bernard Fretchman. New York: Reynal & Company, 1959.

———. *La cérémonie des adieux, suivi de "Entretiens avec Jean-Paul Sartre: Août–Septembre 1974."* Paris: Éditions Gallimard, 1987.

Belloc, Hilaire. *Paris*. London: Methuen & Co., 1929.

Berents, Dirk Arend, J. van Herwaarden, and Marina Warner. *Joan of Arc: Reality and Myth*. Rotterdam: Uitgeverij Verloren, 1994.

Bernstein, Richard. *Fragile Glory: A Portrait of France and the French*. New York: Alfred A. Knopf, 1990.

Binh, N. T., and Franck Garbarz. *Paris au cinéma: La vie rêvée de la capitale de Méliès à Amélie Poulain*. Paris: Éditions Parigramme, 2005.

Birenbaum, Guy. *Nos délits d'initiés: Mes soupçons de citoyen*. Paris: Éditions Stock, 2003.

Birnbaum, Pierre. *The Idea of France*. Translated by M. B. DeBevoise. New York: Hill and Wang, 2001.

Blain, Christophe, and Abel Lanzac. *Quai d'Orsay: Chroniques diplomatiques*. Vol. 1. Paris: Dargaud, 2010.

Blayn, Jean-François, Pierre Bourdon, Guy Haasser, Jean-Claude Delville, Jean-François Latty, Maurice Maurin, Alberto Morillas, Dominique Preyssas, Maurice Roucel, Henri Sebag, and Christian Vuillemin. *Questions de parfumerie: Essais sur l'art et la création en parfumerie*. Paris: Corpman Éditions, 1988.

Brame, Geneviève. *Living and Working in France: 'Chez vous en France.'* Translated by Linda Koike. London: Kogan Page Ltd., 2001.

Braudel, Fernand. *The Identity of France*. Vol. 1, *History and Environment*. Translated by Sîan Reynolds. London: HarperCollins, 1990.

Bréon, Emmanuel, and Michèle Lefrançois. *Le Musée des Années 30*. Paris: Somogy Éditions d'Art, 2006.

Broadway Medieval Library. *The Trial of Jeanne d'Arc: A Complete Translation of the Text of the Original Documents with an Introduction by W. P. Barrett*. London: George Routledge & Sons, 1931.

Brownell, W. C. *French Traits: An Essay in Comparative Criticism*. New York: Charles Scribner's Sons, 1918.

Bruckner, Pascal. *Le paradoxe amoureux*. Paris: Éditions Grasset & Fasquelle, 2009.

——— and Alain Finkielkraut. *Le nouveau désordre amoureux*. Paris: Éditions du Seuil, 1997.

Burr, Chandler. *The Perfect Scent: A Year Inside the Perfume Industry in Paris and New York*. New York: Picador, 2009.

Butzbach, Thierry, and Morgan Railane. *Qui veut tuer la dentelle de Calais?* Lille: Éditions Les Lumières de Lille, 2009.

Callières, François de. *The Art of Diplomacy*. Edited by H. M. A. Keens-Soper and Karl W. Schweizer. New York: Holmes & Meier, 1983.

Caracalla, Laurence. *Le carnet du savoir-recevoir.* Paris: Éditions Flammarion/Le Figaro, 2009.

Chevalier, Louis. *The Assassination of Paris.* Translated by David P. Jordan. Chicago: University of Chicago Press, 1994.

———. *Les Parisiens.* Paris: Hachette, 1967.

Child, Julia, and Alex Prud'homme. *My Life in France.* New York: Alfred A. Knopf, 2006.

Chirac, Bernadette, and Patrick de Carolis. *Conversation.* Paris: Plon, 2001.

Chirac, Jacques. *Chaque pas doit être un but: Mémoires.* Paris: NIL Éditions, 2009.

Clarke, Stephen. *Talk to the Snail: Ten Commandments for Understanding the French.* New York: Bloomsbury, 2006.

Clemenceau, Georges. *Les plus forts.* France: Éditions Fasquelle, 1898.

Cobb, Richard. *Paris and its Provinces: 1792–1802.* London: Oxford University Press, 1975.

Cogan, Charles. *French Negotiating Behavior: Dealing with La Grande Nation.* Washington, D.C.: United States Institute of Peace Press, 2003.

Colin, Pierre-Louis. *Guide des jolies femmes de Paris.* Paris: Éditions Robert Laffont, 2008.

Colombani, Marie-Françoise, and Michèle Fitoussi. *Elle 1945–2005: Une histoire des femmes.* Paris: Éditions Filipacchi, 2005.

Coudurier, Hubert. *Amours, ruptures & trahisons.* Paris: Librairie Arthème Fayard, 2008.

Darmon, Michaël, and Yves Derai. *Ruptures.* Paris: Éditions du Moment, 2008.

Daswani, Kavita. *Salaam, Paris.* New York: Plume, 2006.

Davis, Katharine. *Capturing Paris.* New York: St. Martin's Press, 2006.

Dawesar, Abha. *That Summer in Paris.* New York: Anchor Books, 2007.

DeJean, Joan. *The Essence of Style: How the French Invented High Fashion, Fine Food, Chic Cafés, Style, Sophistication, and Glamour.* New York: Simon & Schuster, 2006.

———. *The Reinvention of Obscenity: Sex, Lies, and Tabloids in Early Modern France.* Chicago: University of Chicago Press, 2002.

Deloire, Christophe, and Christophe Dubois. *Sexus politicus.* Paris: Éditions Albin Michel, 2006.

Descure, Virginie, and Christophe Casazza. *Ciné Paris: 20 balades sur des lieux de tournages mythiques.* Paris: Éditions Hors Collection, 2003.

Dixsaut, Claire, and Vincent Chenille. *Bon appétit, Mr. Bond.* Paris: Agnès Viénot Éditions, 2008.

Downs, Laura Lee, and Stéphane Gerson, eds. *Why France? American Historians Reflect on an Enduring Fascination.* Ithaca, N.Y.: Cornell University Press, 2007.

Dubor, Georges De. *Les favorites royales: De Henri IV à Louis XVI*. Paris: Nabu Press, 2010.

Dumas, Bertrand. *Trésors des églises parisiennes*. Paris: Éditions Parigramme, 2005.

Ellena, Jean-Claude. *Le parfum*. Paris: Presses Universitaires de France, 2007.

Fenby, Jonathan. *France on the Brink*. New York: Arcade Publishing, 1999.

Ferney, Alice. *The Lovers*. Translated by Helen Stevenson. London: Atlantic Books, 2001.

Flanner, Janet. *Paris Was Yesterday: 1925–1939*. New York: Viking Press, 1972.

Fraser, Antonia. *Love and Louis XIV: The Women in the Life of the Sun King*. New York: Nan A. Talese/Doubleday, 2006.

Fulda, Anne. *Un président très entouré*. Paris: Éditions Grasset & Fasquelle, 1997.

Garde, Serge, Valérie Mauro, and Rémi Gardebled. *Guide du Paris des faits divers: Du moyen âge à nos jours*. Paris: Le Cherche Midi, 2004.

Gaulle, Charles de. *The Complete War Memoirs of Charles de Gaulle*. Vol. 1, *The Call to Honor*. Translated by Jonathan Griffin. New York: Simon and Schuster, 1964.

Georgel, Jacques. *Sexe et politique*. Rennes: Éditions Apogée, 1999.

Gershman, Suzy. *C'est la Vie: An American Conquers the City of Light, Begins a New Life, and Becomes—Zut Alors!—Almost French*. New York: Viking Press, 2004.

Giesbert, Franz-Olivier. *La tragédie du président: Scènes de la vie politique (1986–2006)*. Paris: Éditions Flammarion, 2006.

Giono, Jean. *Regain*. Paris: Librairie Générale Française, 1995.

Giroud, Françoise. *Les Françaises: De la Gauloise à la pilule*. Paris: Éditions Fayard, 1999.

——— and Bernard-Henri Lévy. *Women and Men: A Philosophical Conversation*. Translated by Richard Miller. Boston: Little, Brown, 1995.

Giscard d'Estaing, Valéry. *Le passage*. Paris: Éditions Robert Laffont, 1994.

———. *Le pouvoir et la vie*. Vol. 1. Paris: Compagnie 12, 1988.

———. *La princesse et le président*. Paris: Éditions de Fallois-XO, 2009.

Gonnet, Paul. *Histoire de Grasse et sa région*. Le Coteau: Éditions Horvath, 1984.

Gopnik, Adam, ed. *Americans in Paris: A Literary Anthology*. New York: The Library of America, 2004.

———. *Paris to the Moon*. New York: Random House, 2000.

Gordon, Philip H. *A Certain Idea of France: French Security Policy and the Gaullist Legacy*. Princeton: Princeton University Press, 1993.

Green, Julian. *Paris*. Translated by J. A. Underwood. London: Marion Boyars Publishers, 2001.

Greene, Robert. *The Art of Seduction*. New York: Penguin Books, 2003.

Guéguen, Nicolas. *Psychologie de la séduction: Pour mieux comprendre nos comportements amoureux*. Paris: Dunod, 2009.

Guiliano, Mireille. *French Women Don't Get Fat*. New York: Alfred A. Knopf, 2005.

Habib, Claude. *Galanterie française*. Paris: Éditions Gallimard, 2006.

Hennig, Jean-Luc. *Brève histoire des fesses*. Paris: Éditions Zulma, 2003.

Higonnet, Patrice. *Paris: Capital of the World*. Translated by Arthur Goldhammer. Cambridge, Mass.: Harvard University Press, 2002.

Hoffmann, Stanley. *L'Amérique vraiment impériale?* Paris: Éditions Louis Audibert, 2003.

Horne, Alistair. *Seven Ages of Paris: Portrait of a City*. New York: Alfred A. Knopf, 2002.

Hussey, Andrew. *Paris: The Secret History*. New York: Viking, 2006.

Jaigu, Charles. *Sarkozy, du Fouquet's à Gaza*. Paris: Éditions Robert Laffont, 2009.

James, Henry. *A Little Tour in France*. New York: Elibron Classics, 2005.

Johnson, Diane. *Le Divorce*. New York: Penguin Books, 1997.

———. *Into a Paris Quartier: Reine Margot's Chapel and Other Haunts of St.-Germain*. Washington, D.C.: National Geographic Society, 2005.

Jones, Colin. *Paris: The Biography of a City*. New York: Penguin Books, 2006.

Jonnes, Jill. *Eiffel's Tower: The Thrilling Story Behind Paris's Beloved Monument and the Extraordinary World's Fair That Introduced It*. New York: Penguin Books, 2009.

Karnow, Stanley. *Paris in the Fifties*. New York: Times Books, 1997.

Kerbrat-Orecchioni, Catherine. *L'implicite*. Paris: Éditions Armand Colin, 1986.

Kessel, Joseph. *Belle de jour*. Paris: Éditions Gallimard, 1928.

Lafayette, Madame de. *The Princesse de Clèves*. Translated by Robin Buss. New York: Penguin Books, 2004.

Lamy, Michel. *Jeanne d'Arc: Histoire vraie et genèse d'un mythe*. Paris: Payot, 1987.

Laumond, Jean-Claude. *Vingt-cinq ans avec lui*. Paris: Ramsay, 2001.

Lebouc, Georges. *Dictionnaire érotique de la francophonie*. Bruxelles: Éditions Racine, 2008.

L'Enclos, Ninon de. *Life, Letters, and Epicurean Philosophy of Ninon de L'Enclos*. Translated by Charles Henry Robinson and William Hassell Overton. Charleston, S.C.: BiblioBazaar, 2007.

Le Guérer, Annick. *Le parfum: Des origines à nos jours*. Paris: Odile Jacob, 2005.

Le Maire, Bruno. *Des hommes d'État*. Paris: Éditions Grasset & Fasquelle, 2007.

———. *Le ministre: Récit*. Paris: Éditions Grasset & Fasquelle, 2004.

Lemoine, Bertrand. *La tour de Monsieur Eiffel*. Paris: Éditions Gallimard, 1989.

Lévy, Bernard-Henri. *American Vertigo: Traveling America in the Footsteps of Tocqueville*. Translated by Charlotte Mandell. New York: Random House, 2006.

Lilla, Mark. *New French Thought: Political Philosophy*. Princeton: Princeton University Press, 1994.

Lobe, Kirsten. *Paris Hangover*. New York: St. Martin's Press, 2006.

Margolis, Nadia. *Joan of Arc in History, Literature, and Film: A Select, Annotated Bibliography*. New York: Garland Publishers, 1990.

Martel, Frédéric. *Mainstream: Enquête sur cette culture qui plaît à tout le monde*. Paris: Éditions Flammarion, 2010.

Millau, Christian. *Dictionnaire amoureux de la gastronomie*. Paris: Plon, 2008.

Miller, John J., and Mark Molesky. *Our Oldest Enemy: A History of America's Disastrous Relationship with France*. New York: Doubleday, 2004.

Mimoun, Sylvain. *Ce que les femmes préfèrent: Première enquête sur le désir féminin*. Paris: Éditions Albin Michel, 2008.

Minc, Alain. *Une histoire de France*. Paris: Éditions Grasset & Fasquelle, 2008.

Mitterrand, François. *The Wheat and the Chaff*. Translated by Richard S. Woodward, Concilia Hayter, and Helen R. Lane. New York: Seaver Books/Lattès, 1982.

Mitterrand, Frédéric. *La mauvaise vie*. Paris: Éditions Pocket, 2009.

Molière. *Don Juan and Other Plays*. Translated by George Graveley and Ian Maclean. New York: Oxford University Press, 2008.

Moors, Candice, Sébastien Daycard-Heid, and Ophélie Neiman. *Transports amoureux: Les petites annonces de Libération et autres déclarations nomades*. Toulouse: Éditions Milan, 2009.

Morana, Virginie, and Véronique Morana. *The Parisian Woman's Guide to Style*. New York: Universe Publishing, 1999.

Nadeau, Jean-Benoît, and Julie Barlow. *Sixty Million Frenchmen Can't Be Wrong: Why We Love France, but Not the French*. Naperville, Calif.: Sourcebooks, 2003.

Nay, Catherine. *Le noir et le rouge, ou, l'histoire d'une ambition*. Paris: Éditions Grasset, 1984.

Netchine, Ève. *Jeux de princes, jeux de vilains*. Paris: Bibliothèque Nationale de France/Éditions du Seuil, 2009.

Nye, Joseph S. Jr. *The Paradox of American Power: Why the World's Only Superpower Can't Go It Alone*. Oxford: Oxford University Press, 2003.

Ollivier, Debra. *Entre Nous: A Woman's Guide to Finding Her Inner French Girl*. New York: St. Martin's Press, 2004.

———. *What French Women Know: About Love, Sex, and Other Matters of the Heart and Mind.* New York: Putnam Adult, 2009.

D'Ormesson, Jean. *Qu'ai-je donc fait?* Paris: Éditions Pocket, 2009.

Ozouf, Mona. *Les mots des femmes.* Paris: Éditions Fayard, 1995.

Pillivuyt, Ghislaine, Doris Jakubec, and Pauline Mercier. *Les flacons de la séduction: L'art du parfum au XVIIIème siècle.* Lausanne: La Bibliothèque des Arts, 1985.

Pingeot, Mazarine. *Bouche cousue.* Paris: Éditions Julliard, 2005.

Pitte, Jean-Robert. *Bordeaux/Burgundy: A Vintage Rivalry.* Translated by M. B. DeBevoise. Berkeley and Los Angeles: University of California Press, 2008.

———. *Le désir du vin à la conquête du monde.* Paris: Éditions Fayard, 2009.

Pivot, Bernard. *100 expressions à sauver.* Paris: Éditions Albin Michel, 2008.

Platt, Polly. *French or Foe?: Getting the Most Out of Visiting, Living, and Working in France.* London: Culture Crossings, 2003.

———. *Love à la Française: What Happens When Hervé Meets Sally.* Skokie, Ill.: MEP, 2008.

Pochon, Caroline, and Allan Rothschild. *La face cachée des fesses.* Paris: Éditions Jean di Sciullo, 2009.

Powell, Helena Frith. *Two Lipsticks and a Lover.* London: Arrow Books, 2007.

Proust, Marcel. *The Complete Short Stories of Marcel Proust.* Translated by Joachim Neugroschel. Lanham, Md.: Cooper Square Publishers, 2003.

———. *In Search of Lost Time: Swann's Way.* Vol. 1. Translated by C. K. Scott Moncrieff. New York: Vintage Classics, 1996.

Revel, Jean-François. *L'obsession anti-américaine: Son fonctionnement, ses causes, ses inconséquences.* Paris: Plon, 2002.

Reza, Yasmina. *Dawn Dusk or Night: A Year with Nicolas Sarkozy.* Translated by Yasmina Reza and Pierre Guglielmina. New York: Vintage Books, 2009.

Rice, Howard C. *Thomas Jefferson's Paris.* Princeton: Princeton University Press, 1976.

Richardson, Joanna. *The Courtesans: The Demi-Monde in 19th-Century France.* Edison, N.J.: Castle Books, 2004.

Robb, Graham. *The Discovery of France: A Historical Geography from the Revolution to the First World War.* New York: W. W. Norton & Company, 2007.

Roche, Loïck. *Cupidon au travail.* Paris: Éditions d'Organisation, 2006.

Rochefort, Harriet Welty. *French Toast: An American in Paris Celebrates the Maddening Mysteries of the French.* New York: St. Martin's Press, 1999.

Roger, Philippe. *The American Enemy: The History of French Anti-Americanism.* Translated by Sharon Bowman. Chicago: University of Chicago Press, 2005.

Rosenblum, Mort. *Mission to Civilize: The French Way.* New York: Harcourt Brace Jovanovich, 1986.

Rostand, Edmond. *Cyrano de Bergerac*. Translated by Lowell Blair. New York: New American Library, 2003.

Rouvillois, Frédéric. *Histoire de la politesse: De 1789 à nos jours*. Paris: Éditions Flammarion, 2006.

———. *Histoire du snobisme*. Paris: Éditions Flammarion, 2008.

Rowley, Anthony, and Jean-Claude Ribaut. *Le vin: Une histoire de goût*. Paris: Éditions Gallimard, 2003.

Saint-Amand, Pierre. *The Libertine's Progress: Seduction in the Eighteenth-Century French Novel*. Translated by Jennifer Curtiss Gage. Hanover, N.H.: University Press of New England, 1994.

Sarkozy, Nicolas. *Testimony: France in the Twenty-first Century*. Translated by Philip H. Gordon. New York: Pantheon Books, 2007.

Séguéla, Jacques. *Autobiographie non autorisée*. Paris: Plon, 2009.

Sempé, Jean-Jacques. *Un peu de Paris*. Paris: Éditions Gallimard, 2001.

Servat, Henry-Jean. *Bardot: La légende*. Paris: Presses de la Cité, 2009.

Sieburg, Friedrich. *Dieu est-il français?* Paris: Éditions Grasset, 1930.

Simon, François. *Pique-assiette: La fin d'une gastronomie française*. Paris: Éditions Grasset & Fasquelle, 2008.

Sisman, Robyn. *Weekend in Paris*. New York: Penguin Books, 2004.

Stanger, Ted. *Sacrés Français! Un Américain nous regarde*. Paris: Éditions Michalon, 2003.

Steinberger, Michael. *Au Revoir to All That: Food, Wine, and the End of France*. New York: Bloomsbury, 2010.

Stendhal. *The Red and the Black: A Chronicle of the Nineteenth Century*. Translated by Catherine Slater. London: Oxford University Press, 1998.

Stewart, John Hall, ed. *A Documentary Survey of the French Revolution*. New York: Macmillan, 1966.

Suleiman, Ezra. *Schizophrénies françaises*. Paris: Éditions Grasset & Fasquelle, 2008.

Tessier, Bertrand. *Belmondo l'incorrigible*. Paris: Éditions Flammarion, 2009.

Thomas, Dana. *Deluxe: How Luxury Lost Its Luster*. New York: Penguin Press, 2007.

Thomass, Chantal, and Catherine Örmen. *Histoire de la lingerie*. Paris: Éditions Perrin, 2009.

Tiersky, Ronald. *François Mitterrand: A Very French President*. Lanham, Md.: Rowan & Littlefield, 2003.

Tocqueville, Alexis de. *Democracy in America and Two Essays on America*. Translated by Gerald E. Bevan. New York: Penguin Classics, 2003.

Toscano, Alberto. *Critique amoureuse des français*. Paris: Hachette Littératures, 2009.

Turnbull, Sarah. *Almost French: Love and a New Life in Paris*. New York: Gotham Books, 2003.

Vaillant, Maryse. *Les hommes, l'amour, la fidélité*. Paris: Éditions Albin Michel, 2009.

Valéry, Paul. *Regards sur le monde actuel*. Paris: Éditions Gallimard, 1945.

Vereker, Susie. *Pond Lane and Paris*. Oxford: Transita, 2005.

Villepin, Dominique de. *Les cents-jours ou l'esprit de sacrifice*. Paris: Librairie Académique Perrin, 2001.

———. *La cité des hommes*. Paris: Plon, 2009.

———. *Le cri de la gargouille*. Paris: Éditions Albin Michel, 2002.

———. *Éloge des voleurs de feu*. Paris: Éditions Gallimard, 2003.

———. *Le requin et la mouette*. Paris: Plon/Éditions Albin Michel, 2004.

Wadham, Lucy. *The Secret Life of France*. London: Faber and Faber, 2009.

Weber, Eugen. *My France: Politics, Culture, Myth*. Cambridge, Mass.: Belknap Press of Harvard University Press, 1992.

Weil, Patrick. *How to Be French: Nationality in the Making since 1789*. Translated by Catherine Porter. Durham, N.C.: Duke University Press, 2008.

Wharton, Edith. *French Ways and Their Meaning*. New York: D. Appleton and Company, 1919.

———. *Madame De Treymes and Three Novellas*. New York: Scribner, 1995.

White, Edmund. *The Flâneur: A Stroll Through the Paradoxes of Paris*. New York: Bloomsbury, 2001.

Wylie, Laurence, and Jean-François Brière. *Les français*. Upper Saddle River, N.J.: Prentice Hall, 2001.

Zeldin, Theodore. *The French*. New York: Kodansha America, 1996.

ARTICLES

Bensaïd, Daniel. "Mai 1429, naissance d'un mythe: Jeanne d'Arc, la revenante." *Alternative Libertaire* 184 (May 2009).

Ferguson, Patricia Parkhurst. "Is Paris France?" *The French Review* 73, no. 6 (May 2000): 1052–64.

Gagnon, John, Alain Giami, Stuart Michaels, and Patrick de Colomby. "A Comparative Study of the Couple in the Social Organization of Sexuality in France and the United States." *Journal of Sex Research* 38 (Feb. 2001): 24–34.

Galleron Marasescu, Ioana. "Le baiser transport dans la fiction en prose de la première moitié du XVIIème siècle." In *Les baisers des lumières*, edited by Alain Montandon, 31–42. Clermont-Ferrand: Presses Universitaires Blaise Pascal, 2004.

Hohenadel, Kristen. "Paris for Real vs. Paris on Film: We'll Always Have the Movies." *New York Times*, Nov. 25, 2001, 11, 21.

Kaplan, Steven Laurence. "Défense d'afficher . . ." In *Why France?*, edited by Laura Lee Downs and Stéphane Gerson, 73–87. Ithaca, N.Y.: Cornell University Press, 2007.

Vickermann-Ribémont, Gabriele. "Baiser du cœur ou de l'esprit: Le baisemain au XVIIIe siècle français." In *Les baisers des lumières*, edited by Alain Montandon, 55–74. Clermont-Ferrand: Presses Universitaires Blaise Pascal, 2004.

ACKNOWLEDGMENTS

The idea for this book began with a lecture I gave at the New York Public Library in May 2008 entitled "Seduction *à la française*." Nicolas Sarkozy had just marked the first anniversary of his presidency, and a poll had determined that the French people considered him the worst president in the history of the Fifth Republic. I explained to the audience that seduction is a key to understanding France and the French, and that Sarkozy had not mastered the rules of the seduction game.

Paul Golob, the editorial director of Times Books, who years before had edited *Persian Mirrors*, my book on Iran, came up to me afterward. "Elaine," he said, "this is your next book."

So I first must thank Paul, who once again became my editor. He spotted the makings of a book in what was originally conceived as a diverting forty-minute talk and helped shape it into *La Seduction*. His deep knowledge of France and things French (he really does know the difference between a Côte de Beaune and a Côte de Nuits) added a layer of complexity to the text. His editing and reediting improved and refined it.

I also must thank Paul LeClerc, the New York Public Library's director and a scholar on France, who invited me to speak and engaged with me in a lively conversation about the country.

My French adventure had started decades before. James Valone, a warm and wonderful history professor and my academic adviser in college, awakened my passion for French history and persuaded me to pursue it in graduate school. The late Maynard Parker sent me to Paris for the first time as a foreign correspondent for *Newsweek* when I was still in my twenties.

In 2002, the *New York Times* gave me a dream job: Paris bureau chief. Seven years later, Bill Keller and the other editors allowed me to take time off to write this book. Jill Abramson read parts of the manuscript and gave me strategic advice. William Schmidt, whom I have known since our days together in *Newsweek*'s Chicago bureau in the 1970s, was more helpful than he will ever know.

La Seduction was written with the help of a grant from the Woodrow Wilson International Center for Scholars, which hosted me as a public policy fellow. Lee H. Hamilton, Michael Van Dusen, and Robert S. Litwak, who had welcomed me as a fellow when I was writing *Persian Mirrors*, once again made me part of the Wilson Center family.

Princeton University hosted me in the fall of 2010 as a Ferris Professor of Journalism, which gave me access to the awesome resources of the university. A special thanks to Carol Rigolot, the director of the program; her husband, François Rigolot; and Mary Harper for their guidance on France and French literature; and to the Princeton staff: Lin DeTitta, Cass Garner, and Susan Coburn. Thanks also to Brooke Kroeger, who heads the Arthur L. Carter Journalism Institute at New York University, for offering me a perch as visiting scholar.

Once again, Andrew Wylie, the literary agent who makes magic, never sleeps, and responds to every query in record time, and Jeffrey Posternak, his deputy, were faithful, patient partners in the process.

At Times Books and Henry Holt, several people played important roles behind the scenes, including Alex Ward at the *Times* and the marketing and publicity team, especially Stephen Rubin, Maggie Richards, and Maggie Sivon. Emi Ikkanda, Paul's assistant, was helpful in so many ways—organizing photographs, reading the manuscript, coordinating trans-Atlantic communication.

I would like to single out a number of friends for special thanks.

Barbara Ireland, a gifted former *New York Times* editor, spent days, evenings, and weekends reading every line of the manuscript, structuring, shaping, and polishing it and pushing me to find my voice when I was singing in the wrong key.

Bertrand Vannier, a friend and colleague for more than thirty years, carried my manuscript to the beach at Île de Ré; he urged me to make the book shorter and funnier. Michèle Fitoussi, the gifted writer and journalist, shared ideas, gave me leads, and opened doors in the world of French journalism, fashion, and culture. I treasure our friendship.

Basil Katz, a talented journalist and former *New York Times* research assistant, taught me about French cuisine. Jean-Claude Ribaut took up where Basil left off. Walter Wells taught me about French wine. Sophie-Caroline de Margerie took me into her world and taught me about style, beauty, women, and culture. Her husband, Gilles de Margerie, guided me through the minefield of French politics.

Chandler Burr introduced me to the French perfume world and taught me about scent. Gérard Araud, Philippe Errera, and Catherine Colonna schooled me in the ins and outs of French diplomacy. Alan Riding, my mentor in French culture in the *New York Times* Paris bureau, suggested I write more about romance and sex. He saved me from several errors and kept me laughing.

Joyce and Isadore Seltzer, Carol Giacomo, Susan Fraker, Farideh Farhi, Lin Widmann, Geraldine Baum, and Donna Smith were rocks of support, as they were the last time I threw myself into book writing.

Other friends and colleagues read all or part of the manuscript, offering ideas and correcting mistakes, among them Pierre Assouline, Ariane Bernard, Charles Bremner, Marc Charney, Maïa de la Baume, Sybil d'Origny, Maureen Dowd, Hélène Fouquet, Philippe Hertzberg, Julia Husson, Philippe Labro, Frédéric Martel, Sophie Meunier, Jonathan Randal, Shéhérazade Semsar de Boisséson, and Marie-Christine Vannier.

Ed Alcock, a keen-eyed photographer, took many of the photos in the book and helped me locate and choose others. Tom Bodkin, Kelly Doe, Owen Franken, Jeffrey Scales, and Daphné Anglès shared their artistic visions. Ron Skarzenski solved obscure technical problems.

Florence Coupry, a brilliant young journalist, was at my side day after day throughout most of the process. Simply put, she can do—and did—everything. She researched minute facts, translated interviews, resolved logistical and computer problems, found obscure photos, took videos, and watched old French films. Her pursuit of excellence is matched only by her sharp sense of humor. (At particularly stressful moments, she would pull out a hula hoop.)

Sanae Lemoine, a French student and fiction writer studying in the United States, brought a novelist's sensibility to our research. Sarah Sahel and Camille Le Coz, two intrepid French students, cheerfully carried out impossible assignments. Rebecca Ruquist, Elisabeth Zerofsky, Lucie Lecocq, and Samuel Lopez-Barrantes joined our team at crucial moments.

As for the dozens of French men and women—among them politicians, diplomats, artists, writers, chefs, businessmen, merchants, farmers, philosophers, journalists, students, fashion designers, perfume creators, museum curators—who instructed me in French ways and their meaning over the years, their perspectives were invaluable. I am especially grateful to the women in my French women's group, who accepted me, a foreigner, into their ranks and embraced this project.

The most important support came from my family. My daughters, Alessandra and Gabriela, first resisted, then reveled in, the Paris adventure. They learned to speak French, played on French sports teams, and developed a taste for foie gras, *magret de canard*, *steak frites*, and champagne. When I started writing the book, Alessandra played cheerleader, urging me on with notes like, "A safe writer is not a good writer," and "I will treat you to a happy hour and a pedicure when you're done." Gabriela brought home stories about discovering seduction in her everyday life. She used her keen photographer's eye to find beauty in remote corners of France and even offered her legs for the cover photo. (Despite her great legs, the legs belong to someone else.)

My mother-in-law, Sondra Brown, offered hospitality, companionship, and love during my long stints in New York.

Most important was my husband, Andrew Plump. He transferred his work to Paris; joined Darrois Villey Maillot Brochier, a very French law firm, as its only American lawyer; passed the French bar exams; and got to wear a long black robe into French courtrooms. During my book writing, he shared his stories, helped formulate the book's structure, and read over the chapters with lawyerly precision. He is—as he has been since we met—my best editor and best friend.

INDEX

ABOUT THE AUTHOR

ELAINE SCIOLINO is the author of the award-winning book *Persian Mirrors: The Elusive Face of Iran*. She is a Paris correspondent and former Paris bureau chief for *The New York Times*, having previously served as the newspaper's chief diplomatic correspondent and UN bureau chief. In 2010, she was decorated a chevalier of the Legion of Honor. She has also been a foreign correspondent for *Newsweek*, based in Paris and Rome. She lives in Paris with her husband.